THOMAS SHIELDS

AND THE RENEWAL OF

CATHOLIC EDUCATION

SERIES: EDUCATION AND INTEGRAL HUMAN DEVELOPMENT

THOMAS SHIELDS
AND THE RENEWAL OF CATHOLIC EDUCATION

LEONARDO FRANCHI

Foreword by Mary Pat Donoghue

Catholic Education Press
Washington, D.C.

Copyright © 2023

Catholic Education Press
The Catholic University of America
Washington, D.C.

All rights reserved.
The paper used in this publication meets the minimum requirements of American National Standards for Information Science—Permanence of Paper for Printed Library Materials, ANSI Z39.48 - 1992.

∞

Cataloging-in-Publication Data is available from Library of Congress
ISBN: 978-1-9498-2238-0
eISBN: 978-1-9498-2239-7

This book is dedicated to
Ronald (Ronnie) Thumath
(31 December 1955–11 October 2022):
friend, teacher and mentor to many.
Requiescat in pace.

CONTENTS

Foreword	by Mary Pat Donoghue	ix
Introduction	The Master Plan	1
PART I	**Catholicism as an Educational Movement**	23
Chapter 1	Teaching Old Things in a New Way	25
PART II	**Responding to Progressive Thought**	35
Chapter 2	Progressivism and Catholic Education	37
Chapter 3	A Catholic Response to Dewey	50
PART III	**Shields and the Reform of Pedagogy**	67
Chapter 4	Developing a Framework for Reform	69
Chapter 5	Shields's Pedagogy of Catholic Education	92
PART IV	**Forming Teachers in Heart and Mind**	115
Chapter 6	Theological and Pedagogical Formation for Educators	117
Chapter 7	Means of Reform 1: The Catholic Sisters College	135
Chapter 8	Means of Reform 2: Affiliation of Schools	153
PART V	**The *Catholic Education Series***	163
Chapter 9	Textbooks and Readers for Children	165
Chapter 10	The *Catholic Education Series*: Structure and Aims	173
Chapter 11	The *Catholic Education Series*: A Study in Knowledge *and* Method	184
Conclusion	Evaluating Shields's Contribution to Catholic Education	209
Bibliography		227
Appendix:	The *Psychology of Education* Lesson XXV: Educational Principles in the Teaching of Christ and of the Church	241
Index		253

FOREWORD

The nature, essence, and purpose of education is a hotly contested topic these days, and the questions raised by this topic are even more pointed when aimed at Catholic education. This certainly consumes much of my thought and energy as Executive Director of the Secretariat of Catholic Education at the United States Conference of Catholic Bishops.

In the storm of confusion wrought by secularism and "all kinds of strange teaching,"[1] Catholic schools find themselves grappling with the nature of their mission and how to live it out in the world. To many of us, this feels like a new and current problem, but *Thomas Shields and the Renewal of Catholic Education* reminds us that the gospel of Jesus Christ, the foundation for Catholic education, is always at odds with the world. It is a problem that is ever-ancient, ever-new. It makes sense that we should consider the thoughts of the leaders who have confronted it before us.

In this volume, Dr. Leonardo Franchi introduces us to a thinker and reformer of the twentieth century whose methods and insights illumine our challenges in the twenty-first century. In Thomas Shields, we find an educator who deeply believed that the Church's intellectual tradition—which Franchi expertly defines as "the search for meaning through the partnership of faith and reason"—is the true foundation upon which true education rests.

Just as The Catholic University of America was beginning to take its place as a center of thought in the American Church, its own Thomas Shields was encouraging Catholic educators to adopt

---

1 Heb 13:9

the Church's centuries-long tradition of considering new discoveries, weighing them against the eternal truths of the Logos, and retaining what is good. Shields's approach would serve American Catholic education very well.

Indeed, the wisdom of Thomas Shields can be brought to bear on other concerns of the day. The integration of religious formation and academic studies is often expressed as an ideal by Catholic educators, yet there is a struggle to achieve this with authenticity (not to mention the challenge of the fragmented modern curriculum). Shields demonstrates the true confluence of faith and intellectual formation, which rests in an understanding of the relationship between the Creator and ordered creation. Dr. Franchi's own work around the restoration of the liberal arts is another expression of this, making him an excellent guide to a renewal movement of the last century that has tremendous implications for our own time.

Mary Pat Donoghue
Executive Director
Secretariat of Catholic Education
United States Conference of Catholic Bishops

INTRODUCTION

The Master Plan

The present volume explores the contribution of Rev. Dr. Thomas Shields (1862–1921) to the field of Catholic education in the United States of America in the late nineteenth and early twentieth centuries. In bringing Shields's considerable body of work to new audiences, the volume will contribute to the ongoing and much-needed revival of interest in the scholarly basis of Catholic education. Shields, who became a leading figure in the life of The Catholic University of America (hereafter Catholic University), has been described tantalizingly as "an innovator in Catholic education"[1] and "the first major theorist in the U.S. on educational psychology and its application to the teaching of religion."[2] As the present age is also witness to considerable and deep-rooted challenges to Catholic education and, indeed the Catholic understanding of the human person, Shields's work offers some possible pathways for contemporary reform-minded Catholic educators. For this reason, his work merits a fresh study.

My own interest in the work of Shields is an example of academic serendipity. While doing doctoral research on conceptual frameworks in religious education, I came across what was called the

---

1 Robert Anello, "Intellectual Formation for Professionalism in Catholic Education: Catholic Sisters' College, Washington, D.C.," *U.S. Catholic Historian* 35, no. 4 (Fall 2017): 79.
2 John F. Murphy, "The Contribution of the Human Sciences to the Pedagogy of Thomas E. Shields," *The Living Light* 10, no. 1 (1973): 81.

Shields Method of teaching religion.[3] Following some initial exploratory reading I made a mental note to find out more (one day!) about Shields's influence on Catholic education. After a few brief forays into some of his available writing, it became apparent quite quickly that Shields was straddling the intersection of wider educational reform and what seemed to be the Catholic Church's more cautious approach to new insights in pedagogy.[4] I was keen not just to find out how he had approached this important task but also to investigate if his ways of working could be applied successfully to the contemporary scene. This volume is the fruit of that initial encounter.

This introduction is set out in six parts: Intellectual and Ecclesial Contexts, Shields's Life and Work, Shields's Master Plan for Reform, Overview of the Book, A Note on Method, and Acknowledgments. The conclusion will explore, inter alia, the extent to which his many contributions to the mission of Catholic education can still speak fluently to contemporary educators.

Intellectual and Ecclesial Contexts

The influence of religious beliefs on the development of educational thought should be intrinsic to any scholarly history of education. If religion is where we find evidence of humanity's multifaceted quest for identity, meaning, and community, education, as manifested in a host of formal and informal institutions and processes, is where this happens.[5] For the cultural historian and Catholic convert Christopher

3 John L. Elias, "Thomas E. Shields: Progressive Catholic Educator," in *Educators in the Catholic Intellectual Tradition*, ed. John L. Elias and Lucinda A. Nolan (Fairfield, Conn.: Sacred Heart University Press, 2009), 75–102.
4 Throughout the text I use both "pedagogy" and "methodology" as appropriate to context: the former refers broadly to thinking on educational matters more generally and the latter focuses specifically on methods of teaching.
5 To give one example, the Catholic Church's contribution to educational developments, in particular the rise of the European universities and the emergence of forward-thinking teaching congregations in the early modern period and beyond, are essential themes in any serious study of educational

Dawson, it is "the religious impulse which supplies the cohesive force which unifies a society and a culture."[6] While Dawson's conclusion might not be universally accepted today, inadequate, nay poor, is the history of education that marginalizes religion as a sociocultural phenomenon.

Catholic belief has major implications for the choices believers make on earth, including how to think about issues related to human development and formation. More specifically, the Catholic Intellectual Tradition—which I define here broadly as the search for meaning through the partnership of faith and reason—expresses how Catholicism has, from ongoing reflection on the meaning of the Incarnation for humanity's relationship with God, developed a related ecosystem of ideas, beliefs, and social practices.[7]

While Catholicism is in many respects an educational movement (see chapter 1), the term "Catholic education" is commonly used to refer to the work of Catholic schools, colleges, and universities. This definition can and should be expanded to include what happens, both formally and informally, in parishes, sodalities, and lay associations. Catholic education so understood does not stand apart from the Church but acts a place of encounter between its cherished traditions and wider thinking. It is hence freighted with the responsibility to curate and develop the Church's rich intellectual and pastoral traditions.

---

trends. For a secular history of education that gives due recognition to the religious roots of educational structures in the West, see James Bowen, *A History of Western Education*, vol. 2, *Civilization of Europe, Sixth to Sixteenth Century* (London: Methuen, 1975).

6 Christopher Dawson, *Progress and Religion: An Historical Enquiry* (Washington, D.C.: The Catholic University of America Press, 2001), 180.

7 For more on the Catholic Intellectual Tradition, see in particular Robert Royal, *A Deeper Vision: The Catholic Intellectual Tradition in the Twentieth Century* (San Francisco: Ignatius Press, 2015). The website of Boston College has a helpful introductory video on the Catholic Intellectual Tradition at https://www.bc.edu/bc-web/centers/church21/programs/catholic-intellectual-tradition.html. The University of Notre Dame Australia has also recently deepened its commitment to exploration of the Catholic Intellectual Tradition: https://www.notredame.edu.au/about/catholic-intellectual-tradition.

Shields valued and sought to widen the Catholic Intellectual Tradition. His work, while exhibiting high levels of scholarship and a commendable recognition of the importance of effective and accessible resources for the school, cannot be satisfactorily classified as the output of a solitary genius. Granted, there was an element of single-mindedness and dogged determination in the way he operated, but it is vital to locate Shields's contribution to Catholic education in the many and varied contexts offered by the Church and society in which he worked. We note in particular the wider option for universal reform marked out by Pope Leo XIII—although such a trajectory might be illuminated by the always-welcome lights of hindsight— and, as we will see, the awareness in Catholic educational circles of the late nineteenth and early twentieth centuries of the potential of new scientific findings to refresh the pedagogy of Catholic education.

Following the Plenary Council of Baltimore of 1884, the Catholic community in America regarded its expanding network of educational establishments as markers of its unique place in a culture that was not always favorable to Catholicism.[8] As the Catholic population was a mainly immigrant community, Catholic schools understandably became much more than sites of learning, assuming a more general role as centers wherein a so-called Catholic identity was gradually formed.[9] This set of circumstances was ripe for the reception of new thinking in Catholic education.

Shields was not alone in desiring to reform Catholic education. Bishop John Lancaster Spalding (1840–1916), a preeminent figure in the history of Catholic education in America, was instrumental in the foundation of Catholic University in 1887, first as a research center with a papal charter and then as an institution offering undergraduate degrees.[10] Given Shields's interest in higher education and

---

8 Francis P. Cassidy, "Catholic Education in the Third Plenary Council of Baltimore," *The Catholic Historical Review* 34, no. 3 (October 1948): 260.
9 John L. Elias, "George Johnson: Policy Maker for Catholic Education," in Elias and Nolan, *Educators in the Catholic Intellectual Tradition*, 129–30.
10 See the website of Catholic University for more information: https://www.catholic.edu/about-us/at-a-glance/index.html.

THE MASTER PLAN

his related contribution to the life of Catholic University, it is vital to recognize the important work of Bishop Spalding in laying the foundations of Catholic University as a center of new thinking in Catholic education.[11]

Spalding's contribution to Catholic intellectual and pastoral life included a major contribution to the writing of the famous Baltimore Catechism of 1885. This influential volume was written to give Catholic families and pastors the knowledge and language deemed necessary for the effective transmission of the Catholic religious tradition to all, including the young.[12] In other writings, Bishop Spalding's mind and pen roamed freely over a wide spectrum of ideas as he sought to align mainstream Catholic teaching with the many voices and ideas that inhabited the cultural space of the age.[13] For sure Spalding was no esoteric theorist but a pastor with an abiding interest in reminding the wider Church of the importance of inhabiting and contributing to the public square. Moreover, he was always open to engaging with the new ideas that were emerging at that time if they contributed positively to the human condition.

Alongside Bishop Spalding, Rev. Dr. Edward Pace (1861–1938) made a significant contribution to the renewal of Catholic education.

11 "His writings on educational philosophy are unmatched by any US prelate to date. John Lancaster Spalding was without precedent or successor as an American Catholic philosopher of education." Lucinda A. Nolan, "Bishop John Lancaster Spalding: Prelate and Philosopher of Catholic Education," in Elias and Nolan, *Educators in the Catholic Intellectual Tradition*, 48.

12 The initial text of the Baltimore Catechism underwent some revisions in due course. A school of thought had arisen that, despite its orthodox content, the language of the text was too difficult to use with young people. Nevertheless, no alternative text was offered, and the Baltimore Catechism became the key text for catechesis in the US. For more on this, see Bob Rice and Nicholas Stein, "The Catechism of the Catholic Church and Ministry with Youth and Young Adults," in *Speaking the Truth in Love: The Catechism and the New Evangelization*, ed. Petroc Willey and Scott Sollom (Steubenville, Ohio: Emmaus Academic, 2019), 461–73, esp. 469–72.

13 See, for example, John L. Spalding, "Education and the Future of Religion," chap. 5 in *Religion, Agnosticism and Education* (repr., St. Athanasius Press, 2018), 54–69. First published 1902 by A.C. McClure & Co. (Chicago).

Foreshadowing the work and methods of Shields, Pace drew on the traditional body of doctrine permeating the Baltimore Catechism but looked for ways by which teaching methods could be enlightened through study of the so-called Progressive movements in education (see chapter 2 for more on Progressivism). For Pace, the discipline of psychology, in which he was an active and acclaimed researcher-writer, offered some important threads that Catholic educators could use, as appropriate, to improve their methodology.[14] Pace had the honor of giving the homily at Shields's Requiem Mass in 1921, where he highlighted both Shields's academic goals and his focus on correct teaching methods. He paid particular attention to Shields's desire to improve teacher formation, which, he said, became a "directive principle, dominating his thought and deciding the course of his action."[15]

Pace and Shields worked closely together in the period 1908–09 to advance arguments for a Sisters College on the campus of Catholic University.[16] They also co-authored many pieces on multiple topics in the field of Catholic education. Their collaboration was so close that it is no easy task to disaggregate their work. In a PhD dissertation on methods of teaching religion from 1928, Fr. John McMahon suggested that "Dr. Pace came to advocate the principles of the Shields Method from psychology, whereas Dr. Shields came through biology."[17] This might seem like an overly neat way to describe their

---

[14] Pace's desire to be involved in experimental psychology was not universally welcomed by other American Catholic voices, who saw it as too close an embrace of materialism. See John L. Elias, "Edward Pace: Pioneer Psychologist, Philosopher and Religious Educator," in Elias and Nolan, *Educators in the Catholic Intellectual Tradition*, 55–59.

[15] Edward Pace, "Homily, Requiem Mass for Thomas Shields," Thomas Shields Memorial Issue, *Catholic Educational Review* 19 (April 1921): 194–200 at 196.

[16] Rita Watrin, *The Founding and Development of the Program of Affiliation of the Catholic University of America: 1912 to 1939* (Washington, D.C.: The Catholic University of America Press, 1966). See in particular 38–39.

[17] John McMahon, "The Shields Method: Some Methods of Teaching Religion" (PhD diss., National University of Ireland) (London: Burns, Oates and Washbourne, 1928), 132.

scholarly relationship but it does offer a working hypothesis that captures, at least in part, their respective scholarly strengths.

The extent to which one or the other could be deemed the principal author of particular pieces of writing remains a moot point.[18] A biographer of Shields, Justine Ward, while recognizing their differing qualities and temperaments, tended to see Shields as the stronger and more active of the pair.[19] Nonetheless, Pace's contribution to the intellectual life of the Catholic Church in America is, without doubt, significant, and it is possible that the energy he spent in scholarly endeavors was a necessary complement to the more practical, and no less energetic, focus of Shields.

There are also varying perspectives on whether Pace's intellectual leanings could be labeled as primarily conservative or progressive. Such discussions, not unusually, can fail to recognize nuance; a commitment to exploring "new" ways of doing "old" things can too easily lead to sterile debates over the methodology of change. Pace, like Shields, was keen to draw on new insights, no matter their source, in order to advance, as appropriate, the noble cause of Catholic education.[20] Furthermore, Pace had developed a reputation as a distinguished Thomistic philosopher. He sought to align careful philosophical inquiry with the physical sciences, with both, he believed, contributing to the resolution of the many difficulties and problems affecting everyday life.[21] This intellectual marriage, so

18 For example, the *Catholic Education Series*, *First Book* contains a preface by Shields, while *Second Book* and *Third Book* have prefaces by both Pace and Shields.
19 Justine Ward, *Thomas Edward Shields: Biologist, Psychologist, Educator* (New York: Charles Scribner's Sons, 1947), 158.
20 See Fayette Breaux Veverka, "Defining a Catholic Approach to Education in the United States, 1920–1950," *Religious Education* 88, no. 4 (1993): 523–42, for a helpful overview of the current of thought that influenced Catholic education in the United States after the era of Shields.
21 "For Pace, as for other Catholic educators of his time, philosophy was the main unifying discipline in undergraduate education, since it dealt with the basic principles of reality that were studied through other disciplines, including the natural and psychological sciences." Elias, "Edward Pace," 60.

to speak, between philosophy and the sciences was instrumental in shaping Pace's life as an educator.

In 1911 Pace also had the privilege of penning the opening article in the inaugural issue of the *Catholic Educational Review*. Headed "The Papacy in Education" (a title that might give rise to suspicions of ultramontanist tendencies), Pace offered due respect, unsurprisingly, to the Church's contribution to education and culture. Bearing in mind that Pace was writing in an atmosphere in which some Catholics had a firm suspicion, to say the least, of modernism, it is interesting to note Pace's clearly expressed approval of the advances in education with respect to the teaching of religion in school.[22] His rejection of the so-called "rote learning" implied by the Baltimore Catechism (and similar publications) underpinned future ventures in textbook writing and, ultimately, the longer-lasting insights into catechetical methods that, alongside Shields's work, anticipated the work of the catechetical reform movement.[23]

Rev. Dr. George Johnson (1889–1944) continued Shields's work at Catholic University in the field of Catholic education. As Shields had been Johnson's doctoral supervisor, it is no surprise that he saw Shields's work as "outstanding" while admitting that Shields's method had not yet received "universal adoption."[24] While Johnson did not explore why this might have been the case, he expanded the work of

22 "The importance then that modern education attaches to motor processes, is justified in theory and is extremely practical in its consequences. To neglect these consequences in any plan of religious instruction would be, from the psychological point of view, a downright mistake." Edward Pace, "The Papacy and Education," *Catholic Educational Review* 1 (January 1911): 6.

23 "Though there is little direct link between their [Pace's and Shields's] work and the emergence of the catechetical movement in Roman Catholicism in the 1960s, they began the trend of taking secular developments in science, psychology, and education so seriously that future scholars, beginning at the Catholic University and later extending to other universities, introduced considerable changes in the theory and practice of Catholic education." Elias, "Edward Pace," 50.

24 George Johnson, "Character Education in the Catholic Church," *Religious Education* 24, no. 1 (1929): 56.

reform that Pace and Shields had pioneered. For example, Johnson had articles published in *Religious Education,* the journal of the progressivist Religious Education Association, something Shields did not do. Johnson was also the principal author of *Better Men for Better Times,* Catholic University's Commission on American Citizenship's document on Catholic social teaching and citizenship.[25] Johnson's achievements in strengthening the base of Catholic education was considerable and, for some, it was Johnson, not Pace or Shields, who "did the most to shape the direction of Catholic education in the United States."[26]

It is, therefore, on the roads laid out by Spalding and Pace and subsequently developed by Johnson that we can best appreciate the depth and breadth of Shields's contribution to the reform of Catholic education in America.

Shields's Life and Work

Shields's early life is an indispensable source for a mature understanding of his scholarly achievements. It is here that we find the seeds of the energy and determination to succeed that marked his later life, although the success he sought was not for his own reputation but for a renewed awareness of the importance of solid formation for Catholic teachers.

Shields's autobiography, *The Making and Unmaking of a Dullard,* is essential reading for a rounded picture of Shields as priest and scholar.[27] Born in 1862 to a family of Irish American farmers, he was removed from school at the age of nine because his teachers and family thought that he had little or no potential to do well in a formal school setting. Up to that point, Shields's school life has been

---

25 Catholic University of America's Commission on American Citizenship, *Better Men for Better Times* (Washington, D.C.: The Catholic Education Press, 1943).
26 Elias, "George Johnson," 129. See conclusion for more on Johnson.
27 Thomas Shields, *The Making and Unmaking of a Dullard* (Washington, D.C.: The Catholic Education Press, 1909).

unremarkably normal. He reentered school life in 1882 after a period of work on the family farm. Shields had been privately tutored by his parish priest for entrance into the seminary and this ambition came to fruition when he was accepted as a seminarian at St. Thomas Seminary in Minnesota. While a seminarian, Shields published his (now lost) *Index Omnium,* a reference book that brought together the notes and knowledge he had gathered in his studies. This was an early, if rather unsophisticated, expression of the principle of correlation, which would become central to his later thinking. Shields was ordained to the priesthood in 1891 and was sent to John Hopkins University to study natural science. This was the beginning of an academic career that would see him gain a PhD in 1895 with a thesis entitled "The Effects of Odours, Irritant Vapours, and Mental Work upon the Blood Flow."

Shields's early years are contemporaneous with some major developments in Catholic life in America, especially the publication of the Baltimore Catechism in 1885 and the foundation of Catholic University in 1887.[28] Shields was appointed to Catholic University as an instructor in physiological psychology in 1902. He became professor of psychology and education in 1909 but was increasingly keen to explore in greater depth the emerging field of the science of education. In 1904, Shields joined the staff of Trinity College in Washington, an institution run by the Sisters of Notre Dame de Namur for the higher education of women. When Catholic University established a department of education in 1908, Shields happily found a new academic home, where he remained until his death in 1921. Shields was also involved in establishing a number of new academic-professional initiatives: in 1905, the Catholic Correspondence School (the embryo for the future Catholic Sisters College); in 1906 the Catholic Associated Press, later known as The Catholic Education Press; in 1911 *The Catholic Educational Review* (with Rev. Dr. Edward Pace) and the Catholic University Summer School;

---

[28] A summary of the key events of his life is found in the Thomas Shields Memorial Issue, *Catholic Educational Review* 19 (April 1921): 200–21.

in 1912 the School Affiliation Program; and in 1914 the Catholic Sisters College.

Considering his considerable legacy of written work and practical achievements, there is a paucity of secondary literature on Shields. Few scholars—with some notable exceptions as will be noted below—have invested time and energy in serious and suitably contextualized study of his work. Curiously, Catholic University's special collections on Catholic education resources contains limited material on Shields—despite his description on its website as "the foremost Catholic educator in the first quarter of the twentieth century"—in comparison to its more substantial holdings for other important figures, such as Pace. The entry for Shields on Catholic University's special collections website reads as follows:

> A professor of psychology and education at Catholic University from 1909–1921, Shields was perhaps the foremost Catholic educator in the first quarter of the twentieth century. The collection includes the draft M.A. thesis *Dr. Thomas E. Shields and his Educational Theories*; 25 lessons from a correspondence course in the psychology of education which Shields began taking in 1905; a pamphlet containing Shields's 1895 doctoral dissertation, *The Effect of Vapours upon the Blood Flow*; and a lighthearted article in which he discusses coeducation.[29]

This succinct and understated overview of Shields's life and work might seem to belie the claim that he was the "foremost Catholic educator." Thankfully, other studies are available that fill out this snapshot. His close friend and academic collaborator on the place of music in education, Justine Ward, wrote a biography entitled *Thomas Edward Shields: Biologist, Psychologist, Educator*.[30] Published in 1947, it is written in a curiously informal style and has many passages with actual reported speech. What readers make of this style of biography

---

29 https://guides.lib.cua.edu/c.php?g=998602&p=7231392.
30 Ward, *Thomas Edward Shields*, 1947.

is unclear. Despite the author's closeness to the subject, it is still a helpful introduction to Shields as man, scholar, and priest.

In an important retrospective essay on the catechetical scene in America in the early years of the twentieth century, Rev. Professor Gerard Sloyan (1919–2020) argued with some conviction that Shields occupied "first place" in the list of pioneers of catechetical reform. This is a big claim to make—and we note that Sloyan is addressing specifically *catechetical* reform, thus showing the merged identity of catechesis and school religious instruction at that time—and is based on Shields's integration of "new" concepts; for example, learning-by-doing, the laws of apperception, and the use of steps in learning in religious instruction in Catholic schools.[31] Such high praise from a renowned educationalist offered sufficient impetus to new generations of teachers to engage with and learn from Shields's way of working.

To gain a rounded view of the scope of Shields's work, access to other studies on the wider contexts in which he operated is necessary. An early study is a PhD dissertation by Fr. John McMahon with a chapter on the Shields Method alongside studies of other ways of teaching religion; for example, the Sower Scheme, the Yorke Method, and the Munich Method.[32] Harold Buetow's article, "The Teaching of Education at CUA 1889–1966," offers the contemporary reader a broad historical sketch of Catholic University's growing involvement in the field of educational studies.[33] Buetow provided important

---

31 Gerard Sloyan, "The Good News and the Catechetical Scene in the United States," in Josef Jungmann, SJ, *The Good News Yesterday and Today*, trans., abr., and ed. William A. Huesman, SJ (New York: W.H. Sadlier, 1962), 211–28. This important volume contains a condensed version of Jungmann's original text published in 1939, supplemented by a number of reflective essays, of which this is one. Interestingly, Prof. Sloyan's edited collection, *Shaping the Christian Message: Essays in Religious Education* (New York: Macmillan, 1958) does not contain a chapter on Shields despite much of the content being similar in style to Shields's approach. In fact, the introduction, signed by Professor Sloyan, could have come from the pen of Shields himself.
32 McMahon, "The Shields Method," 122–90.
33 Harold Buetow, "The Teaching of Education at CUA 1889–1966," *Catholic Educational Review* 65, no. 1 (1967): 1–20.

details on the substantial shift in pedagogical ideas that were affecting all American schools in the early years of the twentieth century. Rita Watrin's study from 1966 of Catholic University's School Affiliation Program—which Shields founded as a way to foster a corporate identity among Catholic school personnel—is helpful as a guide to the impact of the program on the corporate life of Catholic education in America.[34] Buetow's *Of Singular Benefit: The Story of Catholic Education in the United States,* published in 1970, is an indispensable and well-drawn map of the field. Its comprehensive content befits the claim of the title.[35] John Elias and Lucinda Nolan have a chapter on Shields, written by Elias, in their edited book, *Educators in the Catholic Intellectual Tradition,* from 2009.[36] This scholarly but highly accessible volume has chapters on Pace and Johnson, both penned by Elias, which show how close their ideas were to Shields's thought.[37] There are also chapters on other key figures in Catholic education circles both before, during, and after the time of Shields. Mary Bryce's 1978 article, "Four Decades of Roman Catholic Innovators," includes Shields in a list of influential Catholic educators alongside Edward Pace, Peter C. Yorke, Edwin V. O'Hara, and Virgil Michel.[38] John Francis Murphy offered a critical overview of the thought of Shields in his article "The Contribution of the Human Sciences to the Pedagogy of Thomas E. Shields," published in 1973.[39] In this article Murphy drew on his 1971 doctoral dissertation, "Thomas Edward Shields: Religious Educator" to give a succinct analysis of Shields's thinking.[40] Another helpful doctoral study was written by

---

34 Watrin, *Founding and Development of the Program of Affiliation.*
35 Harold Buetow, *Of Singular Benefit: The Story of Catholic Education in the United States* (London: Macmillan, 1970).
36 Elias, "Thomas E. Shields: Progressive Catholic Educator."
37 Elias also wrote the short biography of Shields on the website of Biola University: https://www.biola.edu/talbot/ce20/database/thomas-edward-shields.
38 Mary Bryce, "Four Decades of Roman Catholic Innovators," *Religious Education* 73, supp. 1 (1978): 36–57.
39 Murphy, "Contribution of the Human Sciences."
40 John Francis Murphy, "Thomas Edward Shields: Religious Educator" (PhD diss., The Catholic University of America, 1971).

Mary Verone Wohlwend—who later took on the task of completing the unfinished *Catholic Education Series*—on Shields's influence on teacher training at Catholic University.[41] Two master's theses, again from Catholic University, round out the picture.[42]

Shields is little known today by scholars of Catholic education, and it is reasonable to ask why this might be the case. The thought of his contemporaries like John Dewey (1859–1952) and St. John Henry Newman (1801–90) are well established in educational-theological circles. Perhaps Shields's work was too localized to travel beyond America, although there is evidence, as we will see, of the impact of his work in the United Kingdom. Given Shields's stellar reputation in the first quarter of the twentieth century, the paucity of secondary studies is striking. This omission might be a blessing in disguise, as the best way for the contemporary educator to learn about Shields's educational ideas is by immersion in the considerable volume of work he bequeathed, much of which is freely available online. There will be a more substantial evaluation of Shields's legacy in the conclusion.

Alongside many articles and book reviews in the *Catholic University Bulletin* and the *Catholic Educational Review*, Shields published a number of important books. Not all academics are natural writers, but Shields, who surely saw his output as necessary for the implementation of the reforms he desired, had a "way with words."[43] His

---

41 Mary Verone Wohlwend, "The Educational Principles of Dr. Thomas E. Shields and Their Impact on His Teacher Training Programme at the Catholic University of America" (PhD diss., The Catholic University of America, 1968).

42 Cf. Thomas Cantwell, "A Comparative Study of the Theories of Self-Activity and Religion according to the Very Reverend Thomas E. Shields and Monsignor George W. Johnson" (master's thesis, The Catholic University of America, 1949); Fumiko Maria Christina Fujikawa, "The Educational Contents and Implications of *The Education of our Girls* by Dr. Thomas Edward Shields" (master's thesis, The Catholic University of America, 1954).

43 The wide reputation of Doctor Shields as an educator was in large measure won by his writings. Beginning at about the time he undertook his university

autobiography, *The Making and Unmaking of a Dullard*, published in 1909, is an invaluable insight into the early challenges he faced from his inability to succeed at school. It is a poignant read but we find therein hints of the grit and eagerness to succeed that would become evident in later life. *The Education of Our Girls*, published in 1907, is where we find the seeds of the future Catholic Sisters College. This book is written in an unusual style. It is not a standard academic text and instead reads in places like the written record of a cozy fireside chat. Despite this stylistic caveat, the underlying ideas about the importance of education for women are clearly and unambiguously expressed.

Shields wrote four theoretical works, each of which included ample practical considerations: *Twenty-Five Lessons in the Psychology of Education* (1906), *The Teaching of Religion* (1908), *The Teachers Manual of Primary Methods* (1912), and *Philosophy of Education* (1917). All contain material which had been part of his university courses or had already been included in journal articles. Shields also found time to write the *Catholic Education Series* (see part 5) for schools: *First Book* and *Third Reader* in 1908, *Second Book* and *Third Book* in 1909, *Fourth Reader* and *Fifth Reader* in 1915, and *Fourth Book* in 1918. The series was unfinished at the time of his death in 1921.[44]

Shields's "Notes on Education" in the *Catholic University Bulletin*, which date from 1907, are important indicators of an ongoing and deep interest in educational matters. He is (along with Pace) highlighting fresh ideas that would bear fruit in the Catholic Sisters College and the *Catholic Education Series*. Shields was very much at home in the emerging academic domain of Catholic education and saw Catholic University and its in-house *Bulletin* as central to the

---

teaching, they placed him almost immediately in the forefront of Catholic thinkers and workers in the field of education. During the short space of less than a score of years he produced a veritable library of pedagogical contributions, witnesses at once to his industry and remarkable literary ability. Patrick J. McCormick, "Doctor Shields as Writer," Thomas Shields Memorial Issue, *Catholic Educational Review* 19 (April 1921): 274.

44 More details about the structure of the *Catholic Education Series* are found in part 5.

urgent mission of educational reform. Shields was, however, keen to establish a new journal focused specifically on Catholic education but without losing the vital connection to wider studies that the *Bulletin* offered. In the "University Chronicle" section of the *Catholic University Bulletin* of January 1911, Shields laid out the scope of the new publishing project:

> An important step forward has been taken by the University in arranging for the publication of a periodical dealing with the problems of education from a Catholic standpoint. "The Catholic Educational Review" will appear in January and each month thereafter with the exception of July and August. It is primarily an outgrowth of the Department of Education which the University Trustees desire to build up; but in its larger scope it will include all that affects the welfare of our Catholic schools, academies and colleges.[45]

This ambitious new venture would place the study of religion at the heart of the mission of Catholic education but not, it seemed, at the expense of a much broader discussion of "methods, historical questions, current discussions, new text-books and courses of study."[46] The new journal, of which he and Pace were initially co-editors, was a concrete development from the work of the *Catholic University Bulletin* and would serve as a key means of disseminating Shields's thought (and that of other scholars too) for the next decade until his death in 1921.[47] It is in the new journal—called the *Catholic Educational Review*—and his monographs that we find the

---

45 Thomas Shields, "University Chronicle," *Catholic University Bulletin* 17 (1911): 90.
46 Shields, "University Chronicle," 90.
47 Catholic University did not offer financial support to the new journal, and it seems that the burden of keeping it afloat fell on the shoulders of Shields and Pace. Over the years, Shields authored around one hundred articles. The *Review* ceased publication in 1969.

key elements of Shields's thinking. Careful reading of his body of work will pay dividends to the scholar wishing to find antecedents of the reforms in catechesis which emerged in the second half of the twentieth century.

It is also important to reflect on the substantial thematic crossover between the content of Shields's articles and books. There are various possible reasons for this, lying somewhere between a lack of time to develop his ideas sufficiently and a conviction that his "discovery" of new scientifically verified methods was the best way to improve Catholic education, and would thus make further theoretical development unnecessary. Nonetheless, Shields's approach could be summarized as follows: religion (meaning the Catholic religion) had to be integrated into the curriculum of Catholic schools, and a reform of methods would ensure the success of curricular integration. Such themes resonated across his writings, and a refreshed understanding of teacher formation was the key to making this happen.

As will become clear in due course, Shields's capacity for work was immense, but his single-minded zeal for reform did have baleful consequences. The reality was that his many commitments—in particular, a dogged determination to keep a very close eye on all aspects of the life of the *Catholic Educational Review*, including the writing of more than one hundred signed articles from 1911 to 1921—became an actual burden on his health.[48]

Given Shields's far-sighted role in aligning Catholic educational thought with emerging insights in the sciences, and his multilayered commitment to Catholic education as academic, author of textbooks and founder of a teacher education institution, it seems fitting that his considerable body of work should now be the subject of fresh scholarly investigation.

---

48 For more background on the journal and the other outlets for Catholic educational thought at the time, see Murphy, "Thomas Edward Shields: Religious Educator," 132–36.

Shields's Master Plan for Reform

The period between 1908 and 1921 saw Shields at the height of his powers. This was when he was intentionally mapping new insights onto the field of Catholic education.[49] Shields's "Master Plan" was comprised of two connected layers. The driver was the realization that the major advances that had occurred in the organization of Catholic schools after the Third Plenary Council of Baltimore in 1884 had not yet brought about a sufficiently robust set of responses to the challenges Catholic schools faced in the formulation of curriculum.[50] Shields saw it as his mission to address this.

The first layer of his reform was the *formulation of a new pedagogy of Catholic education* that sought to align findings from the science of learning with traditional Catholic doctrine. His books and articles are where this theory is set out and it is worth noting in particular the rejection of overly abstract ideas in favor of the practical angle.

The second layer of his reform was to put in place *concrete means for the dissemination of his ideas* using a) the textbooks and readers of the *Catholic Education Series* and b) the proper formation of teachers (both currently serving and future teachers), in dedicated centers. The Catholic Sisters College of 1914, foreshadowed by the Summer Schools and a correspondence course, was the realization of the dream adumbrated in *The Education of Our Girls*. Allied to this was the School Affiliation Program between Catholic University and Catholic schools that would extend the influence of Catholic University to the heart of its associated schools.

---

49 The productive merging of educational theory and practical work was "an almost single-handed attempt at building another invention: a master tool for Catholic education which encompassed teacher training, texts, an affiliation program for schools, and a house organ, the *Catholic Educational Review*." Murphy, "Thomas Edward Shields: Religious Educator," 119.

50 "But the emerging Catholic system, in its concern for external developmental activities during this period, had given less time to translating fundamental Catholic principles into pedagogical practice." Watrin, *Founding and Development of the Program of Affiliation*, 36.

Remarkably, Shields achieved all of this while retaining a substantial teaching load at Catholic University and responding to many other demands on his time and expertise. He was rightly determined that his wide body of scholarship would not remain as monuments on library shelves and hence successfully combined insightful academic work with the writing of innovative school resources. His desire to integrate material from other disciplines facilitated a shift in Catholic education from a predominantly curriculum-centered phenomenon to an allegedly more child-centered approach, but one which, he claimed, remained entirely faithful to the theological and pastoral traditions of the Catholic Church. This synthesis, not wholly accepted in his time, is now in the mainstream of Catholic catechetical and educational thinking.[51] Shields was moving in an atmosphere that was increasingly open to reform of methods in Catholic schools—it is not wrong, therefore, to see his achievements as pioneering in that he actually established concrete means of disseminating his scholarly work in the Catholic Sisters College and resources for schools.

Overview of the Book

The present book does not claim to be a comprehensive biography of Shields. It does, however, plot a path through his principal documented ideas and achievements and relate them, as far as is feasible, to wider developments. The book has eleven chapters set within five parts, accompanied by an introduction and conclusion.

- The introduction sets the scene for the study by presenting some key biographical information and the outlines of the some of the intellectual currents at play. It highlights the core component of Shields's Master Plan for reform.

---

[51] Pontifical Council for Promoting New Evangelization, *Directory for Catechesis* (London: Catholic Truth Society, 2020).

- Part 1, "Catholicism as an Educational Movement," contains a stand-alone chapter titled "Teaching Old Things in a New Way," which sets out the contours of the intellectual climate in which Shields operated and presents Catholicism as a dynamic educational movement.
- Part 2, "Responding to Progressive Thought," explores the relationship between Progressivism and Catholic education, dealing with the work of John Dewey and showing how the Catholic Church responded to the challenges presented by Progressivist thought.
- Part 3, "Shields and the Reform of Pedagogy," examines both Shields's general pedagogical principles and how they relate to Catholic education. This is where we encounter the ideas that drove his ideas for practical reform.
- Part 4, "Forming Teachers in Heart and Mind," considers Shields's ideas on Catholic teacher formation, exploring issues such as culture, vocation, method, and curriculum. The focus is on two concrete means of reform: the Catholic Sisters College and the Affiliation Program.
- Part 5, "The *Catholic Education Series*," explores selected examples from Shields's *Catholic Education Series* to identify how his material for schools reflected, to a greater or lesser extent, his educational ideas.
- The conclusion presents the reader with some further thoughts on Shields's legacy and on what his work means for the contemporary educator.

A Note on Method

Concerning questions of method, my aim is to allow the voice of Shields to speak as clearly as possible. The structure of the book is designed to offer a structure within which to understand better his ways of thinking and grasp, as far as is possible, how he proposed a raft of practical reforms. I have tried to avoid too much biographical detail in the text, focusing instead on the details of his Master Plan. To allow Shields's voice to come through, the text includes some medium to long quotes. On occasion there are quotes in the footnotes when the main body of the text needs enlarging with reference to the sources. Ideally, the reader will seek out the primary material by Shields, which is freely available online, as his work deserves a firsthand reading. I have tried throughout to keep the text accessible by avoiding an overly technical approach.

Acknowledgments

I am grateful to the University of Glasgow for the period of Study Leave in the first half of 2020, which helped bring this work to completion. It was a labor of love. I thank those who offered advice on earlier drafts of this work: Jem Sullivan, Roisin Coll, James Conroy, Bob Davis, and Richard Rymarz.

I am indebted to Joan Stahl, the director of research and instruction at Catholic University Library for her help in arranging access to dissertations on the work of Shields in the library of Catholic University. I offer heartfelt thanks to John Martino of Catholic University Press for his constant diligence, affable availability, and quiet effectiveness. They have helped make this work more complete. My thanks are also due to Greg Black for proofreading the text and to Matthew White for the index. Any remaining weaknesses are my responsibility.

Sancta Maria, Spes Nostra, Sedes Sapientiae: ora pro nobis

PART I

CATHOLICISM AS AN EDUCATIONAL MOVEMENT

CHAPTER 1

TEACHING OLD THINGS IN A NEW WAY

The title of this chapter, "Teaching Old Things in a New Way," is a neat verbal summary of how the Catholic Church's mission in education cannot become fossilized but needs, indeed demands, ongoing renewal. This chapter offers the keys necessary to unlock and engage with the general intellectual currents that influenced the educational scene in Shields's time. It is a study of the "option for reform" that is central to authentic Catholicism and has been expressed in the fluidity of the Church's long-standing educational traditions. While not claiming to be a comprehensive historical study of the Church's educational mission throughout the ages, the chapter reveals how a broad understanding of education has always been central to the life of the Church.

The history of the Church features multiple examples of initiatives—both successful and unsuccessful—to bring its message to all people (evangelization) and develop the faith and religious commitment of the baptized (catechesis). Catholicism's contribution to wider educational history, as found, for example, in the contribution of the post-Reformation teaching congregations to schooling, curricular reform, and teacher formation, is part of the historical record.[1]

1 For example, see Tom O'Donoghue, *Come Follow Me and Forsake Temptation: Catholic Schooling and the Recruitment and Retention of Teachers for Religious Teaching*

The work of Shields is one example of how a confident Catholic culture finds a natural outlet in both explicit and implicit educational initiatives. The religion-education nexus, crucial to Shields's intellectual stance, is central to Catholic thought and requires, in the first place, freedom of religion. As proclaimed in the United Nations document *Universal Declaration on Human Rights*, everyone has the right "to manifest his religion or belief in teaching, practice, worship and observance."[2]

Such high-sounding, indeed lapidary, statements remind us that freedom of religion is essential for a healthy and culturally sensitive polity. Of course, there is scope for varied interpretations of the stated ideals, but the essential point remains clear.

Religious bodies, of course, continue to have much to say about education.[3] This is not surprising, as religions are ways of making sense of the cosmos and of the purpose of life: educational endeavors naturally flow from the religious impulse *pace* the often fraught and tense relationship between modernity and religion.[4] The intellectual phenomenon known as the Enlightenment is often seen as a necessary reaction again the structures of "unenlightened" religious faith, but this view fails to capture both the nuanced and complex intellectual activity that motivated some of the key thinkers of the Enlightenment

---

Orders, 1922–1965 (Bern: Peter Lang, 2004); Francis O'Hagan, *The Contribution of the Religious Orders to Education in Glasgow during the Period 1847–1918* (Lewiston, N.Y.: Edwin Mellon, 2006); Robert Dixon, "The Influence of Religious Teaching Orders on Catholic Schools in Canada Outside of Quebec," *International Studies in Catholic Education* (December 2019). Available online at https://www.tandfonline.com/doi/full/10.1080/19422539.2019.1691828.

2 United Nations, *Universal Declaration on Human Rights* (1948), article 18. https://www.un.org/en/about-us/universal-declaration-of-human-rights.

3 There is a wealth of material on the interaction between religion and education from both academia and the realms of public policymaking at the national and international levels. It continues to be a highly contested domain and, given its nature, will no doubt remain so.

4 Charles Taylor, *A Secular Age* (Cambridge, Mass.: The Belknap Press of Harvard University Press, 2018).

and the flexibility that the Church has often shown when faced with the call to reform its structures and ways of dealing with new thinking.[5] As Charles Taylor has shown, the loss of a sense of enchantment in the contemporary "secular age" has played no small part in removing the soul, if not the appearance, of religion from society.[6] While anthropologists and sociologists will continue to study—as they should—how the religious longing of humanity expresses itself in visible and measurable ways, such as in rituals around food, worship, and family customs, religion is, at heart, a profoundly soulful and social phenomenon with a specific culture emanating from and directed according to its commands and directives.

It is not the case, however, that the religion-education nexus is a space without difficulties. In particular, as we know too well, some expressions of secularism seek to limit or remove the influence and language of religion from the public square in general and education in particular.[7] This is not a new way of thinking. Writing in 1974,

---

5 See, for example, Ulrich Lehner, *The Catholic Enlightenment: The Forgotten History of a Global Movement* (Oxford: Oxford University Press, 2016): 1–2, stating that the reforms and the style of Pope Francis did not fall from the sky but are deeply rooted in the reform movement that found expression in the Councils of Trent and Vatican II, but also in the Catholic Enlightenment. These events all took place in a time of turmoil and have in common the realization that a self-content church that is not dynamically reaching out beyond the pews is doomed to wither away.

6 Our question is how we moved from a condition in 1500 in which it was hard not to believe in God, to our present situation just after 2000, where it has become quite easy for many. A way of putting our present condition is to say that many people are happy living for goals which are purely immanent: they live in a way that takes no account of the transcendent. Taylor, *A Secular Age*, 143.

7 The banner behind which such groups gather is often the language of "inclusion," itself a noble and worthy concept but sometimes twisted to resemble an "exclusivist" ideology. Paradoxically, the concept of "inclusion" flows naturally from Christian anthropology, yet it often depicts traditional Catholic views on marriage, gender, and human sexuality as regressive modes of thinking with which no dialogue is possible.

the British political theorist, Paul Hirst (1946–2003), noted that the advance of secular thinking had already made "the whole idea of Christian education a nonsense."[8] (Similar sentiments are rarely far from the surface of educational thought today.) Hirst's immediate context was the reform of moral education in schools, but his lens is wide enough to include any form of schooling with a defined religious basis. A deeper criticism, that faith schools are sites of indoctrination and not authentic education, has been articulated (in syllogistic terms) by the educational philosopher Michael Hand, who concluded bluntly that these schools should be abolished, not embraced.[9] While this is not the place to engage deeply with such arguments, it is important to address in broad terms the wider issues related to the connections between religion and education.

Discussion of the extent to which religion in general and particular expressions of religion play a part in public life remains a problematic avenue down which to travel. Of course, if "play a part in public life" is interpreted as the Church's desire to receive certain privileges that are not offered to other groups in society, then a right-thinking person would be suspicious of the motivations around such overtures. From a Catholic perspective, what matters is how the Catholic population can contribute positively to the development of civil society. In this vision, lay people are called to be fully involved in contributing to wider secular life; they should not see themselves as "descending" into the world of education and other fields as representatives, so to speak, of the hierarchy.[10]

8 Paul Hirst, *Moral Education in a Secular Society* (Warwick: University of London Press, 1974), 77.
9 Michael Hand, "A Philosophical Objection to Faith Schools," *Theory and Research in Education* 1, no. 1 (2003): 89–99. For a response to Hand's paper, see Douglas Groothius, "On Not Abolishing Faith Schools: A Response to Michael Hand and H. Siegel," *Theory and Research in Education* 2, no. 2 (2004): 177–88.
10 While believers might see the influence of religion on society as a public good, this is not self-evident to those who are not "religious" in the sense of identifying as practicing members of a religious tradition. There continues to be much research on the interface of religion, education, and wider society. See

Catholic education is not just one aspect of the life of the Church; rather, it is of its essence, flowing, as it does, from the liturgy—the lifeblood of the Church.[11] This broadens both the educational vision and mission of the Church beyond the life of specific institutions such as schools, colleges, universities, and seminaries specifically dedicated to the work of human and religious formation.[12] To be part of the Church, therefore, is to let oneself be educated and, in turn, to educate others. The linking of liturgy and education reveals the liturgy, in the words of Romano Guardini, as "a tremendously compelling form of expression, which is a school of religious training and development of the Catholic who rightly understands it, and which is bound to appear to the impartial observer as a cultural formation of the most lofty and elevated kind."[13] There is a need to reclaim and refresh this union.[14]

---

for example: Robert Jackson, "Religion, Education, Dialogue and Conflict: Editorial Introduction," *British Journal of Religious Education* 33, no. 2 (2011): 105–9. A counterview to this narrative is offered by Liam Gearon, "European Religious Education and European Civil Religion," *British Journal of Educational Studies* 260, no. 2 (2012): 151–69. In this field, an interesting (if slightly tangential) demographic study on educational levels was carried out by the Pew Research Center. See *Religion and Education around the World*, 2018, available online at https://www.pewresearch.org/religion/2016/12/13/religion-and-education-around-the-world/.

11 Vatican Council II, Constitution on the Sacred Liturgy *Sacrosanctum Concilium* (December 4, 1963), 14.

12 Stephen J. McKinney, "A Catholic Understanding of Education," in *Reclaiming the Piazza III: Communicating Catholic Culture*, ed. Ronnie Convery, Leonardo Franchi, and Jack Valero (Leominster: Gracewing, 2021), 191–210. Arguments in favor of this wider vision as applied to higher education are also found in John Sullivan, "Catholic Universities as Counter-Cultural to Universities PLC," *International Studies in Catholic Education* 19, no. 2 (2019): 190–203.

13 Romano Guardini, *The Spirit of the Liturgy*, trans. Ada Lane (New York: Crossroads Publishing Company, 1997), 47.

14 See Pope Francis, Apostolic Letter *Desiderio Desideravi* (*On the Liturgical Formation of the People of God*) (June 29, 2022), 62: "I would like this letter to help us to rekindle our wonder for the beauty of the truth of the Christian celebration, to remind us of the necessity of an authentic liturgical formation."

Discussion of the relationship between religion and education is not restricted to debates over the place of a particular subject—religious education (or the equivalent)[15]—on a school timetable, nor is it about the availability of religious worship in schools. Rather, it refers to the extent to which religion, broadly understood, informs educational thought and practice in a plural society. Catholicism claims to illumine and enlighten the human mind, nudging it away from the inclination to sin and toward an openness to the transcendent and a love of God.[16] This has implications for the curriculum, the corporate life of an educational institution, and the professional "identity" of educators in Catholic establishments.

To reiterate, Catholicism is a religious tradition with its own rites of worship, long-standing intellectual and pastoral traditions, and a distinct understanding of the cosmos, which includes a particular vision of the human person. Owing to these multiple and oft-contested perspectives, and in order to identify its many interwoven traditions, it is also in order to describe Catholicism as an educational movement. The British theologian, Nicholas Lash (1934–2020), encapsulated this mission as "the integration of worship and enquiry, of thought and contemplation" which cannot but offer valuable educational opportunities.[17] This "educational movement," therefore, emerges from and is shaped by the cluster of doctrinal formulae, liturgical rites, social practices, and pastoral initiatives that are rooted in and emanate from the life of the Church. It is the *cultus* that supports an ongoing and vibrant "Catholic culture" that should lie at the heart of the believer's daily life and, in turn, encourages believers to share this cultural heritage with others.

---

15 The subject could also be called, for example, religious studies or religious and moral education.
16 Congregation for Catholic Education, *Circular Letter to Presidents of Bishops' Conferences on Religious Education in Schools* (May 5, 2009), 10.
17 Nicholas Lash, "The Church: A School of Wisdom?," In *Receptive Ecumenism and the Call to Catholic Learning: Exploring a Way for Contemporary Ecumenism*, ed. Paul Murray (Oxford: Oxford University Press, 2008), 63–77 at 69.

In this light, a bigger claim can be made for religion's contribution to the development of the expressed culture of society. Christopher Dawson noted that religion's role as a guardian of traditions ensured it both a conservative and a dynamic function as "the great central unifying force in culture" and keeper of moral laws.[18] It is natural to inquire further, however, about what is implied by the term "culture" when viewed through a Catholic lens. There is an obvious danger in a privatized interpretation wherein culture is understood as little more than what my family or community believes and practices at a given point in time. Important as that might be for particular individuals and families, Catholic education as a corporate endeavor can be expressed, for example, in the construction of spaces that, at their best, are accessible oases of learning and relationship-building at the heart of society. An obvious example could be the rise of the medieval university system that emerged from the life and mind of the Church.[19] Alongside such historically conditioned spaces of higher education are more recent initiatives seeking to embed a Catholic culture, or way of life, in society—the Sant'Egidio Community in Rome and the Scholas Occurrentes movement are two contemporary examples of the "Catholic mind" seeking to influence society in direct ways.[20]

18 Christopher Dawson, *Religion and Culture* (Washington, D.C.: The Catholic University of America Press, 2013), 37.
19 For example, in his papal bull of 1451, Pope Nicholas V (1397–1455; pope from 1447) authorized the foundation of the University of Glasgow. The following extract, written in response from an appeal by the then King of Scots, James II (1430–60), for a university to be founded in Glasgow, is a window into the partnership between faith and reason that continues to underpin the Catholic approach to education: "To the end that there the Catholic faith may be spread, the simple instructed, equity in judgement upheld, reason flourish, the minds of men illuminated, and their understandings enlightened." See full text of the bull at the University of Glasgow website: https://www.universitystory.gla.ac.uk/papal-bull/.
20 For information on the Rome-based San Egidio Community see here: https://www.santegidio.org/pageID/1/langID/en/HOME.html. Information about Scholas Occurrentes is available at VaticanNews.va, May 17, 2022.

When we think of fresh ways of presenting ancient messages, it is hard not to alight on the phenomenon of the "New Evangelization" as a backdrop to the life of the Church in the early twenty-first century. Although geared toward restoring in some way the fast-fading colors of Christianity in the industrialized West (or Global North), the New Evangelization is, in some respects, a fresh articulation of a venerable educational principle: the search for a properly ordered relationship between the old and the new. There are strong scriptural reasons to value the interplay between what we have inherited and what we bequeath to future generations. The words of Jesus in Matthew 13:52 are instructive: "Therefore every scribe who has been trained for the kingdom of heaven is like a householder who brings out of his treasure what is new and what is old."[21] This refers to the scribes who are attached to the Old Law but are now called to embrace the New Law. The words of Jesus could also be applied with equal force to all the baptized today as a challenge to develop and renew their inherited faith tradition.

Catholic education is, no more and no less, the working-out of the words of Jesus above by engaging critically with and adding to the current store of human knowledge and skills. This respect for our common inheritance is much more than an unthinking yes to what is already available for study but is open to new and fresh insights that go beyond existing patterns of thought. Such thinking underpinned Pope John XXIII's vision for Vatican II. His address at the opening of the council is an unambiguous reminder to the present age of the interplay between the old and the new: "The greatest concern of the Ecumenical Council is this: that the sacred deposit of Christian doctrine should be guarded and taught more efficaciously."[22] John

---

See https://www.vaticannews.va/en/pope/news/2022-05/pope-chirograph-schola-occurentes-private-association-faithful.html.
21 From the Navarre Bible, which uses the Revised Standard Version translation of the New Vulgate Bible.
22 Pope John XXIII, "Address at the Opening of the Second Vatican Council," October 11, 1962.

XXIII hints here at deficiencies in presentation and educational methods—the "sacred deposit" of faith and its associated traditions need new methods to maintain their vitality. This is as true today as when the council opened in 1962.

Commitment to understanding the correct relationship between the old and the new, so to speak, is the mark of the authentic Catholic educator who cannot and must not be enclosed in a neverending repetition of the same material but is called to exemplify a positive and forward-thinking intellectual vigor. For example, St. Thomas Aquinas shows us how to interrogate inherited doctrine with intellectual tools recovered from the ancients.[23] In so doing, Aquinas as teacher-theologian is refreshing the content and the method of presentation of the Church's teaching so that it can speak to and have fruitful dialogue with new audiences.

The call to dialogue implicit in Catholic education has been more or less explicit at different points in history. As the early Christian community emerged from its Jewish roots and sought an accommodation with Greek thought, profoundly educational implications became visible in the catechumenate and in the early texts from figures such as St. Clement of Alexandria and St. Cyril of Jerusalem.[24] The deep educational imprint of the early Church is still visible today in its commitment to, for example, intercultural dialogue in education, a robust faith-reason partnership, and the desire to show that the baptismal call is not simply another lifestyle choice, but an open invitation to enter into the fullness of life.

What does this line of thinking mean for our evaluation of the Shields's work? An answer begins with a recognition of the elastic

---

23 For more on Aquinas and education, see Jānis T. Ozoliņš, "Aquinas, Education and the Theory of Illumination," *Educational Philosophy and Theory* 53, no. 10 (2020): 967–71.

24 Cf. Clement of Alexandria, "The Instructor," in *The Writings of Clement of Alexandria*, vol. 4, *Ante-Nicene Library Translations of the Writings of the Fathers Down to AD 325*, ed. Alexander Roberts and James Donaldson (Edinburgh: T and T Clark, 1867), 113–349; Edward Yarnold, *Cyril of Jerusalem* (London: Routledge, 2000).

nature of Catholic education as founded on a distinct set of ideas rooted in history but open to dialogue in light of new findings in the sciences. The rise of Progressivism in late nineteenth- and early twentieth-century America—the period in which Shields was at the height of his powers—certainly offered profound cultural challenges to how Catholicism could be expressed in educational terms, and was, therefore, an invitation to deep reflection on the purpose of education. Shields surely drew from some of the insights offered by Progressivism and hence acted as a conduit for reform in the theory and practice of Catholic education. Below we will explore the challenges that wider Progressivism presented to the Catholic educational project, with a particular focus on the work of one its leading lights, John Dewey.

PART II

RESPONDING TO PROGRESSIVE THOUGHT

CHAPTER 2

PROGRESSIVISM AND CATHOLIC EDUCATION

Chapter 2 explores the relationship between Progressivism and educational thought in America in the late nineteenth and early twentieth centuries. It will investigate what this cluster of ideas meant for Catholic education. This is a necessarily brief sketch of the wider field of play on which Shields operated and to which he referred in his work. This is where we can begin to assess the extent to which Shields incorporated new thinking into his well-formed Catholic identity, with chapter 5 offering a fuller treatment of this relationship.

Initial Thoughts on Progressivism

"Progressive" is an emotive term. Few are those who would wish to impede the march of progress, so to speak, if it means a general improvement in a particular situation: the cook wishes to make progress in culinary skills, the student seeks to make progress in attaining knowledge, the amateur golfer makes progress by scoring more pars and fewer bogeys, and so on.

Pope Paul VI noted in *Populorum Progressio* that the Church as a community of believers has a duty to advance the sociocultural conditions in which people live.[1] Drawing on the Church's established body of social teaching, Paul VI placed social progress at the heart of the mission of the Church. In so doing, he was reminding the Church of the implications of Christian faith for the organization of society. His use of "progressive" in this document, therefore, is, on one level, about visible and practical improvement, but placing this direction of travel firmly within his wider religious vision.

To extend the reach of the term "progress" to the larger society, including to education, using associated words like Progressivism and the adjective "progressive" should lead to a deeper examination of what is claimed by this extended use. This is where the waters become slightly muddier; in other words, there is no shared agreement about what we mean by "progress."[2]

In the field of education, Progressivism, in broad terms, refers to how educational methods respond to children's stages of natural development.[3] It recognizes that the development of the human mind requires suitable and appropriate teaching methods if the child is to develop in knowledge and attitudes. As a set of concepts, this is commendable and, of course, essential to Shields's educational thought. More problematically, however, the term "progressive" is now often attached to a raft of ideas expressed chiefly by those whom the Church would see as advocates of cultural relativism. There are progressive policies in economics, law and order, education, and such like, all of which are influenced, to a greater or lesser extent, by the

---

1 Pope Paul VI, Encyclical Letter *Populorum Progressio* (*On the Development of Peoples*) (March 26, 1967), introduction: "The progressive development of peoples is an object of deep interest and concern to the Church."
2 "As is true of the names of many movements, 'progressive' carried a wide range of meanings. Almost everyone in public life was in favor of progress, but the assumptions of what constituted progress were at times contradictory." Gabriel Moran, "Still to Come," *Religious Education* 98, no. 4 (Fall 2003): 496.
3 For a provocative treatment of this approach, see Kieran Egan, *Getting It Wrong from the Beginning: Our Progressivist Inheritance from Herbert Spencer, John Dewey, and Jean Piaget* (New Haven: Yale University Press, 2002).

view that society must gradually discard the inherited impediments to human flourishing which still have the potential to divide society along economic, racial, and cultural lines. In the progressive view, to be a conservative is to remain attached to ways of thinking that benefit the few, not the many, and is, in a sense, to deny the reality of the human person's march toward fulfilment.

Of course, this debate, as cursorily outlined here, has many manifestations and an overly schematic treatment of such deep issues leaves limited space for the informed and nuanced dialogue that should be expected in a mature society.[4] Otherwise, this question can too easily to lead to a poisonous "culture war" mentality in which victory over one's opponents takes precedence over the important search for a shared understanding of complex issues.[5]

In this light, it is essential to nail down the following: What does Progressivism mean in the context of reforms in US schools in the late nineteenth and early twentieth centuries, the timeframe in which Shields was an active scholar and practitioner? Who were its leading thinkers? Did they see themselves as belonging to a unified movement or is such a designation little more than a retrospective label? What effect, if any, did Progressivist thinking have on the life, culture, and curriculum of all schools, not just on Catholic schools? To address such high-level questions, we need a compass, and for this reason, the work of the influential educationalist, John Dewey (1859–1952), will be used as an example of Progressivist educational thought. It

---

4 An excellent introduction to this theme is found in Dawson, *Progress and Religion*.
5 See Francis, Encyclical Letter *Fratelli Tutti* (*On Fraternity and Social Friendship*) (October 3, 2020), 217:
> Social peace demands hard work, craftsmanship. It would be easier to keep freedoms and differences in check with cleverness and a few resources. But such a peace would be superficial and fragile, not the fruit of a culture of encounter that brings enduring stability.... Let us arm our children with the weapons of dialogue! Let us teach them to fight the good fight of the culture of encounter!

is not possible to appreciate the contribution of Shields to Catholic educational thought if there is no related recognition of the work of scholars like Dewey and the scope of wider Progressivist ideals.

Dewey, Education, and Democracy

Historians of education broadly differentiate between European Progressivism and American Progressivism.[6] The former was a fluid grouping of various individuals and charitable associations whose goal was the wider availability of educational opportunities and a better-educated population.[7] The latter had a sharper cutting edge, with ambitions of effecting a radical transformation not just in schools but in society at large. This would be done by a far-reaching transformation of American society, aiming for a rejection of knowledge understood as the foundation of a fixed external world and a related embrace of new educational methods emergent from science and psychology.

At first blush, it might seem that such ways of thinking would sit uncomfortably with traditional religious worldviews. Catholicism claims that there is such a thing as truth (or Truth in the divine person of Jesus Christ), and that the analysis of experiences, while valuable insofar as it helps the person-searcher to come closer to the divine, cannot be the sole energy source of education. Unsurprisingly, the thrust of the Progressive movement in American education at this time, in contrast to the work of the European Progressivist educator Maria Montessori, saw religion as foe, not friend, because

---

6 "In the years leading up to the First World War there were very few progressive schools in Europe; most were in England, where middle-class enthusiasm for voluntary provisions favored the multiplication of independent schools which, if privately owned rather than instruments of a church or society, could engage in progressive activities." James Bowen, *A History of Western Education*, vol. 3, *The Modern West, Europe and the New World* (London: Methuen, 1981), 402–3.

7 For more on Progressivism, see Walter Nugent, *Progressivism: A Very Short Introduction* (Oxford: Oxford University Press, 2010).

religiously conditioned perspectives seemed to reflect the idea of a fixed external world.

Dewey, while advocating ideas that Shields would adapt (as opposed to adopt), did not assign any particular value to the role of religion in education.[8] From his roots in a classical education, Dewey gradually embraced and advocated for a reform of schooling based on the insights arising from scientific experiment and the analysis of subsequent data. In this he was influenced by and carried on the work of the English polymath Herbert Spencer (1820–1903).[9] Opposed to the perceived rigidity of a pedagogy that seemed to bypass the needs of the developing child, Dewey sought to reshape the school as a place where the child's natural curiosity was aroused and social experiences highlighted as a source of educational progress and, ultimately, where a more democratic form of schooling would be made visible.[10]

The American democratic movement was much more than another political voice but became close to a social philosophy aimed at the transformation of American society.[11] For Dewey and the

8 A contemporary parallel might be the tendency by some religious educators to advocate, or at least see some merit in, "worldviews" as an alternative to traditionally religious viewpoints. On the one hand this can be seen as a way to engage in dialogue with those who are far from religion, although it is easy to understand why others would see it as a diminution of the religious aspect of the subject. See Trevor Cooling, with Bob Bowie and Farid Panjwani, *Worldviews in Religious Education* (London: Theos, 2020), 27–28: "A straightforward way of thinking about it is to describe it as constituting both the conscious and the hidden assumptions that people and communities hold. In other words, worldview is constituted by those deeply held, unquestioned beliefs and taken-for-granted ways of behaving that often only come to the forefront of our attention when they are challenged in some way."
9 Egan, *Getting It Wrong*, 15: "Spencer aimed to show how learning and development, and the daily activities of the classroom, were parts of the same laws that shaped the stars above and the earth below."
10 See also the educational theories of Johann Friedrich Herbart (1776–1884). For an introduction to Herbart's work, see https://www.britannica.com/biography/Johann-Friedrich-Herbart.
11 See Royal G. Hall, "The Significance of John Dewey for Religious Interpretation," *The Open Court* 6, article 2 (1928): 331–32: "Democracy was

wider Progressive movement, the intrusion of democratic ideals into education was not simply an expression of radical political activism, but reflected a heartfelt desire to widen the perceived narrowness of the educational methods and, indeed, bodies of knowledge that were predominant in schools at that time. This shift in perspective required classrooms to become "an experimental laboratory of data collection and democratically arrived-at communal judgments resulting in forward-looking actions. Meaning-making occurred through such action."[12] For Dewey, it was the experiences formed in the classroom that would shape the future of American society and thus it was important to get things right from the beginning of the child's life in school.

In such intellectual contexts, it was logical for Dewey to advocate an inductive approach to knowledge, in which critical and accompanied reflection on a host of personal and community experiences would form the primary source material for educational advancement. This pedagogical option would prepare pupils, he argued, for a more active and engaged participation in school and wider society:

> A society which makes provision for participation in its good of all its members on equal terms and which secures flexible readjustment of its institutions through interaction of the different forms of associated life is in so far democratic. Such a society must have a type of education which gives individuals a personal interest in social relationships and control, and the habits of mind which secure social changes without introducing disorder.[13]

---

something more than a mere political arrangement: it has become a social philosophy voicing new attitudes and calling for new interpretations of life."

12 William R. Myers, "John Dewey, God and the Religious Education of the American Public," *Theology Today* 74, no. 2 (2017): 165.

13 John Dewey, *Democracy and Education: An Introduction to the Philosophy of Education* (Delhi: Aakar Books, 2004), 106.

Dewey, therefore, saw the school as a unique environment wherein special attention should be paid to "influencing the mental and moral dispositions of their members" in a way that matched his social philosophy.[14] Of course this ambition, lest we forget, is shared by advocates of Catholic education. For Dewey, the most effective way to influence the development of the child was to create a classroom atmosphere that enabled the child to grow and flourish according to the laws of development.[15] In this way Dewey emphatically positioned the school as a key part of an overall *exit strategy* for pupils with, in his view, overly strong religious influences in their home environment. Arguably, Dewey saw the school as an alternative home, a fertile "training-ground" for the communication of the all-important democratic spirit that pervaded the wider Progressive movement. Consequently, inherited knowledge, so to speak, should only be transmitted selectively; that is, when it served what Dewey saw as its higher democratic purpose:

> As a society becomes more enlightened, it realizes that it is responsible *not* to transmit and conserve the whole of its existing achievements, but only such as make for a better future society. The school is the chief agency for the accomplishment of this end.[16]

14 Dewey, *Democracy and Education*, 21.
15 In his address to the inaugural congress of the Religious Education Association in 1903 Dewey stated as follows:
> It is a question of surrounding the child with such conditions of growth that he may be led to appreciate and to grasp the full significance of his own round of experience, as that develops in living his own life. When the child is so regarded, his capacities in reference to his own peculiar needs and aims are found to be quite parallel to those of the adult, if the needs and aims of the latter are measured by similar reference to adult concerns and responsibilities. John Dewey, "Religious Education as Conditioned by Modern Psychology and Pedagogy," *Religious Education* 69, no. 1 (1974): 7.

16 Dewey, *Democracy and Education*, 22.

Dewey is here veering toward the notion that knowledge has to be "useful," with the corollary that some knowledge, therefore, is "not useful." As Kieron Egan has noted, problems around making inert knowledge alive and relevant to new contexts are not resolved by *excluding* such domains of knowledge from the curriculum.[17] This is always a lazy response to the perennial questions around how to connect in a meaningful way existing bodies of knowledge with the needs of new generations of students.

Dewey seems to be making a full-frontal assault, albeit cloaked in respectable language, on the ideals of education as found in "communities defined by one religion, such as Medieval Christendom or the life of the Jewish villages or shtetels of Eastern Europe"; indeed, any culture in which religion is a "defining collective way of life."[18] He saw schooling not as a complement to the educational responsibilities of the family but as a site of alternative ideas that were both urgent and necessary for the construction of a good society. For Dewey, progress toward a democratic society needed an embrace of democratic ideals, and a society that was overly rooted in expressions of authority in families and churches would be an impediment to this aspiration. This had implications, obviously, for how he saw religious education.

Dewey and Religious Education

Dewey saw value in the multiple bodies of knowledge, traditions, and customs of the human race, while simultaneously questioning the place of organized religion in the educational process. Indeed Dewey saw a school devoid of religious influences as somewhat more advanced than institutions attached to organized religion. Shields was aware of this line of thinking, as we see in his "Notes on Education" in the first volume of the *Catholic Educational Review*:

---

17 Egan, *Getting It Wrong*, 148: "The intentions may be noble and for the best, but the flaw inexorably leads to catastrophe."

18 Thomas Alexander, introduction to *A Common Faith*, by John Dewey, 2nd ed. (New Haven: Yale University Press, 2013): xxx.

"Professor Dewey assures us that the public schools are developing a new and higher form of religion that is devoid of all denominational character."[19] This knowledge sharpened Shields's desire to ensure that Catholic education had a sufficiently robust scientific basis to repel Progressive designs on the intellectual basis of Catholic educational thought.

Dewey's claim that his educational vision is "religious" can be supported in the broadest understanding of the term—in the sense of "religious" meaning shared bonds and obligations—but, crucially, with democracy and the democratic spirit replacing the creeds and commandments of religion.[20] Dewey makes this clear in *A Common Faith*, where he argues that the growth of "knowledge and of its methods and tests" has shaken the foundations behind many of the religious beliefs current in society, which, he claimed, are increasingly "dubious."[21]

Dewey denied that there was such a thing as "religion," preferring to accept the existence of many religions and religious ideas. However, in attempting to separate "religion" from "religious" he fails to convince us that he is not simply forcing a distinction on the basis of inadequate evidence.[22] Referring to particular religions, he

19 Thomas Shields, "The Teaching of Religion," *Catholic Educational Review* 1 (January 1911): 56.

20 As observed by Christopher Dawson:

> Now Dewey, in spite of his secularism, had a conception of education which was almost purely religious. Education is not concerned with intellectual values, its end is not to communicate knowledge or to train scholars in the liberal arts. It exists simply to serve democracy, and democracy is not a form of government, it is a spiritual community, based on "the participation of every human being in the formation of its social values." Thus every child is a potential member of the democratic church, and it is the function of education to actualize his membership and to widen his powers of participation. Christopher Dawson, *The Crisis of Western Education* (Washington, D.C.: The Catholic University of America Press, 2010), 79.

21 Dewey, *A Common Faith*, 30.

22 Moran, "Still to Come," 497. "A distinction in the connotations of the two terms is helpful but the attempt at total separation seems quixotic."

noted that "the differences among them are so great and so shocking that any common element that can be extracted is meaningless."[23] At the end of his essay *A Common Faith* he makes a strong case, unsurprisingly, against the place of traditional religious faith in education and society, favoring instead a commitment to the "common faith of mankind." The following from *A Common Faith* leaves the reader in no doubt about his position:

> The ideal ends to which we attach our faith are not shadowy and wavering. They assume concrete form in our understanding of our relations to one another and the values contained in these relations. We who now live are parts of a humanity that extends into the remote past, a humanity that has interacted with nature. The things in civilization we must prize are not of ourselves. They exist by grace of the doings and sufferings of the continuous human community in which we are a link. Ours is the responsibility of conserving, transmitting, rectifying and expanding the heritage of values we have received that those who come after us may receive it more solid and secure, more widely accessible and more generously shared than we have received it. Here are all the elements for a religious faith that shall not be confined to sect, class, or race. Such a faith has always been implicitly the common faith of mankind. It remains to make it explicit and militant.[24]

The sentiments expressed above merit careful reflection. The use of seemingly "religious" language is noteworthy. Dewey's willingness to employ terms such as "faith," "nature," "values," and "grace" is significant as a marker of the collectivist vision he favored. Such terms, while not owned by religion as such, do resonate with the Catholic Intellectual Tradition and remind us of the human desire

---

23 Dewey, *A Common Faith*, 8.
24 Dewey, *A Common Faith*, 87.

to seek meaning and develop shared bonds. Dewey's "common faith of mankind" is humanistic and religious only in its recognition of the shared quest he outlines and seeks. Ultimately it is a velvet-gloved denial of the validity of religion as a contributing factor in education, although a case could be made, however slight, that the door is open (just) to further dialogue on the aims and nature of education.

Dewey himself addressed the question of a specifically "religious education" in an article published in 1903 in the journal *Religious Education*. Interestingly, the article consists of the text of an address he gave to the first annual convention of the Religious Education Association. The title of the article, "Religious Education as Conditioned by Modern Psychology and Pedagogy" sets out a strong educational rationale for applying new pedagogical and psychological insights to the teaching of religious ideas. The rationale underpinning his approach to religious education comes at the end of the essay:

> The title indicates that it is possible to approach the subject of religious instruction in the reverent spirit of science, making the same sort of study of this problem that is made of any other educational problem. If methods of teaching, principles of selecting and using subject-matter, in all supposedly secular branches of education, are being subjected to careful and systematic scientific study, how can those interested in religion—and who is not?—justify neglect of the most fundamental of all educational questions, the moral and religious?[25]

This suggests that religious education had to be open to being reframed as a critical study of religious ideas and shed pretensions to explicit faith-formation. The tools for this endeavor are the emerging methods of teaching, and this is where we find some parallels with the work of Shields, who would indeed ground his Master Plan on

---

25 Dewey, "Religious Education as Conditioned by Modern Psychology and Pedagogy," 10–11.

similar principles. Shields would be especially attracted by Dewey's clear presentation of the human maturation process—which Shields saw, unsurprisingly, as God-given—and by what psychological theory meant for the integral development of the human person.[26]

Conclusion

Chapter Two has drawn the wider framework within which Shields's work can be understood. This imperative necessitated what might seem to be a detour through the world of Dewey and wider Progressivist ideas.

Essentially, Dewey saw religious beliefs as sociohuman constructs whose roots are found in the cultures in which they originated. Yet we see some common ground in how he places the democratic spirit on the pedestal Christians would offer to scripture and revelation. For Dewey, the ideals and goodwill found in Christianity are best brought to fruition when the social order allows such ideals—shorn of their religious roots and foliage—to flourish.[27]

Dewey's advocacy of a universalist, democratic and increasingly spartan "common religion" might have spared the US from religion-based conflicts but also had the potential to reduce long-standing and intellectually demanding faith traditions to not much more than an abstraction in a democratic society.[28] For the Catholic educator,

---

26 "I shall endeavor to present simply one principle which seems to me of help in this interpretation: the stress laid in modern psychological theory upon the principle of growth and of consequent successive expansions of experience on different levels." Dewey, "Religious Education as Conditioned by Modern Psychology and Pedagogy," 6.
27 Hall, "The Significance of John Dewey," 337.
28 Moran, "Still to Come," 498, puts it this way:
> In some ways, Dewey's search for a religious unity free of the conflicts of religion embodies the best and the worst of United States culture in the twentieth century. Catholics, Protestants and Jews have been able to find a meeting place under the umbrella of "religious." The United States of the past century has been able to avoid most of the religion

any attempt to condense rich religious traditions within the umbrella term "religions" is a step too far. While the social sciences must be valued in any Catholic vision of education, a commitment to empiricism alone could diminish the rich humanistic traditions which have traditionally been cherished and nurtured in the Catholic Intellectual Tradition. In addition, social scientists themselves are not necessarily free from bias so their findings must be treated as critically as the views expressed by humanistic scholars.[29] The encounter between Progressivist educational thinking and religiously conditioned educational aims was always going to be tense, and some might argue that this is still the case.

Ultimately, while Dewey was aware of the need to study matters mystical, moral, and religious, his work presented a major challenge to Catholicism's educational foundations. A response was needed.

---

[29] conflicts that affect much of the world. The drawback is that "religious," standing by itself, tends to become an abstraction or generality. The more conservative or traditional branches of Jewish, Protestant and Catholic religions have never fully embraced an education described as "religious." Let me hasten to add that I don't share their naivete about what the social sciences can do for us, nor their assumptions that these sciences—they really mean psychology—are inevitably innocent of bias or of jaundiced views. They make it sound as if all we need do is turn to psychology to "provide the facts necessary for a positive basis of a constructive movement" (Dewey), and all will be well. Would that it turned out to be that simple? But even as we move beyond their naïve empiricism, and decline such messianic bandwagons henceforth, let us continue to draw critically and creatively upon the insights of the social sciences. Thomas H. Groome, "Remembering and Imagining," *Religious Education* 98, no. 4 (Fall 2003): 518.

CHAPTER 3

A CATHOLIC RESPONSE TO DEWEY

In chapter 3, there is first an examination of the considerable impact the Religious Education Association (REA) had on the developing subject of religious education and the life of schools in America more generally. It then looks at the how the Church responded to emerging democratic ideals—central to Progressivist thinking—and concludes with an examination of catechisms as an educational resource.

The Religious Education Association and Catholic Education

The apparent split between the ideals of Progressivism and religion during the time of Shields was not binary. The formation of the Religious Education Association (REA) in 1903 and its associated journal, *Religious Education*, was a sign of an initial accommodation between Progressivism and some Protestant denominations.

The REA fostered a certain sense of unity and harmony among religiously minded educators, although in its early days it was "predominately Christian in its representation, and heavily mainline Protestant in its beginnings."[1] While there is no record of Shields

---

1 Theodore W. Brelsford, "Editorial Introduction," *Religious Education* 98, no. 4 (Fall 2003): 409.

having a direct working relationship with any of the key people of this association, there are clear lines connecting the educational vision advocated by the REA and the general pedagogical approach promoted by Shields.

The early years of the REA serve as a window into the complex relationship between Progressive thought and religious ideals. The REA's inaugural event was a convention held in Chicago in 1903, during which the president of the REA, Professor William Rainey Harper (1856–1906), an academic and Baptist clergyman, read out a long list of twenty propositions that would serve as a "charter" for its work.[2]

John Dewey was one of the invited speakers. It might seem like a surprise that someone like Dewey—given his well-known distaste for religious forms of schooling—was invited to a gathering of people exploring religious topics.[3] His presence at the gathering is a stark reminder of the importance of the Progressive movement to developments in religious education. There was a belief, however, that the REA's commitment to scholarly study of religious and moral education, by drawing on the scientific work of people like John Dewey, would be a helpful boost to the promotion of inter-religious tolerance, as well as serving to enhance the knowledge base of Christians.[4]

2   For a summary of the life of Professor William Rainey Harper, see the following page from the website of the University of Chicago: https://president.uchicago.edu/directory/william-rainey-harper.

3   I find it amazing that the organizers of the first meeting of the REA should have invited John Dewey to be the keynote speaker. They surely knew the view he held of the church by 1903. It also surprises me that Dewey agreed to give the talk. Although most of the organizers were committed Christians, they had enough distance from the church that they could credibly invite Dewey and that Dewey would accept. But here is where the strength and the weakness of the meaning of "religious" is evident both for Dewey and the REA. Moran, "Still to Come," 497.

4   At the turn of the century there was optimism among REA founders that religious education might nurture inter-religious tolerance and understanding as well as informed belief and commitment. Harper was also

The REA positioned itself, rightly, as the harbinger of fresh thinking in the field of religious and moral education. It made big claims about the work that it could both coordinate and carry out. It was alive with the excitement generated by new ideas and fresh ways of working and there can be little doubt about the sincerity of the Christian and academic commitment of its founders. Interestingly, and despite the claim to have a "universal spirit," there is no mention in the REA's early literature of active engagement with groups with obvious connections to Catholic educational institutions, although Bishop John Spalding (see introduction) was approached to be a member of the original council (he did not take up the offer).[5] This shows a partial opening, at least, toward the world of Catholic education, but it was one that did not advance very far initially.

While we will leave until later a closer examination of the work of Shields in the US context, it is imperative first to take the temperature of the more general response in American Catholic educational circles to Progressivism. Successive popes had challenged to a greater or lesser extent the new ways of thinking that had adversely influenced education and had had a negative effect on family, cultural, and socioeconomic issues.[6] Clearly the intellectual thrust of Progressivism did not lend easily itself to supporting established Catholic

---

motivated by his own passions as a biblical scholar for sharing new insights from modern scientific biblical studies with lay Christians. Harper and other early REA leaders held the conviction that education in communities of faith and other religious associations can and should have rigor and integrity equal to that of education in the schools. He envisioned an organization that would support the advancement of high quality religious and biblical education in a spectrum of contexts, through coordination of existing efforts as well as sponsorship of new initiatives. Brelsford, "Editorial Introduction," 408.

5 Spalding was elected to the REA's original council of religious education but illness might have prevented him from taking up his duties. See Boardman W. Kathan, "Horace Bushnell and the Religious Education Movement," *Religious Education* 108, no. 1 (2013): 50–51.

6 See John L. Elias, "Catholics in the REA, 1903–1953," *Religious Education* 99, no. 3 (2004): 243:

thinking in education.[7] To be clear, the problem lay in the Church's understandable insistence that education had to consider "man's eternal destiny," not just the aspirations toward preparing "a man of culture, good moral character and many-sideness of interest."[8]

Another layer of tension arose from the implications of the Church's catholicity. In other words, it was no easy task to belong to a universal Church while simultaneously endeavoring to be good citizens of America. Catholic bishops had to tread carefully if they wished to avoid exacerbating the precarious position of Catholics in American society.[9] There seemed to be some form of opposition—*pace* Leo XIII's *Immortale Dei*—between a *democratic* (American) and a *monarchical* (Catholic) mindset.[10] As an Irish American Catholic and a scholar open to new ideas, Shields found himself working between these clearly drawn lines, which had at that time the potential to fracture the Catholic Church in America.[11]

The decidedly liberal orientation of the early REA was not conducive to Catholic membership. During this time Catholic liberals or modernists were under attack by the Vatican. The *Syllabus of Errors* of Pope Pius IX in the mid-19th century, Pius X's Encyclical against modernism, and an imposed oath against modernism demanded of priests and seminary professors put the church strongly against liberal tendencies in theology and education. Liberal theologians would again come to the fore only with the emergence in the 1950s of the *Nouvelle Theologie* in France.

7 "This progressive movement in education had overtones unacceptable to Catholic educators; its principles and Catholic philosophy were poles apart. Catholics saw in all these new educational movements an intellectual and social development with religion banished from the schools." Buetow, *Of Singular Benefit*, 170.
8 Buetow, *Of Singular Benefit*, 169.
9 Buetow, *Of Singular Benefit*, 175, offers an outline of how "Americanism" was seen as a possible occasion of a fracture in the universal Church.
10 Murphy, "Thomas Edward Shields: Religious Educator," 1.
11 "The Americanism crisis, the question of the identity of the American Catholic Church, plus the problem of modernism, the early twentieth century heresy, challenged the Church's image of herself." Murphy, "Thomas Edward Shields: Religious Educator," 1. See also Buetow, *Of Singular Benefit*, 175–76. The serious charge of "nativism"—the labeling of Catholics as "un-American"—

Of course, the debates in which Shields and the Church in America were immersed were not unique to America. The papacy of Leo XIII (1810–1903), as George Weigel has suggested, marked the Catholic Church's incipient dialogue with modernity.[12] What Weigel calls the "Leonine Revolution" was, in fact, a determination to use the multiple tools of what we now call the Catholic Intellectual Tradition as a means of persuading others to appreciate the richness and benefits of the Catholic vision of society. His famed social encyclical, *Rerum Novarum*, is but one example of his contribution to developing the Church's engagement with societal ills.[13] Leo's successor, Pope Pius X (1835–1914), prioritized major (and necessary) reforms in catechesis. A country priest at heart, Pius X, like Shields, was determined to deepen the catechetical work of the Church. His now largely forgotten encyclical, *Acerbo Nimis*,

---

could easily have brought about the withdrawal, forced or otherwise, of Catholics from public affairs.

12 George Weigel, *The Irony of Modern Catholic History: How the Church Rediscovered Itself and Challenged the Modern World to Reform* (New York: Basic Books, 2019), 72.

13 Pope Leo XIII, Encyclical Letter *Rerum Novarum* (*On Capital and Labour*) (May 15, 1891). In 1885, Leo XIII wrote one very short encyclical on education, *Spectata Fides*, addressed to the bishops of England. While localized in scope, there is recognition of the wider educational and cultural situation that could endanger children. Referring to voluntary schools in England, as well as elsewhere in Europe, he noted as follows:

> In these schools the liberty of parents is respected; and, what is most needed, especially in the prevailing license of opinion and of action, it is by these schools that good citizens are brought up for the State; for there is no better citizen than the man who has believed and practiced the Christian faith from his childhood. The beginning and, as it were, the seed of that human perfection which Jesus Christ gave to mankind, are to be found in the Christian education of the young; for the future condition of the State depends upon the early training of its children. The wisdom of our forefathers, and the very foundations of the State, are ruined by the destructive error of those who would have children brought up without religious education. Leo XIII, Encyclical Letter *Spectata Fides* (*On Christian Education*) (November 27, 1885), 4.

proposed improved catechetical activity as a way to counter the lack of Christian belief in the baptized.[14] Despite this welcome option for catechetical reform, Pius X did not on the whole share his predecessor's willingness to engage positively with modernity, viewing it essentially as a phenomenon to be opposed.[15]

The tension between modernity and Catholicism came to a head in 1907 with the publication by Pius X of *Pascendi Dominici Gregis*. This encyclical identified a range of targets which had, he claimed, weakened the intellectual cohesion of Catholicism. The papal ire was directed not just at forces outside the Church but at those members of the Church, both lay and clerical, who were lax in their formation and who did not share his position on the importance of strong doctrinal formation.[16]

Pascendi's long critique of the many manifestations of modernism confirmed the papacy's firm stance against the danger to doctrinal and ecclesial cohesion posed by the rise of "new knowledge" and the many ideas clustered around it. Moreover, Pius X's words could also be interpreted as a refusal to acknowledge the work done by scholars like Shields, who were opening up new avenues for Catholic education in America (although there is no evidence of Shields's work having any influence in Rome at this time). Shields surely would have been aware of *Pascendi*'s arguments but clearly he did not see it as a barrier to his heartfelt desire to forge new paths in education. Despite their shared aim—catechetical and educational reform—the methods proposed by Pius X differed

---

14 Pope Pius X, Encyclical Letter *Acerbo Nimis* (*On Teaching Christian Doctrine*) (April 15, 1905), 2.

15 Weigel, *The Irony of Modern Catholic History,* 81: "For all his reformist instincts in terms of the Church's spiritual life, however, Pius X was unwilling to bend even an inch to political modernity."

16 Pius X, Encyclical Letter *Pascendi Dominici Gregis* (*On the Doctrines of the Modernists*) (1907), 2, referring to those who, "feigning a love for the Church, lacking the firm protection of philosophy and theology, nay more, thoroughly imbued with the poisonous doctrines taught by the enemies of the Church, and lost to all sense of modesty, vaunt themselves as reformers of the Church."

from the considered view of Shields. Essentially, Pius X favored the increased use of the genre of the catechism as a means to strengthen religious knowledge,[17] while Shields, as we will see, expressed doubts about the memorization of doctrinal formulae as the principal catechetical method for children.

In 1929, there were some faint signs of change in how the magisterium of the Church saw education. Pope Pius XI's encyclical, *Divini Illius Magistri*, sought to present a definitive response to modernism and the related new currents in educational thinking.[18] He had successfully negotiated a number of difficult political treaties, including the Lateran Pacts of 1929 that established the Vatican city-state. As a noted advocate of humanistic learning, his interest in education (broadly understood) was a spur to his writing what remains, to date, the only papal encyclical on education. In addressing both pedagogical and theological issues, the encyclical is a crucial primary source for understanding the developing papal response to new educational ideas. It is an instructive example of how wider Catholic thinking oscillated between a desire to welcome insights from scientific advances and a stronger desire, it seemed, to prevent such insights from damaging the faith commitment of the ordinary Catholic. As such, the encyclical could be interpreted as a very cautious approval of the pioneering educational reforms done by Shields and others at Catholic University in the early years of the twentieth century. Although there is no direct mention of Shields's work in the encyclical, it is not beyond the bounds of possibility that knowledge of the broad reforming spirit found at Catholic University was known to some members of the Roman congregations.

17 See Pius X, *Catechism of Christian Doctrine* (Dublin: M. H. Gill, 1914).
18 Pope Pius XI, Encyclical Letter *Divini Illius Magistri* (*On Christian Education*) (December 31, 1929). Pius XI was elected bishop of Rome in 1922. His papacy spanned the difficult years between the end of the First World War and the start of the Second World War. His awareness of the diplomatic and political tensions in interwar Europe would have opened his eyes to the possibilities offered by dialogue between opposing parties.

The Church, Education, and Democracy

Dewey's commitment to democratic ideals in the widest sense should not strike the contemporary Catholic as necessarily odd or out of place—far from it. In 2020 the Pontifical Foundation Gravissimum Educationis, in alliance with a number of universities worldwide, set in motion an ambitious project to examine how "democracy" and its institutions could respond to the many new challenges it faces in the early years of the twenty-first century. The goals of the project are set out thus:

> The project aims to start educational trainings capable of transforming democratic practices, informing them of the positive values of peace, solidarity and the common good. In this way, the project wants to support the harmonious co-existence of citizens with different religious faiths, ethical visions and traditions in pluralistic democratic social systems based on the mutual recognition of identities and related legitimate interests.[19]

The extent to which the passage above is a reflection of a specifically Christian educational project is debatable. For some it could be no more than a demonstration of the final arrival of the Deweyan spirit into the Catholic mind. Yet there is scope to take a more nuanced view. An intentional commitment to the development and reform of democratic ideals from a Catholic perspective builds on Leo XIII's encyclical *Immortale Dei*, in which he works through the relationship between eternal truths and the role of states, going so far as to encourage people to look favorably on democratic structures, albeit with the proviso that Catholic doctrine must not be neglected in the building of a fair society.[20] Both apologetic and dialogic in tone,

---

19 Pontifical Foundation Gravissimum Educationis, "Democracy: An Educational Urgency in Pluricultural and Plurireligious Contexts" (2020). Available at: https://www.fondazionege.org/en/progetti/democracy-an-educational-urgency-in-pluricultural-and-plurireligious-contexts:12237/.

20 "Neither is it blameworthy in itself, in any manner, for the people to have

Leo's encyclical highlights the importance of both an active faith and civil engagement without being blind to the temptation toward naturalism and rationalism. Leo's central aim, as always, was "to revive the Church's position as the central moral force in society."[21]

In reality, however, it was not always easy to have such an irenic position. Another practical example of initial suspicion toward new ideas (including democratic ideals) can be found in Pius X's *Our Apostolic Mandate*, issued in 1910 and, therefore, contemporaneous with Shields, Dewey, and American Progressivism.[22] *Our Apostolic Mandate* is a practical application of the principles enunciated in *Pascendi*. Pius X was addressing the French bishops in the context of the work of Le Sillon (The Furrow), a Catholic movement founded by Marc Sangier in 1894 that sought to reform French society in the light of Catholic social principles. While praising the idealism and energy of its leaders, Pius nonetheless cautioned against the way some members of the movement had been too quick to advance a radical agenda, which, he believed, did not serve the Catholic ideal.[23] He was unambiguous about the challenges arising from Le Sillon and his charge, as set forth in the quotation below, could be interpreted today as a preemptive strike against the ideals Dewey would soon advocate:

> To sum up, such is the theory, one could say the dream of the Sillon; and that is what its teaching aims at, what it calls the democratic education of the people, that is, raising to its maximum the conscience and civic responsibility of every one,

---

a share greater or less, in the government: for at certain times, and under certain laws, such participation may not only be of benefit to the citizens, but may even be of obligation." Leo XIII, Encyclical Letter *Immortale Dei* (*On the Christian Constitution of States*) (November 1, 1885), 36.

21 Jay P. Corrin, *Catholic Intellectuals and the Challenge of Democracy* (Notre Dame, Ind.: University of Notre Dame Press, 2002), 62–63.

22 Pius X, Letter to the French Bishops *Our Apostolic Mandate* (August 25, 1910). https://www.papalencyclicals.net/pius10/p10notre.htm.

23 Adrian Dansette and James A. Corbett, "The Rejuvenation of French Catholicism: Marc Sangnier's Sillon," *The Review of Politics* 15, no. 1 (1953): 48.

from which will result economic and political Democracy and the reign of JUSTICE, LIBERTY, EQUALITY, FRATERNITY.[24]

This comment raises many questions about the Church's view of democracy. An initial response to the issues raised by democracy is rooted in the nature of truth itself and brings to the fore questions such as the extent to which believers are bound by laws that are, in Catholic eyes, an offense against truth.[25] While justice, liberty, equality, and fraternity are, lest we forget, rooted in the Christian worldview, the extension of the democratic ideal into the domain of religion and morality could lead to a form of a moral relativism that would then undercut the very ideals necessary for an orderly society. In stark terms, if moral principles are decided by democratic processes, the possibility of objective truth is denied. In such a climate, a cohesive body of doctrine and an associated moral code is increasingly necessary for ecclesial and societal cohesion. A catechism or some central repository of accepted Catholic teaching could be the appropriate means for ensuring the faithful transmission of this heritage when apparently hostile forces are gathering at the gate.

Catechisms as an Educational Resource

Dewey depicted catechism-based religious education as the imposition of an adult understanding of religion onto young people. It was the "grown person's" standard that privileges those who have reached

---

24 Pius X, *Our Apostolic Mandate*.
25 The furor in 2020 over the appointment of Amy Coney Barrett to the US Supreme Court shows once again the tension between those whose beliefs are rooted in a Catholic worldview and the exponents of progressive politics. The editorial board of the *New York Times* had this to say on Judge Barrett's appointment: "When she takes her seat on the bench at One First Street, it will represent the culmination of a four-decade crusade by conservatives to fill the federal courts with reliably Republican judges who will serve for decades as a barricade against an ever more progressive nation." https://www.nytimes.com/2020/10/26/opinion/amy-coney-barrett-supreme-court.html.

majority. Doubtless, Dewey would see any model of education which leaned heavily on a catechism (or any compendium of propositions for that matter) as inimical to the democratic spirit in education, not just in matters religious. Nonetheless, he is happy to pass a particularly negative judgment on a catechism-based approach to religious education:

> Once admit the rightfulness of the standard, and it follows without argument that, since a catechism represents the wisdom and truth of the adult mind, the proper course is to give to the child at once the benefit of such adult experience. The only logical change is a possible reduction in size—a shorter catechism, and some concessions—not a great many—in the language used.[26]

Dewey's words might seem attractive as a helpful articulation of the importance of getting the language and tone of educational literature right. He seems unaware, however, that the Catholic Church had already recognized, in principle at least, the pedagogical deficit brought about by using "adult language" for children. Dewey is also unaware, it seems, of the various genres, or styles, that fell under the heading of "catechism," leading to his rather harsh and one-sided understanding of religious instruction as a book-tied process obviously lacking in warmth, humanity, and community spirit. In the wider Catholic tradition, the genre of "catechism" did not necessarily imply a question-and-answer approach, although this would have been the impression given by the Baltimore Catechism, which was the standard catechism for Catholics in America at that time.[27] It is thus reasonable to suggest that Shields's understanding

---

26 Dewey, "Religious Education as Conditioned by Modern Psychology and Pedagogy," 7.
27 For more on the circumstances around the publication and diffusion of the Baltimore Catechism, see David Malloy, "The American Hierarchy, The Propaganda Fide, and Composition of the Baltimore Catechism," *Records of the American Catholic Historical Society of Philadelphia* 103, no. 2 (Fall 1992): 35–46.

of a catechism-based education did not reflect this more general history of the catechism as a genre and that he fell into the same trap as Dewey in seeing catechisms in overly monochrome tones.

In contrast, the famed Catechism of the Council of Trent (also known as the Roman Catechism, published in 1566), in its combination of doctrine and methodological guidance, served as a teaching manual for priest-catechists in the turbulent years known as the Counter-Reformation or the Catholic Reform.[28] The Council of Trent (1545–63), often unfairly depicted as the harbinger of hard-nosed responses to a prevailing spirit of reform, had mandated an adaptation of catechetical methods to better serve the needs of children. To do this, it issued guidance to parish priests on how to catechize all their parishioners effectively:

> [They] shall at least on Sundays and solemn festivals either personally, or if they are lawfully impeded, through others who are competent, feed the people committed to them with wholesome words in proportion to their own and their people's mental capacity.[29]

The words "their own and their people's mental capacity" are crucial, recognizing both the limitations of the priest-catechist and the limitations of the people to be catechized. This is not the place to reflect speculatively on what such limitations might have been, but we can at least identify therein some understanding, however limited,

[28] The aim of the *Roman Catechism*, as stated in its Preface, was to offer a conspectus of the Catholic theological tradition in the context of broader spiritual development. Significantly, the *Roman Catechism* offered clear direction on teaching methodology. In keeping with the approach of the Canons and Decrees of the Council of Trent on preaching and teaching, it recommended a differentiation according to age and capacity. This is another important sign of an increasingly sophisticated understanding of how catechesis should be developed. Leonardo Franchi, *Shared Mission: Religious Education in the Catholic Tradition* (London: Scepter, 2017), 51–52.

[29] Session 5, chapter 2, "On Preaching," in *Canons and Decrees of the Council of Trent*, trans. H. Schroeder (Rockford, Ill.: Tan Books, 1978), 26–28.

of the dynamic processes of human growth and maturation—and what they mean for education—that propelled the work of Dewey and Shields.[30]

Regarding sacramental worship, the Council of Trent also stressed the importance of adapting material to the "audience":

> That the faithful may approach the sacraments with greater reverence and devotion of mind, the holy council commands all bishops that not only when they shall first, in a manner adapted to the mental ability of those who receive them, explain their efficacy and use, but also they shall see to it that the same is done piously and prudently by every parish priest, and in the vernacular tongue, if need be and it can be done conveniently, in accordance with the form which will be prescribed for each of the sacraments but the holy council in a catechism which the bishops shall have faithfully translated into the language of the people and explained to the people by all parish priests.[31]

In this guidance, "mental ability" is identified, alongside the "vernacular tongue," as key components of a catechesis that is accessible to a wide range of people. While the language is clearly ecclesiastical-clerical in tone, there is recognition of the importance of experience and community as essential parts of the catechetical process. The examples from Trent and the Roman Catechism bring to light the awareness in Catholic circles of the importance of good methodology for the success of the educational enterprise. How much of this was lost, forgotten, or ignored in subsequent years is

---

30 While Shields was always quick to praise the advances in pedagogy he encountered, he rarely mentioned John Dewey's influence, although he did pen a favorable review of one of Dewey's texts, *Schools of Tomorrow*. See Thomas Shields, review of *Schools of Tomorrow*, by John and Evelyn Dewey, *Catholic Educational Review* 16, no. 11 (November 1918): 344–46.

31 Session 24, "Decree Concerning Reform," chapter 7, "On Sacraments," in *Canons and Decrees of the Council of Trent*, 197.

up for debate; we can say, however, that Progressive movements in education, as exemplified by Dewey—and to some extent Shields himself—were not offering methodological insights that would have been foreign to informed Catholic ears, even if their starting points were not aligned with the intellectual and spiritual frameworks presented by Catholicism.

Conclusion

Dewey's oeuvre in general, with its desire to foster a democratic spirit, can be interpreted as a movement toward the socialization of American society through education. The sharing of experiences in the classroom would, in this view, take the child away from individualism and closer to a shared democratic mindset. Interrogated by a Catholic "worldview," the Deweyan vision does aim to foster social cohesion and a sense of shared humanity—which is clearly a good thing—but pushes this too far so as to usurp individual freedom by marginalizing the insights of religion for the betterment of the human condition.

For the Catholic educator, Dewey is an example of how new thinking in psychology can positively influence educational methods and is hence a field worthy of study. His contribution to educational thought is of universal significance as a response to rapidly changing sociocultural conditions and the advance of scientific knowledge, but he committed the methodological flaw of breaking the link between noble aspirations for a democratic "good society" and what is, for Catholics, that society's scriptural foundation.[32] In a sense

---

32 See Richard John Neuhaus, "The Real John Dewey," *First Things* (January 1992):

> Dewey's great mistake was to think that he could break those truths away from their necessary and continuing dependence upon biblical religion. He lived in a time when the best and the brightest were miseducated to believe that traditional religion was simply beyond the pale of plausibility for the truly enlightened. The cultural hegemony of that rationalist dogma is no longer very secure. Indeed it is collapsing all around us.

Dewey's work was the harbinger of contemporary debates on the compatibility of religious ideas and scientific knowledge. His desire to loosen society and its structures from the influence of religious ideas—motivated by a passionately evangelizing attitude toward the democratic spirit—played no small part in creating multiple sources of authority, which is a marker of postmodernity.[33] But that is another tale for another time.

Shields's ambivalence toward the REA might suggest, however, a possible aloofness with respect to other traditions of Christianity, reflecting the reality of his status as an established figure rooted in his Catholic heritage and, in turn, not inclined to reach out in practical ways to people espousing other ways of thinking. His packed schedule of teaching, writing, and administration might have been a limiting factor. Shields, however, was convinced that the new pedagogical insights of the time, when examined in light of Catholicism's intellectual tradition, actually manifested the veracity of the teaching methods of Jesus as recounted in the gospels and thus sought confirmation from science of what he already "knew" from faith, which is an interesting position. In this tense cultural and political climate, Shields was one of the principal advocates of intellectual dialogue between such new thinking and classic Catholic theology. Chapters 4 and 5 will offer a deeper examination of how Shields sought to forge a new path through this ever-growing field.

It is curious that Shields rarely mentioned Dewey and his work by name. Neither did he become involved in organizations such as the REA, when it seems that such a body would have given his ideas a courteous hearing at least. The story of the REA, like all scholarly bodies, is complex, nuanced, and open to multiple interpretations. Its continued existence, and the ongoing significant impact of the

---

33 "In retrospect, given the cultural context of his time, a religiously educated 'common' faith was an illusionary liberal hope; instead, in retrospect, what we've come to call postmodernity (with its multiple authorities) was inevitable." Myers, "John Dewey, God and the Religious Education of the American Public," 15.

journal *Religious Education*, suggest more success than failure. Sociologists of religion and historians of education will continue, rightly, to explore the extent to which religious forms of schooling have made a valid contribution to social cohesion. The history of the REA will be central to such ongoing scholarly endeavors in the American context and elsewhere.

In the linking of the scholarly and the practical, Shields mirrors the work of John Dewey and other lights of the Progressive movement who were not content simply to write about education but wished to set in motion a true reform of systems and curricula, the desired effect of which would be a transformation of the child's experience in school. Shields was, therefore, a figure who straddled the apparent gap (to put it crudely) between Progressive ideals and Catholicism's vision of society. The following chapter will examine the extent to which his educational vision sought to reconcile what seemed to be divergent intellectual and cultural currents.

PART III

SHIELDS AND

THE REFORM OF PEDAGOGY

CHAPTER 4

DEVELOPING A FRAMEWORK FOR REFORM

An important characteristic of Shields's writing is his love for the concrete and the practical, which was doubtless linked in part to his experience of growing up on the family farm. Shields's educational principles, as set out in his many articles and books, offer a set of keys to support and guide the theory and practice of Catholic education in light of new knowledge about the psychology of education. The best examples of Shields's guidance in pedagogical matters are found in articles written between 1909 and 1911 in both the *Catholic University Bulletin*'s "Notes on Education" section and the *Catholic Educational Review*. A more substantial treatment of his ideas is found in *The Teacher's Manual of Primary Methods*, published in 1912 as volume 3 in the Catholic University Pedagogical Series, and *Philosophy of Education*, published in 1917 as volume 5 of the same series.[1] Both volumes build on an earlier work, *Twenty-Five Lessons in the Psychology of Education*, published in 1906.

While his commitment to the inherent value of academic research is obvious in his ample body of scholarly work, this was

---

1 Shields was the author of volume 1 of the Catholic University Pedagogical Series, *The Making and Unmaking of a Dullard*, and volume 2 of the series, *The Education of Our Girls*. Planned future volumes included works by Shields and other authors.

not at the expense of efforts to offer practical examples to guide practitioners. In chapter 4 there is an examination of the principles that Shields saw as essential to any good educational system. To illustrate Shields's attempt to inform Catholic education with fresh ideas, there now follows an exploration of Shields's pedagogical principles, ending with an example of the highly practical advice he offered to the teaching profession.

Shields's Pedagogical Principles

Principle 1—From the Static to the Dynamic

Shields saw Catholic education as a process involving many actors: family, clergy, teachers, and academics are all called to draw from the Church's intellectual and pastoral sources in support of their specific roles in the mission of education. Catholic thinking in education demands a dialogue with wider learning, which was crystallized in Shields's positive response to the many valuable educational insights emerging from Progressive thought.

Shields argued that it is the role of the teacher *in loco parentis* to communicate knowledge in a way that is suited to the child's capacity to understand what is being taught. In *Philosophy of Education,* Shields uses the example of a rosebush to show how a teacher, using wholly didactic methods, would explain its shape and structure, etc.[2] Following this, he then claims that the rise of the biological sciences demands no less than a fundamental change in methods of teaching.[3] Shields does not offer an immediate example of how new thinking would affect this particular lesson, which is unfortunate, but does provide an explanation of how the new methods—attributed to Thomas Huxley's *Evolution and Ethics*—would use the traditional tale of "Jack and the Beanstalk" as an educational parable. Doing this

---

2 Thomas Shields, *Philosophy of Education* (Washington, D.C.: The Catholic Education Press, 1917), 48.
3 Shields, *Philosophy of Education*, 47–48.

would show education as a response to what he calls, elliptically, the "cosmic process."[4]

Advances in science had challenged the notion that all of creation had come straight from the Creator's hand without any process of change or evolution. Shields's ideas are close to and seem to draw on the principles of doctrinal development as set out by St. John Henry Newman's *An Essay on the Development of Christian Doctrine*, first published in 1878, although there is no direct evidence of any formal link between them.[5] Newman's insights are normally employed in the context of theological developments, but his arguments as employed in *An Essay on the Development of Christian Doctrine* could be applied to the Catholic Intellectual Tradition: what matters is not change for change's sake but change understood as the fruit of an organic development that enlarges and sheds lights on what has gone before. All of this is part of a chain of events in which, Shields claimed, the study of history has increasingly shed light on how "a knowledge of the past is indispensable to an understanding of the process of becoming in which they [scholars] seek the key of the present and the indications of the future."[6]

Shields, therefore, acknowledged the importance of fostering positive change in educational methods but also argued that only a profound understanding of the history of education could adequately prepare the teacher to grasp fully the process of development that takes place in the mind of the child.[7] It is through an intentional

---

4 Shields, *Philosophy of Education*, 52.
5 Shields, *Philosophy of Education*, 52.
6 Shields, *Philosophy of Education*, 53. See also Thomas Shields and Edward A. Pace, *Twenty-Five Lessons in the Psychology of Education* (Washington, D.C.: The Catholic University of America, 1906), 41–42, where he again pairs Darwin with Newman. This volume is a set of lessons from a correspondence course for teachers (probably religious sisters) and was based on the premise that progress in understanding the scientific basis of education was actually beginning to reveal the pedagogical truths at the heart of the Catholic education system.
7 "The present concept and method of education are a growth and outcome

historical focus that it becomes possible to detect and appreciate the emergence of the school as an institution generated by the complex and interconnected webs made up of multiple familial and sociocultural traditions.[8]

The so-called processes of development that the teacher must consider come from the "reign of law" applicable to humanity as a whole. This idea is so powerful and profound that it demands no less than a change of attitude among everyone having an interest in education. The "reign of law" is of such conceptual potency that it has radically changed the meaning, purpose, and aims of education and the related role and responsibility of the teacher:

> The teacher has ceased to be a mere purveyor of facts; his function is to minister to the growing mind, to guide the complex processes of development that are taking place in the minds and hearts of his pupils. He has come to realize that the process of education as it takes place in the mind of the pupil is a vital process which is governed in all its phases by the laws of life and mind.[9]

This shift in the understanding of the role of the teacher, expressed by Shields in Deweyan language, cannot but have significant implications for how material is selected and taught in class. It places the human person squarely at the center of the educational process but not in a way that overemphasizes the self-esteem of the learner—a temptation into which it could easily fall. It is in this important context that our knowledge of the past becomes indispensable to a nuanced and informed understanding of the present.

---

of the past, and we shall understand them fully only by learning what has been their history and by studying the influences that have been playing on the minds of teachers, compelling them to change their methods." Shields, *Philosophy of Education*, 60.
8 Shields, *Philosophy of Education*, 322–23.
9 Shields, *Philosophy of Education*, 145.

For Catholic educators, according to Shields, the life of the mind ("conscious life") is nurtured by four clear sources:

> First in the direct revelation of the truth and beauty and goodness of God that reaches the individual through Revealed Religion; second, in the truth and beauty and goodness of the Creator as reflected in Nature; third, in the concrete embodiment of human thought and action; fourth in the manifestations of the human mind and heart through the arbitrary symbols of speech.[10]

We note here Shields's unsurprising commitment to the theological foundation of Catholic education as the articulation of "Revealed Religion." The focus on truth, beauty, and goodness is a reminder of the dynamism of education: the three transcendentals must be embodied in the life and action of the human person and not remain simply as objects for philosophical reflection, important as that might be. What is also clear is that Shields was conversant with the intellectual developments of his age and that he integrated many new insights and thinkers into his classes at Catholic University. Murphy notes as follows:

> When students entered Shields's intellectual world, they found it populated with strange bedfellows by Catholic 1906 standards. Since he was comfortable with the scientific thought of his day, he referred his classes to Darwin's Origin of Species, and the work of men such as James Spencer, and Huxley. The Catholic University professor's study on psychology stressed the words "growth," "adjustment," "plasticity," "dynamic," which were the terms of the emerging secular progressive educators.[11]

Shields sees no value, and only harm, in laying his religious faith to one side when discussing scientific advances. While this could be a potential barrier to his thought migrating into (contemporary) secular

---

10 Shields, *Twenty-Five Lessons*, 36.
11 Murphy, "Contribution of the Human Sciences," 83.

discussions on educational reform, it offers evidence of the bridges uniting the Creator and the created, the educational importance of the Incarnation of God in Jesus Christ, and the network of relationships that give life to communities. As such, it is a presentation of the foundations of a truly Catholic understanding of education that offers a hand of welcome to genuine scientific progress.

Principle 2—Plasticity

Another key feature of Shields's educational vision was his understanding of plasticity:

> It means the power to change and dominate environment quite as much as the power to dominate and change the individual. Indeed, plasticity as a vital power should include this positive faculty, this ability to change environment in many ways so as to make it meet the needs of self. Adjustment means change both in the individual and in his environment, and education, to be efficient under present conditions, must develop in each individual this two-fold power.[12]

Plasticity offered an invaluable means of equipping pupils to deal in an effective way with all of the social, economic, and cultural challenges they would inevitably face in life. It was not enough just to know and revere the past, as could easily be inferred, albeit incorrectly, from his appreciation of the history of education; neither was it sufficient to be adaptable to what was already known in the present moment—what mattered ultimately was the human person's ability to adapt and adjust oneself successfully to new circumstances, whatever these might be and whenever they might arise.[13]

Education was the environment in which plasticity was realized. Indeed, an essential mark of a good school is how effectively it

12 Shields, *Philosophy of Education*, 66.
13 Shields, *Philosophy of Education*, 67.

promotes plasticity in its pupils. It is not enough simply to replicate former / current pedagogical approaches—each pupil in the school should be fully supported on the journey to human flourishing, which plasticity should facilitate, with the teacher as the cornerstone of this vital process.[14] This is especially important in the early years of school when the child is most pliable.[15] The importance of the teacher's role in this process is such that Shields makes a point, curiously, of describing what the teacher should *not* do:

> Those teachers who fail to recognize the fact that their function is to minister to the process of growth and development in the mind of the child, proceed with their work after the manner of architects and builders. They delve in the mines of truth and make their bricks of knowledge with which they proceed to build up stores of information in the minds of pupils. In this procedure the intelligence of the pupil is used to recognize the several parcels of knowledge, to attach to each of them an appropriate label, and to store them away in the memory in accordance with any system that will enable him to find them whenever a future need arises.[16]

Shields is arguing here against a view of teaching as the ability simply to effect a successful transfer of knowledge from the mind of the teacher to the mind of the child. He claims that such "memory load" actually makes authentic assimilation of knowledge difficult.[17] While Shields agrees that the memory grows in power when exercised, an overworked or overloaded memory is of little lasting educational benefit:

14 Shields, *Twenty-Five Lessons*, 47.
15 "The plastic period of individual life is the period of the mental development and it is confined to the morning of life." Shields, *Philosophy of Education*, 131.
16 Shields, *Philosophy of Education*, 108.
17 For more on the importance of a rounded education, see James Schall, *Another Sort of Learning* (San Francisco: Ignatius Press, 1988).

In like manner, in all efficient education, the teacher supplies abundance of suitable material, prepared to meet the needs of the pupil's developing mind. The pupil is surrounded by favorable conditions and he is thus enabled during the short years of his school life to come into the possession of the rich inheritance prepared for him by the conscious efforts of the race. But he and only he can build the mental structures. There is no royal road; he must, by his own efforts, aided by all suitable extrinsic helps, pass step by step through the long series of developmental phases which will finally bring him to the highest level of civilization attained by his race.[18]

This extract offers an interesting interplay between the effort of the teacher to provide what Shields calls "thought material" (see below) and the desire (or ability) of the child to put in the mental effort required to improve in knowledge, although it is possible that we could be moving close here to a Pelagian view of learning that stresses personal effort above the promptings of grace. Shields makes use of powerful imagery to argue firmly against the overload of memory as a general educational principle and is not shy in repeating his view that teaching methods must move from the "didactic" to the "organic" if plasticity is be realized.

Principle 3—Adjustment

Shields makes big claims for the notion of adjustment. The young child entering school for the first time cannot just be parachuted into a desk in a class full of strangers (who would wish that anyway?) but needs a smooth, supportive passage from the family home to the more formal school environment.[19] The necessary process of adjustment

---

[18] Shields, *Twenty-Five Lessons*, 133.
[19] See part 1 of Thomas Shields, *Teachers Manual of Primary Methods* (Washington, D.C.: The Catholic Education Press, 1912). Here Shields provides a considerable amount of practical detail, most of which is not explicitly religious in

consists of an aggregation of activities designed intentionally to mimic the structure of home—"the wellspring of authority"—while simultaneously introducing the child to the wider community of the school with its need for friendship and cooperation.[20] Religion, unsurprisingly, is both the binding force in the adjustment process and the element that will most easily help the child absorb the atmosphere of the school.[21] Shields, unlike Dewey, saw the school as an extension of the life and culture of the home.

As an institution working to support the educational mission of the family, the school soon "became the means of enlarging and perfecting the educative process itself."[22] The nurturing instincts

---

its nature. For example, on p. 31, Shields tells us that the child must not be allowed to sit still for a long period of time. Much of this advice need not detain us here, but it is worth mentioning that, for Shields, a sense of loving order (which is God-given) is crucial for the success of the home-to-school adjustment process. See also chapter 7 (pp. 51–67), entitled "The Child's First Day in School," for a highly detailed, step-by-step guide for teachers. NB: The *Teachers Manual of Primary Methods* was published in 1912 as volume 3 of The Catholic University Pedagogical Series. It is a collection of crisply written chapters with a strong practical focus. Even when the chapter headings suggest rather more abstruse topics, he often proffers practical advice, concrete examples, and direct recommendations. Given this commitment to enhancing practice, it is right to see this text as the foundation stone of his desire to prepare teachers for service in Catholic schools.

20 Shields, *Teachers Manual of Primary Methods*, 30.
21 Shields, *Teachers Manual of Primary Methods*, 31, asserts that

religion, above all things else, binds the home and the school together and makes of them parts of a larger whole. Just as in our travels the sun, the moon, and the stars accompany us and make us realize that there are bonds which bind together the most distant lands, and as the Catholic who on his journey in foreign lands enters a Catholic church and assists at Mass realizes that he is in his Father's home, and for the time being ceases to think of color and race, national boundaries and intervening oceans, so the properly taught child on entering school brings with him God, Jesus, Mary and Joseph, his Guardian Angel, and all the inhabitants of the spiritual world.

22 Shields, *Philosophy of Education*, 321.

inherent in family life had to be present in the life of the school if it (the school) were to be a successful partner to parents in adjusting the individual child to, in Shields's own words, "the institutions on which Christian civilization rests. These are chiefly the home, the state and the church."[23]

Shields's lofty ideals about the contribution of Christianity to family life were not, of course, unique to him and remain fundamental to any authentically Catholic understanding of education.[24] At the same time, he did not see life in the home as immune to reforming insights originating from beyond the Church. He thus anticipated Pius XI's observations in *Divini Illius Magistri* that the family is not a perfect society "since it has not in itself all the means for its own complete development; whereas civil society is a perfect society, having in itself all the means for its peculiar end, which is the temporal well-being of the community."[25] In other words, the family needs the support of civil society if it is to discharge its important responsibilities effectively.[26] If the home is truly to be a school of life, the findings of the educational sciences on human behavior and development should surely influence the raising of children.[27] In

23 Shields, *Philosophy of Education*, 277.
24 See Vatican Council II, Declaration on Christian Education *Gravissimum Educationis* (October 28, 1965), 3, which speaks of the three "authors of education" as family, civil society, and the Church.
25 "Nevertheless, the family is an imperfect society, since it has not in itself all the means for its own complete development; whereas civil society is a perfect society, having in itself all the means for its peculiar end, which is the temporal well-being of the community." Pius XI, *Divini Illius Magistri*, 12.
26 Pius XI, *Divini Illius Magistri*, 12.
27 Shields had very traditional views on the roles to be played in family life by the husband and the mother: in brief, the former was oriented (externally) toward the world of work outside the home; the latter, even if she had experience of the workplace after leaving school or college, was oriented toward the building of a home. As a corollary, Shields believed that a woman's education had to prepare her satisfactorily for the important role she would play in building a family home and raising children. For more on this, see Shields, *Philosophy of Education*, 289–90.

other words, as teachers needed to be well trained to be successful practitioners, so too do those who have the responsibility of forming homes and raising children if they are to carry out the responsibilities of homemaking and parenthood appropriately.[28]

The process of adjustment demands of both parents and pupils a cooperative spirit and an appreciation of the importance of play for child development. It also involves an appreciation of the communicative power of both spoken and written language, including what Shields describes as essential thought material. Referring to the pupil, Shields observed:

> He must grow, day by day, towards an understanding of the great fundamental truths that will later on serve him in adjusting himself to God and to his fellow man. He has, as yet, little or no ability to derive food material for himself from nature and still less power to derive nutriment for mind and heart from books.[29]

The dependence of the human child on others for the supply of basic human needs is a metaphor, of course, for the human dependence on God. Similarly, the maturing child in the school requires the necessary fostering of copious thought material through the provision of educational resources of high quality. The purpose of such an approach is not just to entertain the class and respond to each child's predilections and need for stimulation but, crucially, to introduce the child to the truths that will be developed in time into a vivid spiritual inheritance.[30]

---

28 "Those who undertake the work of teaching should be familiar with advances made in the educational sciences, but should we not demand with at least equal justice that those who take upon themselves the responsibility of founding homes and bringing children into the world should learn how children are to be brought up?" Shields, *Philosophy of Education*, 294.
29 Shields, *Philosophy of Education*, 41.
30 Shields, *Philosophy of Education*, 42.

Principle 4—Correlation

In the project of correlation, religion is the capstone and demands to be the fulcrum around which the curriculum revolves:

> Religion, to be effectively taught, must be interwoven with every item of knowledge presented to the child and it must be the animating principle of every precept which he is taught to obey. Without thorough correlation of religion with the other subjects of the curriculum, it can never take its proper place in the developing life of the child. It will remain a mere garment to be donned on Sunday and laid aside Monday morning when the real business of life is undertaken. The proper correlation of religion with the other subjects of the curriculum does not imply that religion should not be taught as a separate study when the right stage of mental development for the systematic teaching of separate branches is reached, but it does require that in the early phases of the child's development, such as those usually found in the first and second grades, the teaching of religion be so intimately interwoven with every truth that is presented to the child as to leave but little room for separate formal religious instruction.[31]

Religion, therefore, is not necessarily an extra subject on the timetable as such but, as a body of knowledge and social practices, informs and shapes the school curriculum without making the other curricular domains simply annexes to it. There is flexibility in how and when religion becomes a discrete subject, but Shields is of the view that in the early years of formal education (grades 1 and 2), religion should be woven into an integrated curriculum. It is only in grade 3 that religion emerges as a subject alongside other subjects.

31 Thomas Shields, "Correlation in the Teaching of Religion," *Catholic Educational Review* 1 (May 1911): 425.

This synthesis is not an easy task to accomplish but it is the role of the teacher to make this happen and to "lay the foundations of Letters and Sciences, of Aesthetics, Institutions and Religion."[32]

Correlation does not happen automatically but involves a high level of teaching skill. An early example of correlation in practice is Shields's own *Index Omnium*, an early work, published in 1888 (when he was sixteen years old), which was, in effect, both a study plan and reference book. In this book, it is said (there are no known copies available) that he gathered all the necessary facts and information available to him at that point in his educational journey, painstakingly cross-referenced and checked. This, it is reasonable to argue, is clear evidence of a mind that needs to see patterns and connections and is a curtain-raiser to his later work on correlation.[33]

As experienced teachers of young children will verify, frequent changes of activity are essential to maintain their interest, but this is not in itself a path to curricular fragmentation. On the contrary, it could offer scope for an increased range of thought material that should, ideally, be both a contributor to and evidence of correlation. Multiple examples of thought material are found in the textbooks and readers of his *Catholic Education Series* (see part 5). Essentially, the principle of correlation demanded the integration of knowledge, but for Shields it means the influence of religion across the whole curriculum. How this is achieved is not easy to articulate. It requires initially some trial and error but essentially demands a collegial attachment to the vision of the Catholic school and the unifying principle of religion.

32 Shields, *Teachers Manual of Primary Methods*, 42; Shields, *Twenty-Five Lessons*, 113.
33 "The *Index Omnium* served its chief purpose in its effect upon his own mind as he composed it; for he found that when he had entered a thought under all the possible headings under which it might be of use, he had already developed a habit of thinking of each subject in a rich and fecund way and of correlating it with everything else that he knew." Ward, *Thomas Edward Shields*, 94–95.

*Principle 5—The Relationship between
Mental Development and Mental Growth*

Shields differentiated between mental development and mental growth.[34] The distinction is important for him: the former refers to the process that makes the mind of the child into the mind of the adult; the latter is the gathering, or accumulation, of knowledge. If teachers are to do their job effectively, they must ground their approach firmly in the necessary insights from the discipline of psychology. This requires a definite ordering of material so that the content is taught at the appropriate moment for the developing child. Otherwise, the mind of the child might suffer as "arrested mental development may easily result from excessive and untimely mental growth. This is particularly true in the early stages of the educative process."[35] In simple terms, thought (or mental) development is no less than the ability to absorb, think through, and engage critically with all manner of subject matter.[36] In Shields's view, there is little value in the development of the memory as the primary pedagogical instrument, despite its favored status in other educational systems.[37]

To avoid the pitfall of an unbalanced approach to the provision of thought material, and also in order to foster mental growth in

---

34 Shields, *Philosophy of Education*, chapter 7. This is a very technical chapter exploring growth and development with concrete examples from biology.
35 Shields, *Philosophy of Education*, 131.
36 Building on the distinction between accumulation of knowledge and thought development (see above), Shields identifies four stages of thought development: 1) the function of memory; 2) thought development in textbooks; 3) collateral reading; and 4) dramatization. Chapter 15 of *Philosophy of Education* provides a good amount of detail on this way of working.
37 "When the aim is erudition, the exact form will be committed to memory by frequent repetition. This method prevails in China and it has held sway for long centuries among the Hindoos. And while it does not find many champions among our modern educational thinkers, it still prevails to no small extent in many of our class-rooms." Shields, *Teachers Manual of Primary Methods*, 186.

DEVELOPING A FRAMEWORK FOR REFORM

pupils, Shields proposed a fivefold educational plan under the following headings: aesthetic, institutional, religious, literary, and scientific.[38] This plan expands and gives life to the four sources of "conscious life"; that is, revealed religion, nature, thought / action, and speech. The fivefold pathway (or set of instincts) is designed to promote a broad-based education with a strong focus on attaining a fluent cultural knowledge. The curriculum as so planned would forge an apparently liberal path, which should allow for sufficient balance between the demands of mental growth and development and, crucially, prepare pupils for specialization as and when appropriate.[39]

In this context, Shields is especially sharp in his comments on practices like memorizing the catechism in the classroom:

> Swallow a catechism, reduced to a verbal memory product. Pack away the essence of morals in a few general laws and rules, and have the children learn them. Some day they may understand. What astounding faith in memory cram and dry forms![40]

This statement is clearly in line with Dewey's ideas on the value of catechism for young people. It is a rejection of so-called traditional catechetical methods—and the ways of working with the Baltimore Catechism—that would have been very much in vogue in his day.[41] It shows a desire to forge of a new way of thinking in order to reform catechetical methods according to new insights from the sciences. Shields is not content, however, simply to aim his fire at the teaching of religion. Other subjects too have suffered from the use of dry

---

38 Shields, *Twenty-Five Lessons*, 113, diagram.
39 "Culture, or a liberal education, demands a symmetrical development along these five lines, and in so far as an individual falls short of this his culture is defective and his education insufficient. Specialization should follow culture; it should not precede it and it cannot dispense with it." Shields, *Twenty-Five Lessons*, 120.
40 Shields, *Philosophy of Education*, 110.
41 See also Shields, *Twenty-Five Lessons*, 76, where he again notes that overuse of the memory in catechesis fails to recognize the laws of mental development.

teaching approaches, which, to use his forceful expression, "result in dead accumulations instead of living growth."[42]

These are strong words, and Shields argues that the best way forward involves both a *looking back* and a *looking forward*. In this apparent state of tension, he foreshadows the vivid debates around the two hermeneutical keys—*ressourcement* and *aggiornamento*—that fed into and colored the life of the Church in the twentieth century, especially in the years following Vatican II.[43] As noted above, Shields looks forward by placing his trust in scientific advances that will, he believes, lead educators toward the adoption of new, evidence-based teaching methods. Shields is hence aligning himself with aspects of the Progressive movements in education. Where he differs fundamentally from Dewey and his ilk, however, is in the belief that such advances would, in fact, corroborate the teaching methods of Jesus as recorded in the gospels.[44] This places Shields squarely in the camp of those who valued inherited traditions while still having the leeway to question educational traditions if new knowledge emerged.

While admitting that memorization is not unique to the domain of religion, he is wholly unconvinced that it can lead to the formation of a "robust Christian character," which is one of the chief ends of a Catholic education.[45] For primary school pupils, Shields held that

42 Shields, *Philosophy of Education*, 111.
43 "The Council revolved around the twin axes of *ressourcement* and *aggiornamento* and the fruit of its deliberations was a set of documents which made, and continue to make, a deep impact on contemporary Catholic life." Franchi, *Shared Mission*, 124. See also Henri de Lubac, *The Splendor of the Church* (San Francisco: Ignatius Press, 1986) and Yves Congar, *Diversity and Communion* (New London: Twenty-Third Publications, 1985) for examples of how the so-called Catholic intellectual revival informed thinking in ecclesiology. It is also helpful to consider how reform of ecclesiology is related to developments in catechesis and education.
44 "Psychology and pedagogy demand a return to the method of teaching which was employed by the Master, who so frequently spoke of the truths which He came into the world to impart to the children of men, but which He refused to announce to those who were not ready to assimilate them and render them functional in their lives and conduct." Shields, *Philosophy of Education*, 111.
45 Shields, *Teachers Manual of Primary Methods*, 187.

"the pupil's growth in knowledge should not be advanced beyond the point where such growth is necessary or helpful to mental development."[46] In other words, the acquisition of knowledge is, at its best, a contributor to the integral development of the human person and is not, and never can be, an end in itself.[47] Shields illustrates this point by linking it to the educational journey of each pupil: those pupils who are more likely to leave school as young teenagers ("eighth grade") should have their mental growth advanced; that is, a greater acquisition of knowledge in a shorter timeframe so that they can play a part in adult life when they leave school. Conversely, those who are likely to progress to higher education should, he argues, be afforded many opportunities for substantial mental development, thus inferring that the amount of knowledge offered to this group will be reduced but will be subject to a greater level of critical analysis. All of this has implications, as we will see, for the design of a school curriculum and the criteria employed for the selection of textbooks and other resources.

We can summarize Shields's thoughts on how to promote and sustain effective mental development thus: the child must be adjusted to receive the social inheritance of the race; schools must avoid simply requiring the child to replicate existing ways of thinking, and teachers should promote a wider understanding of self-determination in regard to changing environments, encouraging children to search for the underlying principles of the laws to which they are exposed.

There is much to ponder in all of this. The Deweyan focus on experience is the overall context for the necessary processes of adjustment and growth. Plasticity, adjustment and correlation are the means by which children, in their interaction with the environment and other people, become, essentially, well-adjusted people, which is

---

46 Shields, *Philosophy of Education*, 131.
47 "The study of the child is just begun; and it offers more problems than solutions. But it has already thrown considerable light on the question of mental development. As a result, we know that education does not consist in loading the memory with details nor in forcing the pupil to learn things that are devoid of interest." Shields, *Twenty-Five Lessons*, 32.

the object of the educational process.[48] Shields is bringing the world of educational psychology to the heart of Catholic pedagogy. He is not blind to the problems arising from rigid applications of false norms—like the overuse of the memory—which have often driven all teaching, including religious instruction.[49] The child, therefore, must be suitably *guided* in the search for educationally valid experiences, and not left to search for them without help. The selection of such experiences by the teacher is fundamental, as mistakes in this regard will have deleterious developmental effects.[50]

The role of the teacher, for Shields, is much more than that of a facilitator in the background. The process of *selecting* the experiences through which the child will be guided is, in fact, an intentional didactic act in itself. This then offers a particular lens through which to view Shields's pedagogical vision: education is the search for truth and is too important to be left to the unguided mind of the child. While the Deweyan influence comes through in the importance offered to "experiences," Christian anthropology reminds Shields (and us) of the reality of the human person as both *graced* and *flawed*: we need grace to open our eyes to truth as our flawed human nature is not guaranteed to reach truth otherwise, despite the importance of what is offered to the faculty of reason in the Catholic Intellectual Tradition.[51]

48 Role-modeling is crucial and Shields reminds the reader of the importance of using the saints as examples of holiness. See Shields, *Philosophy of Education*, 156.
49 "Thus the rigid observance of the Puritanical Sabbath has arrested the religious development of many a child and it has given to the world multitudes of men who avoid church and who find in themselves no response to the abundant blessings which religion has to offer." Shields, *Philosophy of Education*, 144–45. A similarly hard line is taken against those who insist on memorization of catechetical formulae.
50 "And, on the other hand, if he is led into experiences for which he is not prepared, or into experiences that will turn his development into wrong channels, the result will be either an arrest of mental development or a development of those characteristics which will unfit him either in the present or in the future to take his place as an efficient member of a civilized society." Shields, *Philosophy of Education*, 153–54.
51 See *Catechism of the Catholic Church* (Vatican City: Libreria Editrice Vaticana,

While Shields offered substantial material on what he saw as important educational principles, it was sometimes hard to glimpse what this could actually mean in practice. On the other hand, he was at times very keen to offer direct advice to teachers on the actual practice of teaching. An example of such explicit advice follows.

Sense Training: An Example of Practical Advice

Shields was not content to rest on his scholarly laurels but sought to support teachers with various aids and suchlike. *The Teachers Manual of Primary Methods,* chapter 8, is a prime example of a text with solid practical aims. At just over eight pages long, the chapter is not a demanding read but offers an invaluable insight into how Shields envisaged his ideas working out in practice. It is far from being a detailed theoretical study of methods but gives the distinct impression of being designed to be read by teachers as they prepare lessons: one could easily imagine the book lying well-thumbed and slightly chalky on a teacher's desk on a daily basis.

The title of the chapter is "Sense Training in the First Grade." It opens with a short introductory section followed by more substantial sections: The Milkweed Lesson, The Fruit Lesson, and a short final section on drawing. The focus is on the awakening of the senses as the place where the knowledge of God will enter:

> His [the pupil's] senses must be quickened to perceive the beauties of nature and the details of her marvellous adjustments, and he must be taught to see both himself and the Creator mirrored in the phenomena that hold his senses captive and delight his imagination.[52]

1993), § 286: "The existence of God the Creator can be known with certainty through his works, by the light of human reason, even if this knowledge is often obscured and disfigured by error."

52 Shields, *Teachers Manual of Primary Methods,* 68.

Successful implementation of a strategy as outlined above requires teachers to be resourceful in arranging stimuli and other suitable thought material (resources) for the pupils. Running through this proposed set of lessons is the important thread of religiosity because pupils need reminding that the elements of nature are reflections, no less, of the grandeur of God. This is why the truths of life and existence must be presented in a manner suited to the pupils' stage of development.

Following this, the first of two lessons are presented: "The Milkweed Lesson," starting from observation of colored pictures of the plant and some ripe pods, leads, through questions, to a discussion of reproduction in nature. Shields opines that this lesson "prepares their minds also for the reception of many biological truths."[53] This is followed by "The Fruit Lesson," which has five core elements: sense training, assimilation, imagination, results, and sensory motor drills. Each element is part of a process that brings nature to life for the child, part of which is the handling and eating of the fruits (apples, pears, lemons, oranges, and grapes) the teacher has provided. The use of images of apples hanging from trees is an opportunity for the teacher to write the word "apple" on the board, thus linking the written word with the other senses. Finally, drawing is introduced as the foundation of sensory motor skills. Interestingly, in recommending that the child use chalk on a blackboard, Shields advocates the predominance of the arm, not the wrists and fingers, in the process, giving quite precise instructions on, for example, the arm movements the teacher must teach if the child is to form letters correctly.[54]

In noting the level of instructional detail offered, it becomes clear that in Shields's work we see a confluence of reason, scientific

---

53 Shields, *Teachers Manual of Primary Methods*, 70.
54 "The movement should be a large one; circles or flowing curves should be attempted before straight lines. In these early muscular exercises, rhythm is a very important factor and should not be neglected by the teacher. Some simple music should help the child at the blackboard." Shields, *Teachers Manual of Primary Methods*, 75.

advances, and religious faith. This reflects his sincere conviction that his ideas were truly the best methods for Catholic schools to adopt. Indeed, it is this commitment to forging a fresh path for Catholic educators through the thickets of pedagogical innovations that makes Shields's work worthy of study today. The level of detailed methodological guidance offered suggests an innate self-confidence that his ideas were universally valid. Yet, there may also be a possible lack of trust in the ability of teachers to work out, for example, appropriate lesson sequences for themselves. This might seem an apparently harsh judgment, but it merits mentioning. The reality, however, might be more nuanced. There is no need to experiment with methods if we already know from science what "works." The teacher needs to be directed toward this body of evidence and offered suitable means of support if she is to be, to use a contemporary term, a research-informed practitioner.

Conclusion

To bring about authentic reform in any activity related to the life of the Church, it is wise to avoid a "Year Zero" approach that too easily dismisses what has gone before as "unfashionable" or "irrelevant." Shields's radical agenda was centered on Catholic school reform and on devising the means to achieve this, such as revised textbooks and improved teacher formation.[55] Such a multiple-track approach has been described as "educationally progressive, yet theologically orthodox or conservative."[56]

---

55 Shields's efforts in religious education were channeled through the existing forms of his day and of his church: the Catholic parochial school staffed by sisters, the same form he experienced as a child. His incursion into the emerging educational psychology did not cause him to challenge the Catholic school system; his concern was primarily for the learning process in the child, and his psychological contribution was to aid the child's growth as a Catholic. Murphy, "Thomas Edward Shields: Religious Educator," 80.

56 Elias, "Thomas E. Shields: Progressive Catholic Religious Educator," 76.

What are we to make of this apparent contradiction in approach? Is Shields trying to square the circle of keeping orthodox doctrine at the heart of his mission while embracing wider insights in psychology and biology in line with the broader progressive movements in education? Bearing in mind that educational thinkers like Dewey were not wholly attracted to the notion that religion had a central role to play in education, are we on safe ground to claim that Shields enjoyed both "having" and "eating" his cake?[57]

Shields's initial studies were in biology, physiology, and zoology at Johns Hopkins University and these fields of interest, alongside the work on psychology from Pace, are not incidental to his later work: in fact they are foundational to his contribution to Catholic education in that his mind and heart saw the data emerging from experimental science as signs of God's providence, which the faithful educator could not ignore. To the twenty-first-century reader, this is not a controversial position, but in the context of the ecclesial mood of his time, it was, for sure, an innovative way of thinking about Catholic education.

Shields's educational principles emerged from his desire to unite concepts like plasticity, adjustment, correlation, and mental growth / development. He saw this way of working as scientifically valid and applicable to all domains of knowledge. The commitment to a broad education, while laudable and necessary, also needs religion.[58]

---

[57] Chapter 1 explored the Progressive movement in education with reference, inter alia, to John Dewey and the Religious Education Association of America, founded in 1903.

[58] In the teaching of Religion, therefore, one of the first things to be attended to is to adjust the matter and form of instruction to the needs and capacity of the child, and if we are considering the children in the first grade this necessarily implies a careful study of the child in the home and in the process of being transplanted from the home into the school. And the second consideration leads to the study of the religious content to be presented in its relations to the other elements of the curriculum in the first grade. Thomas Shields, "Notes on Education," *Catholic University Bulletin* 15 (1909): 475.

DEVELOPING A FRAMEWORK FOR REFORM

Shields saw science as the exploration of a world created through laws and patterns that revealed the delicate hands of a creator. His work could be a call to Catholic educators to adopt a professional humility that welcomes, indeed promotes, a wider dialogue across all domains of scholarship.[59] This also poses a risk that new findings could continue to challenge established ways of working. McMahon, writing in the late 1920s, had already noted some psychological shortcomings in the Shields Method, especially around the classification of fundamental instincts: letters and sciences, aesthetics, institutions, and religion.[60] There is now ample scope for contemporary psychologists to return to the work of Shields and Pace to ascertain the extent to which their findings and practical proposals are in line with the most recent research.

---

59   The more that scientific literacy and discoveries become part of our common worldview, the more a sense of their relation to the Catholic faith becomes essential for us to be compelled by the beauty, goodness and truth of the Catholic faith. In our scientifically literate culture, ignoring science, or offering only shallow reflections upon it, leads to the impoverishment of evangelization and catechesis and to the scorn of a world that needs the gospel. Christopher Baglow, "A Catholic History of the Fake Conflict between Religion and Science," *Church Life Journal*, May 4, 2020, https://churchlifejournal.nd.edu/articles/a-catholic-history-of-the-conflict-between-religion-and-science.

60   "Modern psychology would not accept this classification of fundamental instincts." McMahon, "The Shields Method," 143.

CHAPTER 5

SHIELDS'S PEDAGOGY OF CATHOLIC EDUCATION

In chapter 5, we will see first how Shields's reforms were linked to more general Catholic thinking on educational reform. Following this, there is an exploration of his claim that the teaching methods of Jesus were an advanced form of pedagogy. The chapter then sets out some key features of Shields's pedagogy of Catholic education by looking at one lesson from *Twenty-Five Lessons in the Psychology of Education*. It ends with some key features of his educational vision.

Shields and New Thinking in Catholic Education

Central to enquiries in the Catholic Intellectual Tradition is the question of how to interpret processes of change in the Church and, related to this, the extent to which earlier periods in the life of the Church are somehow normative for future generations of believers. In other words, are doctrine and liturgical practices "better" or more authentic the closer they are to the time of Jesus Christ and the early Christian community? While this might be an attractive option for some, to rush down this road too quickly brings the risk of depicting the story of Christianity as one of the gradual corruption of an early idealism.[1]

---

1 There is a line connecting the monastic and cathedral schools of the early medieval period with contemporary education, but it features many chinks

As noted in the preceding chapter, St. John Henry Newman offered a set of keys for interpreting the process of doctrinal change in the Church. For Newman, the Church, as a living organism, had to be open to authentic *development* of its doctrine. To illustrate his position, he proposed "Seven Notes" to ascertain whether so-called "doctrinal developments" were indeed authentic or were simply corruptions, to a greater or lesser extent, of an original ideal. The "notes" are preservation of type; continuity of principles; power of assimilation; logical sequence; anticipation of its future; conservative action upon its past; and chronic vigor.[2] While this is not the place to critique the Newmanian method per se, the sevenfold test remains a relevant set of analytical tools for contemporary educators, although it will engender much discussion about how each "note" can be applied to particular situations in the Church and its educational traditions. Shields's openness to new insights from the sciences encouraged him in the mission to strengthen Catholic education, principally through reform of methods. It is wholly credible that Shields would have argued that the new pedagogical insights from science—which he claimed were confirming the value of the teaching methods of Jesus as recorded in the gospels—passed the Newmanian tests of authenticity.

Shields's approach to reform is reflected to some extent in contemporary catechetical pedagogy. The *Directory for Catechesis* published in 2020 by the then Pontifical Council for Promoting New Evangelization—now part of the Dicastery for Evangelization—had no hesitation in recommending ways of working that would be very much in harmony with Shields's approach:

---

and curves. Shields was of the view that scholars of education, no matter their religious / cultural stand, could not simply ignore the contribution made by the Church to civilization through its educational structures. See Shields, *Philosophy of Education*, 305.

2 John H. Newman, *An Essay on the Development of Christian Doctrine*, rev. ed. (1989; repr., Notre Dame, Ind.: University of Notre Dame Press, 2005), chapter 5. We cannot be sure of the extent to which Newman's work influenced Shields.

> Thanks to the research and reflections of the human sciences there have arisen theories, approaches and models that profoundly renew educational practices and make significant contribution to an in-depth understanding of people, human relationships, society and history. Their contribution is indispensable. Pedagogy and didactics in particular enrich the educational processes of catechesis.[3]

As is evident from the *Directory,* the intersection of religion and education is integral to the success of the project of Catholic education. It requires, now as always, rigorous theological, cultural, and professional formation, both initial and ongoing, of its corps of teachers: *where* this formation takes place, *how* it operates, and *what* is to be studied are, rightly, issues of genuine and necessary debate across the Church. Closely related to this academic-professional debate is the related and complex matter of the faith formation of young people in the Catholic school: in other words, to what extent is the school and, especially its religious education curriculum, an expression of *catechesis*?

The Church's official documents on school-based education rightly distinguish between catechesis and the wider subject of religious education available in its curricula.[4] The *Directory for Catechesis* describes the relationship as "one of distinction in complementarity," drawing on earlier magisterial teaching on the religion-culture nexus.[5] Nonetheless, a clear separation of both concepts does not capture the

---

[3] Pontifical Council for Promoting New Evangelization, *Directory for Catechesis*, 180. This important extract is part of a subsection entitled "Catechetical Pedagogy" located within chapter 5, "The Pedagogy of the Faith."

[4] "The distinction between religious instruction and catechesis does not change the fact that a school can and must play its specific role in the work of catechesis. Since its educational goals are rooted in Christian principles, the school as a whole is inserted into the evangelical function of the Church. It assists in and promotes faith education." Congregation for Catholic Education, *The Religious Dimension of Education in Catholic Schools: Guidelines for Reflection and Renewal* (April 7, 1988), 69.

[5] Pontifical Council for Promoting New Evangelization, *Directory for Catechesis*, 313.

potential richness that religious education—sometimes called "religious studies" or "religious instruction," although each term has different emphases—can, at its best, offer the Church.[6] This complementarity, which was not fully highlighted and appreciated until the final quarter of the twentieth century, was not part of the Catholic world—which saw Catholic schooling as a profound union of catechetical and educational aims—inhabited by Shields.[7] It is important to bear this in mind as we read Shields's aspirations—at the heart of Shields's mission to reform Catholic education was a desire to advance the formation of teachers in order to enable them not just to be excellent in professional qualities but also equipped as effective catechists. Indeed, it is reasonable to posit that Shields saw the teacher's catechetical function as integral to her professional life. In this position, he was at one with the established wider thinking in the Catholic educational circles of the time. Shields surely would not have recognized the distinction between catechesis and religious education as developed by the Congregation for Catholic Education in the final years of the twentieth century.

The contemporary scholar can see in Shields's output a profound attachment to the school's role in the explicit religious development of the child. We will explore in the conclusion how Shields positioned his pedagogy as a form of school-based catechesis within an integrated curriculum and explore the extent to which this model of Catholic education is viable (or not) for the contemporary Church.

The Advanced Pedagogy of the Gospel

As already noted in chapter 4, Shields used concepts such as plasticity, adjustment, correlation, and mental growth / development as the building blocks of a pedagogy of Catholic education. Although

---

6 Franchi, *Shared Mission*, 20.
7 The present volume will use "religious education" as the preferred term for the religious formation of children in Catholic schools, while acknowledging that Catholic education today recognizes both areas of overlap and distinction between school-based religious education and catechesis more generally, whether in a school setting or elsewhere.

he was drawing on new knowledge, his clear starting point is that the undeniable advances in the science of education were, in fact, confirming the validity of the teaching methods of Jesus as recorded in the gospels.[8] The alignment between science and the gospel lends a sense of originality to Shields's work, especially when combined with his commitment to disseminating his ideas through the preparation of teachers and the writing of school textbooks. In this light, we can talk with some confidence about a "Shields Method" but it might be a step too far to propose that he formulated a particular *theory* of Catholic education. The reason for this is that he did not have the intellectual space to develop his ideas sufficiently because, in his final decade, much of his energy was expended in establishing the Catholic Sisters College and the *Catholic Education Series*.

Shields was fond of presenting his ideas through schema. This way of working seemed to offer Shields an opportunity to organize his thoughts in an orderly fashion and an opportunity for some initial correlation of ideas. He proposed two such frameworks for coming to an understanding of the teaching methods of Jesus. The first is articulated through three core elements:

1. the dogmatic content of His teaching, which is subsequently developed by systematic theology;
2. the divine personality of Jesus is shown by the way he lived his life. This has been formulated in moral theology and exemplified by the religious character of teachers in their commitment to a life of virtue and their zeal for salvation of souls; and
3. the teaching principles of Jesus, as shown in the gospels, have flowed into the liturgy and sacramental system of the

---

8 "He (Jesus) constantly appealed to the emotions and instincts, to the love of parent for offspring, to physical appetites, to human ambitions, to the desire for wealth and power, and He makes these purely human tendencies lift the soul into an understanding of the higher truths of revelation." Shields, *Philosophy of Education*, 319.

Church but somehow seem to have lost their connection to the teaching of doctrine.[9]

Shields also offered the following four-part division (or phases) in the teaching of Jesus:

1. an appeal to observe familiar phenomena in the natural world;
2. an appeal to human emotions;
3. a comparison between the people of the Kingdom of God with those "dwellers of the lower planes of life"; and
4. an obligation that his followers live in conformity with their dignity as children of God.[10]

These schema, as we will see later, offered a framework for his series of religion textbooks and readers and are also helpful signposts for contemporary teachers wishing to refresh their pedagogical approaches. Of course, the appeal to emotions and human experiences, which might have come across as radical in his day, would not be unfamiliar to those conversant with post–Vatican II thinking on catechesis and religious education.

The use of such schema, or frameworks, was designed to help teachers navigate the field of religion and education, strewn as it was with new knowledge and ideas that were not always helpful to the Catholic educator. Shields had always been keen to communicate his findings in concrete terms, including in his courses of study lessons that contained clear practical aims. In an early work, *Twenty-Five Lessons in the Psychology of Education*, published in 1906, Shields bequeathed the text of a correspondence course he had conducted with teaching sisters. He is described in the book as "Assistant Professor of Physiological Psychology," thus emphasizing his credentials in the field. In the final lesson of the course (Lesson

---

9 Shields, *Philosophy of Education*, 68.
10 Shields, "Notes on Education," 71.

XXV), Shields describes his key educational principles, giving examples of how each principle is embodied in Catholic teaching. (Please see the appendix.) Lesson XXV thus forms a helpful and necessary bridge between his scientific thought and his theological / educational mission.

The final lesson, as a summary of the study course, offers a helpful overview of Shields's position on the pedagogy of Catholic education, even though it is representative of a stage in his career when he was just starting out as a writer. Here he strives to align key pedagogical principles with the Church's educational traditions, ending characteristically on a polemical note. There is no reason to suppose that his thinking changed much from 1906 until the end of his career, as the ideas adumbrated above are scattered throughout his subsequent work.

Key Features of Shields's Pedagogy of Catholic Education

The final lesson from *Twenty-Five Lessons in the Psychology of Education* (reproduced in the appendix of this book) shows the early shape of Shields's ideas. Looking back on his work as a whole, and in order to show the depth and breadth of Shields's pedagogy of Catholic education, there now follows a presentation of its principal features, arranged according to four broad themes.[11]

Theme 1—The Mission of Catholic Education

Drawing on his wider understanding of pedagogy, Shields summed up the ultimate aim of the Catholic educational project as follows:

> Christian education, therefore, aims at transforming native instincts while preserving and enlarging their powers. It aims at bringing the flesh under the control of the spirit. It draws upon

11 This is the present author's arrangement of Shields's themes, not that of Shields himself.

the experience and wisdom of the race, upon divine revelation and upon the power of divine grace in order that it may bring the conduct of the individual into conformity with Christian ideals and with the standards of the civilization of the day. It aims at the development of the whole man, at the preservation of unity and continuity in his conscious life; it aims at transforming man's native egoism to altruism; at developing the social side of his nature to such an extent that he may regard all men as brothers, sharing with them the common Fatherhood of God. In one word, it aims at transforming a child of the flesh into a child of God.[12]

While this statement reads like a charter, or mission statement, for the life of an institution dedicated to Christian education, we cannot help but note the robust theological language used.[13] Few would be the Catholic schools today with the confidence to use such terminology, although such robust expressions of Catholic identity might not have been uncommon in the Catholic schools of Shields's own time. Perhaps the chosen tone is an implicit recognition of the major challenges facing the wider Christian community from progressive ideas, thus prompting Shields to strengthen the language used as a possible counterweight to the more general, and at times fractious, educational atmosphere of the time. Interestingly, there are some hints above of the hand of friendship being offered to those wedded to the progressive view. For example, the inclusion of phrases like "experience and wisdom of the race" is a quasi-Deweyan term, as is

12 Shields, *Philosophy of Education*, 180.
13 Some Catholic schools today expend much energy in the writing of attractive mission statements. For the most part, these offer helpful indications of what makes the school's mission unique, although there is also a risk of their becoming little more than examples of corporate marketing blurbs. Yet there is still a place for a fairly condensed piece of text that seeks to capture the essence of Catholic education in general and of particular schools. Shields's work has many passages which could be adapted as informative mission statements.

the pithy pairing of "egoism to altruism" and the desire to develop the "social side" of human nature.

Underpinning this broad statement of educational principles is the recognition that the human intellect, left to its own devices, is an inadequate means for becoming educated. Indeed, Shields goes so far as to argue that education is also a "protective" mechanism that protects the child from "undesirable and obsolete instincts."[14] It is no surprise that the inspiration for the reforming approach to Christian education adopted by Shields is found, as he claims, in the gospels. The call to take up the cross and to love God with all our being constitutes nothing less than vivid "positive formulations of the ultimate end of education." The Church is responsible for communicating the "divine commission" to all.[15] The task of the "divine commission," reflecting the reality of the Church as an educational movement (see chapter 1) is no less than the building of a new civilization:

> The unchanging aim of Christian education is, and always has been, to put the pupil into possession of a body of truth derived from nature and from divine revelation, from the concrete work of man's hand, and from the content of human speech, in order to bring his conduct into conformity with Christian ideals and with the standards of the civilization of his day.[16]

For Shields, therefore, knowledge is never the end of the Catholic educational process. Rather, the purpose of knowledge acquisition is to "nourish the conscious life of the pupil and this is sought to the further end of securing desirable conduct."[17] To the nonbeliever, none of what Shields proposes is obvious. This is unsurprising as Shields's starting point is divine revelation and the truth of the

---

14 Shields, *Philosophy of Education*, 167.
15 Shields, *Philosophy of Education*, 169.
16 Shields, *Philosophy of Education*, 171.
17 Shields, *Philosophy of Education*, 174.

gospels. Yet while he does attempt to frame the call to good conduct and virtue without direct reference to religion, he always falls back on the divine foundation of law.[18]

Theme 2—A Catechetical Framework of Catholic Education

In assessing Shields's work in Catholic education, we enter a field replete with challenges that did not exist in his time. One of these challenges is the extent to which the Catholic school can be a channel for the explicit faith formation (catechesis) of pupils. This has already been alluded to above. Although Shields advocated a broad-based liberal education, Shields also saw Catholic education as primarily a catechetical endeavor, unlike more recent Catholic teaching which tends to see school-based religious education and wider catechesis as related but distinct concepts.[19]

The contemporary Church has relied on the genre of catechetical directories as sites of information about catechesis (see introduction), and we find therein the latest thinking about practice. The *Directory for Catechesis*, published in 2020, makes clear that catechesis must be influenced by positive developments in the sciences.[20] There is no room for a neofideistic approach that places the Church's catechetical mission—which is for all people, not just children— somehow apart from other ways of understanding the world. In particular, the catechist is called to accompany people in discerning God's presence in their lives, not just to tell the gospel story. In so

---

18 Shields, *Philosophy of Education*, 176: "It is the purpose of education, in the widest acceptation of the term, to substitute for instinct the control of intellect and free will so as to secure action in conformity to the laws of nature and to the dictates of divine will."
19 Congregation for Catholic Education, *Circular Letter*, 17.
20 Of course, deeper study of the Church's own engagement with the world of science belies any binary split between religion and science. For a concise introduction to this topic, see Fr. Andrew Pinsent, "A Catholic Understanding of Science," in Convery, Franchi, and Valero, *Reclaiming the Piazza III: Communicating Catholic Culture*, 113–28.

doing, the processes of evangelizing and educating interact creatively with each other, with the gospel message presented as the key to a fully integrated life.[21]

There is more than an echo in the *Directory for Catechesis* of the methods adopted by Shields in the series of textbooks and readers that, as we will see in part 4, explored aspects of nature and the family before presenting stories from the gospel. The *Directory* also reminds the Church that the complexity of human nature needs the expertise afforded by psychology if the catechetical mission is to be successful.[22] In many ways, the *Directory* is a belated "imprimatur" on the approach adopted by Shields. Issued almost a hundred years after his death, it is evidence of how the Church does not wish to live apart from but as part of and leaven to the world. It is important to consider the extent to which contemporary catechetical and wider educational processes embed such ways of working today, perhaps drawing as appropriate from the work of Shields to develop a rich pedagogy of Catholic education that recognizes and values the distinction and complementarity between catechesis and school-based religious education.

21 Pontifical Council for Promoting New Evangelization, *Directory for Catechesis*, 179, describes it thus:
> In the journey of catechesis, the principle of *evangelising by educating and educating by evangelising* recalls, among other things, that the work of the catechist consists in finding and drawing attention to the signs of God's action already present in the lives of persons and by using these as an example, present the Gospel as a transformative power for the whole of existence, to which it will give full meaning.

22 "Pedagogy and didactics in particular enrich the educational processes of catechesis. Together with them, psychology also has an important value, above all because it helps one to grasp the motivational dynamics, the structure of the personality, the elements relating to problems and pathologies, the different stages of development and developmental tasks, the dynamics of religious maturation and the experiences that open human beings to the mystery of the sacred." Pontifical Council for Promoting New Evangelization, *Directory for Catechesis*, 180.

Theme 3—Faith, Reason, and the Philosophy of Education

A partnership between faith and reason is essential to the successful operation of Catholic education. Pope St. John Paul II, drawing on the work of St. Thomas Aquinas, opened the encyclical *Fides et Ratio* with the now oft-repeated words: "Faith and reason are like two wings on which the human spirit rises to the contemplation of truth."[23] Following a short preamble on the need to contemplate truth, John Paul titled the introduction "Know Yourself," which he goes on to interpret as a call to philosophical reflection on truth.[24] Drawing from this invitation to integrate faith and reason into the wider life of the Church, schools, if they are to engage in the important search for truth and meaning, must do so equipped with the best methodological approaches the human mind can offer. This is a recognition of the truths that lie at the heart of science. It is faith working alongside reason that will uncover those things that obscure the journey to human flourishing.[25] When applied to

23 Pope John Paul II, Encyclical Letter *Fides et Ratio* (*On the Relationship between Faith and Reason*) (September 14, 1998).
24 In the present Letter, I wish to pursue that reflection by concentrating on the theme of *truth* itself and on its *foundation* in relation to *faith*. For it is undeniable that this time of rapid and complex change can leave especially the younger generation, to whom the future belongs and on whom it depends, with a sense that they have no valid points of reference. The need for a foundation for personal and communal life becomes all the more pressing at a time when we are faced with the patent inadequacy of perspectives in which the ephemeral is affirmed as a value and the possibility of discovering the real meaning of life is cast into doubt. John Paul II, *Fides et Ratio*, 6.
25 In this respect, Aquinas's thoughts on teaching are worth recalling: see *De Veritate*, q.11, St. Isidore E-Book Library, https://isidore.co/aquinas/english/QDdeVer11.htm. See also Dennis Doyle, "Thomas Aquinas: Integrating Faith and Reason in the Catholic School," *Catholic Education: A Journal of Inquiry and Practice* 10, no. 3 (2007): 348:

> Aquinas believed that the Incarnation was something to which human beings could not reason on their own, but he also thought that it would

education, specifically Catholic education in schools, the call to cherish reason and faith is revelatory. Catholic education needs the contribution of reason if its schools are to be sites of meaningful learning and human flourishing—a Catholic educational institution is not a place of refuge from wider intellectual and social currents.

For Shields, successful Catholic schools were not simply the fruit of prayer and divine guidance. It is from the exercise of reason that we learn the importance of educational tools such as judicious planning and the formulation of clear sets of aims, all of which require serious human initiative and endeavor. Given Shields's own tremendous capacity for hard work, it is easy to portray his contribution to Catholic education in neo-Pelagian terms. Yet we also need to recapture the importance of work to the human condition—in the Catholic mind, it is in work well done that we contribute fruitfully to the ongoing phenomenon of creation. Shields recognized that his project to reform Catholic education would not fall fully formed from the sky but needed hard graft and an ability to overcome the obstacles that impede change.

Shields's use of the term "Philosophy of Education" as the title of one of his monographs is not a claim that he is establishing a new branch of the academic discipline of philosophy. His aim is more practical and, possibly, of more use to his readers because his concern is to offer practical insights into the actual work of education.[26]

---

not flatly contradict human reason if it were true. Jesus Christ is the example of how the divine and the human can fit together. Ancient wisdom still had much to offer Aquinas, but he needed to reinterpret it with this most crucial of points, the Incarnation, in mind. Throughout various nooks and crannies of the *Summa*, Aquinas is applying to many theological questions the principle of Incarnation, that the eternal and invisible are present and active within the finite and the visible.

26 "The philosophy of education, as a branch of applied science, is not concerned directly with the establishment of fundamental principles in any department of philosophy. Its business is to apply the truths and principles established by pure philosophy to the practical conduct of the educative process." Shields, *Philosophy of Education*, 23.

Philosophy of Education is a substantial volume of twenty-three closely argued but accessible chapters. Part 1 (chapters 1–9) is titled "The Nature of the Educative Process," part 2 (chapters 10–16) is titled "Educational Aims" and part 3 (chapters 17–23) is titled "Educative Agencies." It is the closest he comes to developing an academic theory of education in a single volume. Despite a publication date of 1917, it consists of the teaching material Shields collected from 1895 until 1910. Some of it had been used in teaching sisters; extracts had already been published in the *Catholic Educational Review* in 1916. It is not clear if the material underwent any substantial revision before being published as a complete volume.[27]

Philosophy of Education makes no reference to religion in the title. This could be significant insofar as it reveals an attempt to integrate Shields's insights on Catholic education into wider educational thinking, leading to a conclusion that education in itself deserves robust supporting theories that are valid for all, not just Catholic, schools. Alongside this observation, it is evident that Shields is offering a fresh set of lenses through which to improve the foundational principles of specifically Catholic education.[28]

The importance of uniting insights from the applied sciences to education—a leitmotif in his body of work—is encapsulated thus:

> It is the problem of education to develop the individual to precisely that stage of completeness at which he can most successfully live in the service of humanity, and at the same time enjoy a normal

---

27 Shields, *Philosophy of Education*, 10.
28 The author is to be commended for the tenacity with which he holds to Christian moorings and for the faithfulness with which he everywhere recalls the position for which the Church stands. He enjoys the distinction of producing the first philosophy of education in English from a Catholic viewpoint, a distinction that will be far less prized by him than the assurances, which we hope will be many, that he has in this inspiring and vigorous work eminently served the Catholic cause. Patrick J. McCormick, review of *Philosophy of Education*, by Thomas Edward Shields, *Catholic Educational Review* 13 (May 1917): 459.

> healthy life; and so to inspire the young with love for humanity, and so to educate their instincts and ideals that, when the rights of the individual and the race come into conflict, the right of the race shall be given precedence. Education of the young, thus understood, is plainly not only the most moral and vital work we do, but the most inclusive; for in a sense it involves all other practical activities. Nothing else requires so profound knowledge, nor so earnest thought, as the training of the child.[29]

We are offered here the unambiguous understanding of education as the promotion of human flourishing. It is good education that will lay the groundwork for a healthy society in which the rights of all are paramount. It is a call to look beyond self-interest. Yet, as a Catholic educator, Shields is not content with a philosophy of education that denies the final destiny of the human person; in fact, he uses the term "Christian philosophy" as a way of showing individuals their worth as children of God and their development of a spiritual inheritance as children of God.[30] This allows the Christian to be "born again" and function effectively as a member of a civilized society.[31] Crucially, it requires a shift of teaching methods from the didactic to the organic (as noted above) to allow this spiritual inheritance to be communicated in a vital way. As necessary food is offered for the

---

29 Shields, *Philosophy of Education*, 40.
30 "But Christian philosophy would carry the thought one step further by adding to the worth of the individual as a member of an earthly society his worth as a child of God and as a member of the kingdom which endureth forever." Shields, *Philosophy of Education*, 40. For more on the issues presented by terms like "Catholic philosophy of education" vis-à-vis "philosophy of Catholic education," see Leonardo Franchi and Robert Davis, "Catholic Education and the Idea of Curriculum," *Journal of Catholic Education* 24, no. 2 (Fall 2021): 104–19.
31 Shields made clear his view that the Protestant Reformation dried out the Church's long-standing educative principles, "thus leaving the descendants of confessors and of martyrs wandering in exterior darkness, where, like the Children of Israel, they were compelled to make bricks without straw." Shields, *Philosophy of Education*, 320.

healthy growth of a child's body, so the child's soul must be opened to its unique spiritual inheritance.[32]

For Shields, this approach is rooted firmly in the gospel, where food is often used as a symbol of spiritual nourishment.[33] The elements of humanity's spiritual diet must also be well balanced if it is to have a positive effect. In other words, mental life requires substantial nourishment. Illustrating this by means of a diagram, Shields shows how God is the source of all four elements in this particular schema.[34] Any separation of the elements is liable to harm the educative process and this, he claims, is the error into which American state education has fallen. Shields accepts the good intentions of those behind the reforms of state education, but maintains that the elimination of God and revealed religion from their schemas can only lead to educational impoverishment.[35]

Theme 4—Curriculum, Religious Instruction, and Character Formation

While religion lies at the heart of the curriculum in the Catholic school—as demanded by the principle of correlation—other branches of knowledge must be intentionally arranged around it.[36] The structure and content of the curriculum are foundational to a properly nuanced and well grounded understanding of the aims of Catholic education. Shields was happy to admit that Catholics should be interested in curricular developments in other types of schools, but argued that their ways of working could not be simply replicated in Catholic schools owing to the nonconvergence of their respective

---

32 Shields, *Philosophy of Education*, 41.
33 Shields, *Philosophy of Education*, 41.
34 Shields, *Philosophy of Education*, 44.
35 Shields, *Philosophy of Education*, 44–45. Shields offers many examples of how religion has influenced human culture and civilization: Homer, the Vedas, the Psalms, etc.
36 Shields, *Philosophy of Education*, 398.

educational aims. In fact, he claimed, somewhat controversially, that the "ultimate aim of Catholic education is higher than that of the state schools" as Catholic schools include all the "legitimate aims of the state school," but also aim to provide a Catholic education, unlike state schools.[37]

This way of thinking leads to a pivotal question: What is the curriculum in the Catholic school supposed to achieve? What does it look like? Shields avoids offering a short answer by suggesting that important questions about the aims and content of a curriculum can only be settled with reference to the new knowledge emerging from the field of genetic psychology.[38] Furthermore, and drawing from the history of Christianity, Shields stresses the artistic side of life and its influence on the human person's emotional development. For example, the beauty of the Church's liturgy, its miracle plays, and its rescuing of ancient art and literature, all show the unity of creation and knowledge as essential antidotes to curricular fragmentation. The inclusion of religion and morality in secular knowledge was a means to developing a system of integral education in Catholic schools.[39] For many Catholic educators today, the so-called "Catholic curriculum," admittedly a complex term, is a means of presenting the transcendentals of truth, beauty, and goodness to a wide and diverse audience.[40] Such contemporary thinking on the nature of the

---

37 Shields, *Philosophy of Education*, 412. In 1918, after the publication of *Philosophy of Education*, the bishops of Scotland agreed to transfer their network of Catholic schools to the state with some safeguards for religious education and the appointment of key staff. In all other aspects, they were governed like any other state school, an arrangement that continues to the present day. I wonder what Shields would have said about this political arrangement. For more on this, see Francis O'Hagan and Robert Davis, "Forging the Compact of Church and State in the Development of Catholic Education in Late Nineteenth Century Scotland," *Innes Review* 58, no. 1 (2007): 72–94.
38 Shields, *Philosophy of Education*, 401.
39 Shields, *Philosophy of Education*, 403–4.
40 See, for example, André Gushurt-Moore, *Glory in All Things: Saint Benedict and Catholic Education Today* (Brooklyn: Angelico Press, 2020): 103–22.

curriculum in Catholic schools is a legitimate and necessary development of Shields's work.

Shields has been described, with some justification, as the "Catholic educator closest in spirit to John Dewey."[41] Like Dewey, Shields welcomed the turn away, in broad terms, from education understood primarily as the mere memorization of facts toward the valuing of personal and communal experiences as the raw material for study.[42] He was particularly keen to reform religious instruction. Seemingly aiming his fire, albeit cautiously, at catechetical texts like the Baltimore Catechism, Shields spoke of relieving "needless burdens" on the memory, thus enabling it better to serve "the needs of the growing mind."[43] Crucially, and in line with the insights of the 2020 *Directory for Catechesis* (see above), Shields afforded the teacher the responsibility of selecting which "experiences" should be selected for lessons and also of encouraging pupils to reflect on the layers of meaning contained therein. Furthermore, such reflection was not a primarily mystical or spiritual enterprise but required practical outlets.[44] For the avoidance of doubt over the practical aims of education, Shields proposed clear and partly measurable outcomes, such as participation in the Church's sacramental life allied to a commitment to devotional and penitential practices. Developing this practical outcome further, Shields saw definite educational value in studying the lives of the saints. If religion is to be taught *and* practiced, it is the example of the saints as role models that acts as a bridge between the teaching of doctrine and the experiential nature of education. In other words, the saints are those who "do" what is taught in a religiously inspired curriculum, not just those to whom we pray for special intentions.

---

41 Elias, "Thomas E. Shields: Progressive Catholic Religious Educator," 76.
42 Shields, *Philosophy of Education*, 407: "The business of the curriculum, therefore, is chiefly to supply to the children the right kind of experiences."
43 Shields, *Philosophy of Education*, 66.
44 "Education is not a mere knowing or remembering: it is preeminently a matter of doing." Shields, *Philosophy of Education*, 408.

If the essence of education is authentic character formation, leading in turn to a hoped-for improvement in personal conduct, an understanding of the proper processes of mental assimilation demands that the truths of doctrine can and must be adapted to suit the natural stages of human development. Shields, therefore, proposed that Catholic doctrine be presented in concrete forms to develop the child's intellect until the child / adult can comprehend, so to speak, more abstract truths. The journey from concrete to abstract, a staple of progressive education, demands that elements of the truth be shared gradually, drawing on the importance of imitation and correlation as the fundamental principles of pedagogy.

Shields admitted to caution in proposing changes to methods of teaching doctrine. Given the sacredness of content, poorly understood and implemented methodological change could do more harm than good to the child. This suggests that Shields was aware of the radical nature of his reforms and that his zeal was, on paper at least, tempered by the desire not to upset the wider teaching force and educational establishment, not least in the Church itself.[45]

Unsurprisingly, Shields emphasized the importance of intelligibility as the foundation of new methods. Doctrinal truths cannot be

45   The text-book in use is for the most part a catechism of Christian Doctrine cast in the dryest of didactic forms and completely isolated from all the other subjects of the curriculum. The thought is abstract in the extreme and it is couched in language for which the child has no preparation either proximate or remote. There is no attempt made to build up in the child-mind vigorous apperception masses capable of aiding in the assimilation of the religious thought. The book seems designed solely for the production of a verbal memory product and as if there were a consciousness somewhere that this was the only end possible of attainment. The whole stress is laid on the form of question and answer which will facilitate a teat of the capacity of the pupil's memory. On the practical side the work is no better. The content is not shaped so as to lead directly or immediately to conduct or to the formation of habits of thought and action. Back of this method there seems to be an incredible belief in the power of memorized formulae to translate themselves at a later period into vital elements in the conduct of the adult. Shields, "Notes on Education," 157.

simply dropped from on high into the memory of the pupil. Teachers must use all legitimate human means to facilitate growth in knowledge and assimilation in line with the pupils' stages of development. Nonetheless, it seems right to point out that a commitment to reform does not mean the discarding of so-called "old" methods. The first Christian believers had to preserve the records of the life of Jesus and then of the teachings of the apostles—as they lived in an essentially oral culture, the early Church had no option but to use the faculty of memory if they wished the traditions of the Church to be maintained and passed on. Again we note the importance of balance; perhaps Shields was too quick to deny the value of the memory in religious instruction, caricaturing it as an ancient tool that was of decreasing value the more we learned about how people learn. It is also reasonable to suggest that the move away from the use of memory in catechesis in the years following Vatican II went too far, thus prompting John Paul II, in his apostolic exhortation *Catechesi Tradendae*, to highlight in particular the need to value memorization in certain contexts.[46]

Conclusion

Shields portrayed the Church as an "infallible teaching agency" that gains its authority from the passages in the Gospel of Matthew known as the "Great Commission."[47] Thus inspired, Shields

46 Shields, *Twenty-Five Lessons*, 76: "An overuse of the memory in catechesis contradicts the laws of human development." Compare this statement with the sentiments expressed by John Paul II in his Apostolic Exhortation *Catechesi Tradendae* (*On Catechesis in Our Time*) (October 16, 1979), 55:

> The final methodological question the importance of which should at least be referred to—one that was debated several times in the synod—is that of memorization.... A certain memorization of the words of Jesus, of important Bible passages, of the Ten Commandments, of the formulas of profession of the faith, of the liturgical texts, of the essential prayers, of key doctrinal ideas, etc., far from being opposed to the dignity of young Christians, or constituting an obstacle to personal dialogue with the Lord, is a real need, as the synod fathers forcefully recalled.

47 Shields, *Philosophy of Education*, 298.

emphasized that the effective teaching of religion was essential for developing the authentic religious culture of the school.[48] Indeed, how could it be otherwise? The explicit teaching of Catholic doctrine in an age-appropriate manner was the sine qua non of the Catholic culture of the school. His ideas are, therefore, double-edged in his support for the explicit teaching of doctrine and for such doctrine to underpin and shape the wider curriculum.

In devising, promoting, and using such an approach to teaching, Shields saw himself as wholly in line with the mission of the apostles and, ultimately, with the teaching mission of the Church. In his description of the Church's way of teaching, however, there is a tendency to eulogize the history of Christian education throughout the ages.[49] This does not necessarily detract from the value of his insights into how Jesus actually taught—far from it—but it merits mention here.

Nonetheless, there is an assumption that life in the home is normally smooth, orderly, and peaceful: the life of the school should

---

[48] Two important works offer ample and innovative insights into his developing understanding of religious education (understood as a distinct curricular subject): *Twenty-Five Lessons in the Psychology of Education*, published in 1906, and *The Teaching of Religion*, published in 1908. Shields brought the key points from these works together in "Notes on Education," a regular column he penned in the 1909 volume of *Catholic University Bulletin*. All of this work predates the final publication of *Philosophy of Education* in 1917; we bear in mind, however, that *Philosophy of Education* consisted of material that had been published in earlier articles.

[49] But all down the ages it was the Sacramental system of the Church and her liturgy that kept the vital truths of Christianity vividly before the minds of the people and that rendered them fruitful in their lives. To the Liturgy, as a means of popular instruction, were added in time the resources of the fine arts. Poetry and music lent their beauty and eloquence, while painting, sculpture and architecture joined in the building of great cathedrals which spoke eloquently to the hearts and minds of the unlettered children of the forest no less than to the cultivated mind of the philosopher and of the theologian. Shields, "Notes on Education," 74.

While Shields is correct in a broad-brush fashion, there is a lack of nuance in this description.

aim to replicate this irenic ideal. Yet can we be sure that there is not an element of wishful thinking in the portrait of home that we find here and on which Shields's ideas are predicated? In the conclusion to this book, some further thought will be given to such matters.

The claim that the teaching methodology of Jesus was a forerunner of what was only uncovered by progressive thinkers in the late nineteenth and early twentieth centuries is not without controversy, to say the least.[50] Does this argument serve only to place faith above reason, with the sciences seen simply as the way to uncover, or find proof of, what is already made clear by revelation? This challenges the notion of free and open inquiry and disciplinary autonomy. Of course, on another level, it offers an open window into a confident Catholicism, which saw science not as a threat but as a handmaid to a greater understanding of the human condition sought by faith. Perhaps Shields was (unintentionally) blurring the lines between doctrine and pedagogy, failing also to inquire as to the extent to which the pedagogy of Jesus, far from being unique to Him, might have been rooted in the Jewish understanding of education, especially in the use He made of parables.[51]

Furthermore, if the teaching methods of Jesus were truly well developed, as Shields claimed, why did they become less common over time? When did this shift in practice happen and who was responsible? Given the Catholic Church's high profile in educational matters throughout the ages, is it really a credible position to

---

50 "The faithful Christian brings the findings of science to the feet of the Saviour and there examines their validity in the light of the method employed by the Teacher of mankind." Thomas Shields, "Fundamental Principles in the Teaching of Religion," *Catholic Educational Review* 1 (April 1911): 340.

51 For more on this, see R. Steven Notley, "Reading Gospel Parables as Jewish Literature," *Journal for the Study of the New Testament* 41, no. 1 (2018): 40. "I have tried to demonstrate that the gospel parables belong to a larger landscape of emerging Jewish thought. These didactic short stories give voice to the hopes and concerns that one can hear elsewhere in Second Temple Jewish literature. They also exhibit the early literary developments of a genre that is evinced only in the NT and rabbinic literature."

adopt what seems to be a hermeneutic of gradual decay until the arrival of more scientifically based methods in the late nineteenth century? On the other hand, one could also argue that the teaching methods of Jesus as recorded in the gospels had gradually become covered by layers of human traditions that needed reform in order to restore their original freshness and dynamism. Nonetheless, Shields's embrace of an "organic" pedagogy is essential to ensure that the laws of life and growth underpin all teaching, therefore making it a truly vital process, notwithstanding the need for a delicate balancing act between creativity and tradition.

As a practical thinker, Shields was not content simply with the writing of scholarly articles and monographs—important as this was—but was keen to disseminate his findings to as many educators as possible. At the heart of the methods advocated by Shields is the role of the teacher. She (or he) is the key figure, responsible for making the transition from home to school smooth and meaningful. Apart from the "homely" aspect, the teacher requires sufficient pedagogical knowledge to instill the foundations of spoken (first) and written language. In addition, the focus on cooperative play, carefully planned by the teacher, is not aimed at the immediate gratification of the child, but is a preparation for the "serious aspects of living."[52] The high level of skill required of the teacher obviously requires good training, both in facilitating worthwhile educational experiences and in direct instruction as and when required.[53] Shields's ideas on the formation of teachers will be the focus of part 4.

---

52 Shields, *Teachers Manual of Primary Methods*, 40.
53 There is increasing evidence of the effectiveness of direct instruction in schools. This dovetails with the work of Shields in replacing some well-established teaching practices with more evidence-based reforms. See, for example, Adam Boxer, ed., *The researchEd Guide to Explicit and Direct Instruction: An Evidence-Informed Guide for Teachers* (Woodbridge, UK: John Catt Educational, 2019).

PART IV

FORMING TEACHERS IN HEART AND MIND

CHAPTER 6

THEOLOGICAL AND PEDAGOGICAL FORMATION FOR EDUCATORS

Chapter 6 adopts a broad understanding of "formation" as a process relevant to all stages of a teacher's career, not just the preservice phase. Shields's vision of teacher formation was, unsurprisingly, fundamental to his wider thinking on education. At the core of his ideals were the study of history, philosophy, and psychology. Without well-formed teachers, the Master Plan to reform Catholic education would be of limited effectiveness. Shields, as a practical person, was not content with the mere formulation of theory but desired to establish some practical means of reform.

Key Principles of Catholic Teacher Formation

The role of the teacher is crucial in driving forward improvement in educational quality. It is hence essential that all the means of teacher formation—whether located in the academy or organized by professional associations—are of sufficient academic and practical quality to address more general, internationally recognized challenges to teacher development, such as recruitment and training. Running through such concerns is the recognition of the power to change lives for the better that rests in the hands of the teacher. Such a universal claim takes on particular resonances when applied to Catholic schools. In a discussion of the life and work of (Fr.) George Johnson, Dr. Shields's successor as dean of the Catholic Sisters College at Catholic University, John Elias noted that alongside the raft of essential professional qualities required of teachers was the important matter of personal holiness.[1] The conjoining of personal holiness and professional excellence helpfully encapsulates the very high bar that prospective and serving teachers in Catholic schools are called to attain.[2] It is not a one-off target for a particular year but a mission for life, requiring commitment from individual educators to what should be ongoing formation in a supportive community of faith, scholarship, and practical wisdom.[3] Shields was insistent that the level of preparation available for teachers henceforth must be of a piece with that offered to other professions, such as physicians, lawyers, and clergy.[4]

---

1 "To hand on this human heritage and culture they must have the pedagogical skills that come through training and practice. Catholic school teachers need something deeper than personality: they need holiness of life." Elias, "George Johnson," 114.

2 "Whoever undertakes to educate children must be duly prepared for the task. And the preparation must be no less thorough than that which is given to the physician, the clergyman and the lawyer." Shields, *Twenty-Five Lessons*, 36.

3 There is much written on the relationship between religious faith and scholarship in the modern academy. The intersection of academic freedom and research integrity with a life of religious faith are central to these debates. For a wide-ranging summary and evaluation of these matters, see James L. Heft, *The Future of Catholic Higher Education* (Oxford: Oxford University Press, 2021).

4 See Thomas Shields, "Survey of the Field (The Cultural and Vocational Aims in Education)," *Catholic Educational Review* 10 (June 1915): 49:

> What has been said of the doctor, the lawyer and the priest should apply with equal force to the teacher, the writer and the artist. Hence the professional callings are pre-eminently vocations and the preparation for these vocations must be one of the chief aims of education. If society is to be preserved from sinking into mere sensual indulgence and from

He had no qualms about highlighting the need for colleges and universities to offer suitable professional-vocational training—allied to concomitant spiritual formation—for those intent on joining the professions. This level of ambition is as relevant today as it was then, the corollary being, of course, the need for universities, dioceses, and other professional bodies to devise and make available suitable opportunities for such rigorous integral formation.

Catholic teacher formation—understood as the career-long process that prepares and supports teachers academically, pastorally, and spiritually for work in Catholic schools[5]—is, has been, and always will be a critical component of the mosaic of features underpinning a successful Catholic school. There is some evidence from the contemporary Church, both in its magisterial documents on education and in the literature produced by particular churches and their educational agencies, concerning how this could be done, but clear templates setting out the priorities for Catholic teacher formation are not yet widely available.[6] Of course, the arrival of what could be perceived as overcentralized guidelines—which could potentially diminish or replace local initiatives in the field—might not be universally welcomed, for a number of educational and cultural reasons.

Shields was determined to refresh and breathe life into the vital contribution of the Church of the early twentieth century to the formation and preparation of its prospective and serving teaching

---

> disintegrating, the professions must be supplied with men who are not only possessed of the technical skill required, but whose souls have been so strengthened and uplifted that the end and aim of life for them must remain forever in the order of social service.

See also Shields, *Twenty-Five Lessons*, 36.

5 Other terms are also used for this process: "Catholic teacher education," "Catholic teacher preparation," and "Catholic teacher training."

6 Richard Rymarz and Leonardo Franchi, *Catholic Teacher Preparation: Historical and Contemporary Perspectives on Preparing for Mission* (Bingley, UK: Emerald, 2019), 143–53 offers a summary of recent magisterial thinking on Catholic teacher formation.

personnel.[7] His wide reading included not just the insights from contemporaneous progressive thinkers but ideas about education gleaned from major figures in the history of Christian thought, including St. Augustine of Hippo and St. Thomas Aquinas.[8] The historical angle is a reminder to readers both then and now that the need for the proper formation of teachers is not a new concern.[9] If Shields's desire for a research-informed teaching profession were to be successful, it would require a teaching force that was prepared to embrace innovative insights from the sciences while remaining comfortably at home in the inherited philosophical, theological, and cultural traditions of the Church.[10]

The *Lineamenta* (guiding principles) for the 2015 World Congress on Catholic Education—which marked the fiftieth anniversary of *Gravissimum Educationis,* Vatican II's Declaration on Christian

---

[7] America was not unique in rethinking its attitudes to Catholic education. Much interesting work was also carried out in France. It is not always clear how much Shields drew from the European context, but the parallels between Shields's mission and the initiatives taken by some teaching congregations in France is striking. For a helpful overview of the French situation, see Eleanor L. Rivera, "Cultivating the Spirit: Catholic Educators, Primary Educators and Pedagogy in Early Third Republic France," *Paedagogica Historica*: *International Journal of the History of Education*, published online, February 4, 2022. https://www.tandfonline.com/doi/abs/10.1080/00309230.2022.2032770.

[8] "Historically, the noblest example is presented to us in the training which Our Savior gave his disciples. In the treatises left us by such men as St. Augustine and St. Thomas Aquinas we find excellent direction for the teacher. More recently, the religious orders of the Church have emphasized the importance of training." Shields, *Twenty-Five Lessons*, 36.

[9] For an indication of what Augustine and Thomas Aquinas can offer Catholic teacher formation, see Rymarz and Franchi, *Catholic Teacher Preparation*, 21–34.

[10] There is a parallel here with St. John Henry Newman's desire to place holiness and intellectual refinement as partners, not foes, for the educated layperson. See John Henry Newman, "Intellect, the Instrument of Religious Training," (sermon, 1856), *Works of John Henry Newman*, collected by the National Institute for Newman Studies, available at https://www.newmanreader.org/works/occasions/sermon1.html. This text was written as part of his preparation for the opening of the Catholic University of Ireland and, therefore, a ready partner for Shields's desire to include teacher formation in the Catholic University of America.

Education—did not shirk from acknowledging the host of contemporary challenges faced by the Church in its commitment to providing excellent formation for Catholic teachers. While rightly suggesting that the mission of Catholic teacher formation seems to need renewal in every generation, the *Lineamenta*'s immediate priorities can be summed up as follows: i) the difficulty in finding people who are suitable for the mission of Catholic education; ii) the uniformity of training processes, which apparently fail to appreciate the distinctive elements that should be part of the prospective teacher's initial formation; and iii) the perceived status of the Catholic teacher when state schools often offer better conditions of service than those present in Catholic schools.[11]

It is not unfair to say that the apparent challenges outlined in the *Lineamenta* are not new. Shields for one had already recognized the importance of a rounded and robust formation for teachers in his time. His repeated stress on the transformative power of new classroom methods needed, as is still the case, a corps of teachers who were themselves open to continuous theological and pedagogical formation. In other words, teachers had to be immersed in the emerging thinking in pedagogy and curricular reform—mere credentialism or membership in a teaching congregation was not enough to be a successful teacher. Three themes encapsulate Shields's thinking on the processes of teacher formation: culture and vocation, correct method, and curricular content. I will explore each of these in turn below.

Principle 1: Culture and Vocation

Shields regarded teacher formation to be a research-informed and scientifically valid educational process, not simply the passing on of the received wisdom of practicing teachers. Programs of teacher

---

11 Congregation for Catholic Education, Instrumentem Laboris *Educating Today and Tomorrow: A Renewing Passion, Lineamenta* (April 7, 2014). It is worth noting that some countries have arrangements with the state for full or partial funding of Catholic schools. We always need to be cautious in drawing an overly sharp state-Catholic binary.

formation were, therefore, the foundation on which Catholic education was built.

At the Requiem Mass for Shields, Pace noted as follows:

> From long experience he had reached the conviction, which abided with him always, that the future of Catholic education, its worth and its success, depended on the preparation of Catholic teachers. Whatever else might be done to win support for our schools, to improve their facilities, quicken the interest of parents or increase vocations for the religious life, the center and pivot was and must be the teacher, her training and qualifications. This conviction roused him, filled him with eagerness, stirred him to a holy impatience. It became for him a directive principle, dominating his thought and deciding the course of his action. It became, finally, the standard by which he appraised every idea, proposal and movement, whether in the field of education or in the broader field of the sciences in which education takes root and from which it draws its vitality.[12]

This retrospective analysis of Shields's mission places teacher formation at the heart of the Master Plan, which had been brewing in Shields's mind for some time. In an article from 1909 addressed to seminary professors, Shields offered a summary of key educational principles for the benefit of the future priests who were his immediate audience. This is, in a sense, a prelude to future work in which he would set out in practical detail the lines that the process of teacher formation should follow. The principal point (as noted above) was the teacher's ability to discern the laws of mental growth / development and work with these natural processes to ensure that the educational experiences offered to pupils were aligned methodologically to what science had discovered.[13]

---

12 Pace, "Homily, Requiem Mass for Dr. Thomas Shields," 196.
13 "It is not sufficient to understand in a general way that the mind grows and then take our chances on having our method fit in more or less perfectly

Similarly, an article in 1910 on the place of the university in the training of primary teachers demonstrated how the increasing professionalization of education in the late nineteenth century demanded new insights into its scientific bases.[14] Shields made special mention of the training colleges of Scotland, including the fact that the Sisters of Notre Dame de Namur had established a training college for Catholic women (not necessarily future teaching sisters) in 1895 in the lee of the ancient University of Glasgow (founded in 1451).[15] This decision allowed the new college to breathe and be

> with that growth. The mind develops in definite ways—according to laws that are, in part at least, already formulated." Thomas Shields, "The Teaching of Pedagogy in the Seminary," *Catholic University Bulletin* 11 (1905): 445. This article was published in the same year (1905) in which he launched the Catholic Correspondence School (for religious sisters). In 1906, he published *Twenty-Five Lessons in the Psychology of Education*, which substantially developed issues around method. This book would in turn feed into a stream of further monographs and articles on method as applied to various aspects of the curriculum, not least the teaching of religion.

14 Thomas Shields, "The University and the Training of Primary Teachers," *Catholic University Bulletin* 16 (1910): 578–87. This article, interestingly, uses teacher training models in late nineteenth- and early twentieth-century Scotland as an inspiration for reform in the US. Referring specifically to Scotland, Shields claims as follows:

> Their need of contact with the universities became increasingly evident with the new demands that were being made upon the primary schools through the development of the sciences and their application to the every-day affairs of life. It became evident that the professional or trade aspect of the education given to the primary teacher was emphasized at too early an age. A broader cultural basis was necessary, but how was this to be attained? Shields, "The University and the Training of Primary Teachers," 579.

15 The first edition of the *Catholic Educational Review* in 1911 has a short, unsigned (was it from the pen of Shields?) feature on the proposed teachers college at the Catholic University of America:

> The central idea in this undertaking is to afford Catholic teachers an opportunity of securing under Catholic auspices the professional and academic training which they need in order to make the schools under

informed by the academic air of the university.[16] His plans for the Catholic Sisters College were designed to offer similar opportunities for teaching sisters in America.[17] The establishment and development of the Catholic Sisters College was to become his overriding passion, perhaps to the detriment of his wider scholarly work and, ultimately, his physical health.[18]

To deal with the formation processes of teachers in light of science is to enter a field that oscillates between two broad understandings of teacher formation: on the one hand, the importance of a liberal education, with little explicit focus on professional qualifications, and, on the other, a preference for a professional-vocational approach linking higher study with the gaining of practical skills. Shields's commitment to the scientific basis of pedagogy, and his desire to improve practice and a concomitant willingness to offer detailed advice to teachers, strongly suggest an informed

---

their charge as efficient as possible. Besides this immediate benefit to the teachers themselves, the Institute will contribute largely toward the co-ordination of all our Catholic schools, and will thus be of service to the entire Catholic body. See "The Teachers Institute," *Catholic Education Review* 1 (January 1911): 75.

16 Thomas Fitzpatrick, *No Mean Service: Scottish Catholic Teacher Education, 1895–1995: A Centenary Celebration* (Bearsden: St. Andrews College, 1995).

17 At first there was no campus, nor facilities for housing nor classrooms during the normal academic year, A Benedictine Convent nearby provided a setting for the 1911–1912 semester. By November 1911, Shields had bought fifty-seven acres to form the new campus. In April 1913, the University's Board of Trustees approved the government of the new college and called it "The Catholic Sisters College." In 1914, it was constituted as a separate corporation but to be affiliated with the University so that its students would be eligible for University degrees, and by September 1914, it had moved to its own campus, with a portable building combined for chapel, lecture hall, and dining room. Murphy, "Thomas Edward Shields: Religious Educator," 147.

18 Murphy, "Thomas Edward Shields: Religious Educator," 147. See also pp. 144–45 for details of correspondence by Shields about the significant difficulties he encountered with some teaching congregations at various stages of his plans.

predilection for the professional-vocational framework. Yet alongside this vital eye toward the practices that supported effective teaching in schools, Shields also recognized that the necessary vocational thrust of teacher formation had to be grounded in a wider and more intellectually refined base:

> Today more than ever before we need an education that will lay broad and sure foundations for future intellectual development. We need an education in theory and principle which will send our young men and young women forth from the schools with plasticity and power to meet any and every concrete situation that may arise in our rapidly changing social and industrial environment. Premature industrial training can only result in arrest of development, in rigidity of mental structure, and in a lowering of the industrial efficiency of the nation. We should by all means have vocational schools, but these should be for youths and not for children; they should presuppose an adequate cultural development and demand it of the schools that are rightly charged with the physical, moral and intellectual formation of our young people.[19]

Although this lengthy excerpt deals primarily with the educational culture of schools, its main points are also applicable to higher education. Shields sees both liberal and professional-vocational models as partners in the integral formation of the teacher. In other words, he is an advocate of a broad liberal education as the intellectual base supporting subsequent specialized training, which would incorporate applied study of such key educational concepts as "plasticity" and "development." Catholic schools, and by extension Catholic colleges and universities, therefore, should value so-called vocational training as an extension of, not a replacement for, its liberal base. Furthermore, Shields was adamant that Catholic schools

---

19 Thomas Shields, "Survey of the Field (Vocational Training)," *Catholic Educational Review* 7 (April 1914): 359.

must use every opportunity to improve the life of the school so that pupils would benefit from an education that was as good as, if not better than, that offered by its state counterparts.[20] A commitment to developing the relationship between liberal and vocational education was, and remains, necessary for improvements to happen.

Principle 2—Correct Methods

In Shields's educational vision, the choice of method is the key to an effective and meaningful classroom experience for pupils and teachers. As successful educators know, how teaching is planned, organized, implemented, and evaluated is not a succession of acts without a common thread. Good teaching is much more than the application of instinct and imitation—which are not to be too quickly discarded—but the practical outcome of the study of and reflection on the laws of mental growth and development.

The importance of the "individual in community" was central to Shields's thought. He could not overestimate the importance of "educated teachers" working in harmony for the benefit of the pupils.[21] The unity of purpose, heart, and mind necessary to build a solid system of Catholic schools would not be a product of legislation alone but the unleashing of the collective power of teachers. In this ambition he placed much trust in the members of the teaching force, acknowledging both their abilities and the need for ongoing formation:

---

20   What is demanded is that the Catholic schools meet the needs of the time as effectively as the public schools meet them. Just as the Catholic schools in the past taught the secular branches so that they might be able to teach religion and morality in a vital way, so they must now teach vocational subjects that they may continue to develop religion and morality in the hearts and lives of our children. Shields, "Survey of the Field (Vocational Education)," *Catholic Educational Review* 9 (April 1915): 295–96.

21   Franchi and Davis, "Catholic Education and the Idea of Curriculum," 108.

We have difficulties to face and we are surrounded by dangers, but we can rely upon our army of trained and devoted teachers to adhere steadfastly to Catholic ideals and whatever wandering beyond the line may occur in the storm and the stress, we may be sure of a speedy return as soon as the danger is realized. We need unity and strength in our educational system, but the unity must come rather from a recognition of common fundamental principles than through legislative enactments or coercive measures and our strength will be abundant when we turn to general use [of] the educational power that is now locked away in the brains of individual teachers scattered through the teaching communities of this country. We need our own textbooks and our own educational literature and when that need is fully realised there will be at hand an abundant supply of both the one and the other and the quality will not be inferior to the best that is produced by the hired teachers in a state school system.[22]

Shields, to be clear, recognized the many good efforts that American state schools had undertaken to prepare pupils to be good citizens but saw the aim of the Catholic school as resting on a higher, supernatural plane. He was keen to foster unity among the teaching profession but, at the same time, was suspicious of uniformity as, in his mind, the educational atmosphere around American state schools was not supportive of the principles underlying Catholic education. Shields regarded Catholic education as an enhancement to an educational system that is wholly occupied with preparation for citizenship (even as the particular nature of Catholic education, paradoxically, makes more secure the pupil's capacity to adjust to the demands of the state).[23] It was, therefore, urgent to ensure that the Catholic schools had all of the resources and support they required to be true to their educational mission and, from that faith-filled

22 Thomas Shields, "The Catholic Educational Association," *Catholic University Bulletin* 15 (1909): 88.
23 Shields, *Philosophy of Education*, 32.

base, play a leading role in the formation of both good Catholics and good American citizens. Teachers henceforth needed all manner of support, including that of printed resources, such as teaching manuals and textbooks. While the provision of such material was essential for all Catholic teachers, it was especially important for those charged explicitly with the teaching of religion:

> The teacher of religion who would be faithful to the Divine Model, must take into account natural phenomena, human emotions and passions, the figures and prophecies of the Old Testament and their fulfilment in the New. He must seek to make the Saviour live in the imagination and in the heart and he must call to his assistance every resource of art. This plan will be carried out as far as may be in the series of text-books of Religion which are here under discussion.[24]

Given this high ideal, the provision of textbooks (see part 5) was, in his mind, not only for the benefit of the pupils; rather, it was part of the ongoing support mechanisms for teachers. In a sense it was a recognition that pupils *and* teachers formed an educational and ecclesial community and, therefore, deserved the support of the wider Church community.

There were also some very practical considerations facing Shields—there were many teachers who would welcome the opportunity of greater formational opportunities but other issues, such as geographical location, were an obstacle to participation in related events such as symposia. Furthermore, the human tendency to grow rusty in our ways of working needed to be addressed if teachers were to remain abreast of new thinking in the field:

> It has often been said by those in a position to know that no matter how thorough the normal training of a teacher may have been, three years of actual work in the schoolroom will find her settling

---

[24] Shields, "Notes on Education," 75.

into a rut unless she keeps her mind alive and her spirits refreshed by contact with the world outside the schoolroom. Furthermore, it is evident that she will rapidly become wooden in her methods and stereotyped in her knowledge unless she keeps abreast of her profession by frequent contact with current educational thought and literature. To avoid a deterioration of this sort every influence is brought to bear to induce the teachers to attend educational conventions and lectures, from time to time, on educational topics by educators who are supposed to have something vital to impart. Many of our teachers, however, are so situated as to be unable to take advantage of these sources of help except at very rare intervals. The only hope of such teachers is the educational literature that may be placed within their reach.[25]

The temptation to lukewarmness and professional staleness, as noted above, is not unique to teaching. As human vices, they can afflict any person in any role. Shields sees particular value in the community of educators as a source of inspiration and a counterweight to the perceived professional ennui that he lamented above. In encouraging a cycle of conventions and lectures designed to raise teacher formation toward a higher academic plane, while keeping a constant eye on how to improve classroom practice, he manifested a farsighted attachment to linking "theory" and "practice." Shields's solution to problems created by teacher location—to find innovative ways to connect knowledge and practice in a set of written resources—remains an interesting response today.

Principle 3—Curriculum Content

For Shields, deep theoretical and practical knowledge of educational science alongside excellent personal-social qualities were the material that made the teacher a link in the golden chain that

---

[25] Shields, "Catholic Educational Literature," *Catholic University Bulletin* 15 (1909): 663–64.

transmits knowledge and cultural inheritance to new generations.[26] If the importance given to methods were to have the desired positive effects, careful study of the roots of such methods would, of course, be needed. Knowledge of the cultural history of educational institutions and the critical awareness of the broad field of educational philosophy would also be required. Teacher formation programs, therefore, needed clear direction with respect to actual program content. To this end, and drawing on the general principles set out above, Shields developed a teachers curriculum based on three pillars: philosophy of education, psychology of education, and history of education.

Philosophy of education is the predominant strand in this curricular project. It is proposed as a "branch of applied science," which, ideally, imports insights from "pure philosophy" into the realm of the school. It facilitates the building of knowledge and good habits in the pupils.[27] From psychology there emerges a necessary focus on the mental processes and faculties of the child, while history of education provides a form of "control" upon the conclusions, however tentative, drawn from philosophy and psychology.[28]

---

26 Shields, *Philosophy of Education*, 413.
27 Shields, *Philosophy of Education*, 23.
28   Parallel to the history of philosophy is the history of education; and not simply parallel but interacting and intertwined. If we would understand in its fulness the meaning of modern thought, we must trace its development from the beginning to our own day. And if we would fully appreciate modern theories and methods of education, we must follow their historical growth. And more than anything else, if would realize in a very concrete way what the Church has done for education we must read over and over the story of those ages in which the Church was literally the teacher of the nations. Shields, "The Teaching of Pedagogy in the Seminary," 446.

See also Shields, *Philosophy of Education*, 22: "The philosophy of education, the psychology of education and the history of education are linked together in their services to the teacher and interwoven with each other as the basis of

For Shields, philosophy of education must seek to suppress humanity's sinful instincts and open the mind of the human person to the life of grace. The need for reform was urgent owing to the plethora of educational literature promoting a vision of education "wholly at variance with Catholic ideas and ideals of life."[29] Within this complex state of affairs, Shields concluded that so-called Catholic philosophy must underpin the life of the school.[30]

Shields, therefore, did not see dialogue with and openness to new ideas as a means of replacing the foundations of Catholic education. Of course dialogue, if it is to be meaningful, is a robust process and can lead to both agreement and disagreement on many issues among interlocutors. Consequently, the formation of teachers for Catholic schools had to be grounded in an all-encompassing Catholic vision of the human person that allowed teachers to engage in external dialogue with a degree of confidence in their own traditions.[31] Hence the importance afforded to the philosophical foundations of Catholic education.

Furthermore, Shields was open to finding common ground between Catholic and other theories of education. The point of intersection is biology: those who have accepted the evidence from biological research can more easily see education as, to use the words of Shields, "a process by which society seeks to perpetuate

---

his professional training. On this basis rest the other branches included in the curriculum of the normal school and the teachers college."

29 Shields, *Philosophy of Education*, 24.

30 "It is, therefore, a matter of the utmost importance to Catholics that the philosophy of education employed in the training of Catholic teachers be not only technically efficient, but that it be such that as draws from the pure fountains of Catholic philosophy wholesome principles of life." Shields, *Philosophy of Education*, 25. For more on the place of philosophy in religious education, see Richard Pring, *Challenges for Religious Education: Is There a Disconnect between Faith and Reason?* (Abingdon: Routledge, 2019).

31 Shields cites St. John Baptiste de La Salle as an example of an educator who combined holiness of life with important innovations in the training of teachers. See Shields, *Philosophy of Education*, 415.

its institutions and its life and to adjust each generation of children to the environments into which they must enter at the close of the school period."[32] Interestingly, Shields saw the three pillars of teacher formation—philosophy, psychology, and history—as a means of liberation from the perceived restraints of the so-called "craft" model of teacher formation.[33] They form the core elements of the academic, not the professional, curriculum for prospective teachers. The necessary academic-professional binary—if we can call it that—is, for him, a means to the proper application of scientifically valid methodology in the classroom.[34]

In drawing from the field of science, Shields's scope is the reform of educational methods in all schools, not just in Catholic schools. Nonetheless, he was also insistent that the differences between Catholic and state schools were not just in the educational principles on which they were based. There had to be clear light in the following: curriculum material (both in content and its interpretation), selection / training of the teaching force, and the teaching methods employed.[35]

Ultimately, the aim of the Catholic school goes beyond the promotion of good citizenship: prospective teachers, whether they be in a normal school or a teachers college, required a firm grasp of the importance of Catholic education as a means of transforming young people into "children of God."[36] For this to happen, the prospective

---

32 Shields, *Philosophy of Education*, 32.
33 "Freedom from this bondage could only be attained through a liberal education which would enable her to comprehend the great underlying principles of the art of teaching to be found in the philosophy, psychology and history of education." Shields, "The University and the Training of Primary Teachers," 581.
34 "Pure science leads to discovery, while applied science aims at invention. Applied science presupposes pure science and is limited by its development. Invention may lag behind discovery; it rarely, if ever, overtakes it and from the nature of the case, it never can transcend it." Shields, Philosophy of Education, 22.
35 Shields, *Philosophy of Education*, 31.
36 Shields, *Philosophy of Education*, 157.

teacher needs a set of appropriate academic qualifications and personal qualities, which he has no hesitations in delineating as follows:

> Before entering the professional school in which a beginning is to be made in acquiring the difficult art of teaching, the candidate should possess at least an elementary knowledge of general psychology, a good working knowledge of genetic psychology and mastery of a goodly share of the social inheritance of the race, and he should have realized in himself a worthy personality.[37]

The bar is, obviously, set very high. One can only speculate on how many prospective candidates for teaching would make these preentry standards today. It seems right, however, that a high threshold should be set given the importance of education for the building of a good society. The many personal qualities required suggests, of course, that the pool of candidates with the knowledge and aptitude for teaching would be small. Shields seems to make this pool even more select with his view that Catholic schools should be staffed mainly by members of teaching congregations. The idea that the majority of teachers in Catholic schools would be lay people, as is the case today, is not part of his thinking. Certainly, the contribution of the congregations to Catholic schooling cannot be underestimated, but that is not the same thing as saying that "the Church finds that her educational aims are best achieved through the organization of her teachers into religious communities which are governed by the counsels of perfection."[38] This is another debate for another time.

Conclusion

Shields's decision to turn his mind and energy to meaningful reform of Catholic teacher formation is another indication of a character that was determined to make a practical difference to education.

37 Shields, *Philosophy of Education*, 157.
38 Shields, *Philosophy of Education*, 425.

Not content with mere tinkering with existing practices in teacher formation, and doubtless inspired by the example of such influential figures as Jean Baptiste de La Salle and Julie Marie de Biliart, Shields's pioneering spirit, exemplified in his desire to ground his wider pedagogical ideas in the domains of psychology, philosophy, and history, needed a new arena in which to take his reforming zeal to a higher and more influential level. Such an ambition stemmed from his conviction that existing methods of teacher formation were simply inadequate for those who were charged with the responsibility of teaching in Catholic schools.[39]

Shields understood the importance of vocational-professional training for prospective teachers but was equally adamant that such training needed to be built on a wider cultural formation. His commitment to explicit instruction and detailed textbooks seems to favor, at least in part, a *training* paradigm and not a commitment to broader cultural formation for prospective teachers. Yet he sought to forge, at least in theory, a middle way between cultural and vocational education. As a Catholic educator, Shields saw both cultural and vocational education as ways to implement what was, in essence, a deeply theological vision of education. By this he understood Catholic education as a means to seek truth through study and immersion in the life of a Catholic educational community. To what extent the culture and curriculum of the Catholic Sisters College reflected this noble ambition is important, as we will see below.

---

39 Patrick J. McCormick, "Dr. Shields, First Dean of the Catholic Sisters College," Thomas Shields Memorial Issue, *Catholic Educational Review* 19 (April 1921): 265–68.

CHAPTER 7

MEANS OF REFORM 1: THE CATHOLIC SISTERS COLLEGE

For Shields, the priority for teacher formation was first the establishment of a dedicated university center followed by the fostering of active links between schools and Catholic University. Chapter 7 explores this ambition in three stages: Shields's early thinking on institutional reform, the Catholic University Summer School and, finally, the Catholic Sisters College itself.

Shields's Early Thinking on Institutional Reform

Late nineteenth-century America saw much debate on how to reform Catholic education. Following the Third Council of Baltimore of 1884, all aspects of Catholic education were in the mainstream of Catholic thinking, including the proper formation of teachers.[1] The first rector of Catholic University, Fr. John Keane, had already outlined his ambitions in this regard in 1888 in an article on the history of the Catholic universities of France, where he set out his

---

1 For a plentiful supply of background information on the Third Council of Baltimore, see Cassidy, "Catholic Education in the Third Plenary Council of Baltimore."

views on how Catholic University could be the national standard-bearer for the education of both clergy and teachers.[2] Fr. Keane anticipated Shields's thinking on how both a university education and school-based ("normal") training were essential and complementary pathways for the prospective teacher. In this regard, Keane and Shields were not outside the mainstream of educational thought—across the US more generally, the early years of the twentieth century saw a rise in the numbers of established chairs of pedagogy.[3] This was a testament to the increasing and long-overdue importance afforded to research into the scientific basis of how people learn and the related importance of pedagogy as a domain worthy of study in the academy.[4]

Fr. Keane's position was developed in turn by Bishop John L. Spalding, himself a noted contributor to the area of religious education.[5] Picking up on the prevailing winds of much-needed educational reform and recognizing the importance of a satisfactorily rigorous approach to teacher formation, Bishop Spalding opined that knowledge of a subject did not translate into a corresponding ability to impart such knowledge successfully to others. The good teacher had to combine a satisfactory level of subject knowledge with correct teaching

[2] "The religious orders and congregations established for that special work stand already in sore need of helpers in so wide a field, and these must be prepared for their important task, not only by specially wide and profound studies but also by the normal training that will fit them to impart knowledge success-fully." John Keane, "The Catholic Universities of France," *Catholic World* 47, no. 279 (June 1888): 295.
[3] "By 1903, eighteen New York private colleges had chairs of pedagogy." Buetow, *Of Singular Benefit*, 187.
[4] The American Catholic History Research Center and University Archives webpage at "History of CUA–Growth (1904–1928)" does not mention Shields at all despite noting the formation of Sisters Colleges at Catholic University and elsewhere at this time. https://cuexhibits.wrlc.org/exhibits/show/the-heritage-of-cua/growth--1904-1928-/the-university-expands.
[5] Nolan, "John Lancaster Spalding."

methods if schools were to be sites of authentic human formation.[6] This necessitated a reform of thinking about how to prepare young people for the profession.[7]

Shields was, therefore, moving in circles that were keen to reform the training of Catholic teachers. In this charged atmosphere, he placed his own substantial reserves of energy and prowess at the service of the wider community. Inspired by the Scottish example of teachers colleges situated close to a university campus (see chapter 6), Shields thought this proximity would have academic benefits. Shields was explicit in his praise for the Scottish "way" of training teachers as developed in the second half of the nineteenth century.[8] The closeness of the training college to a university campus would allow students (future teachers) "to comprehend the great underlying principles of the art of teaching to be found in the philosophy, psychology and history of education."[9]

6   A hundred years ago it was generally accepted that to know a thing was to know how to teach it, but now it is plain to all that knowledge is not necessarily skill, and that the teacher, besides knowing what he teaches, should also have the ability to impart his knowledge. This special skill is the result of a knowledge of right methods, and of the training which will give power to awaken and interest the mind, to command attention, and thereby to bring the pupil's whole spiritual being under the teacher's influence. John L. Spalding, "Normal Schools for Catholics," Catholic World 51, no. 301 (April 1890): 88.

  For a summary of the issues around teacher training and the establishment of the Catholic Sisters College at the Catholic University, see "The Catholic Sisters College," *Catholic Educational Review* 7 (May 1914): 437–44.

7   Shields recognized the role of Bishop Spalding in the development of normal schools following the Third Council of Baltimore. See Thomas Shields, "Teachers College of the Catholic University of America," *Catholic Educational Review* 6 (November 1913): 314–37.

8   For a more general study of the history of teacher education in Scotland, see Rachel Shanks, ed., *Teacher Preparation in Scotland* (Bingley, U.K.: Emerald, 2020).

9   Shields, "The University and the Training of Primary Teachers," 581.

Crucially, Shields was committed to advancing the education of women and, in particular, to increasing their numbers in institutions of higher education. His own view is encapsulated in an article from 1913 in which he dealt in broad strokes—and not uncontroversially—with the effect of the Protestant Reformation on women's education, comparing in unfavorable terms women's higher education in Italy with the diminished reality of women's roles in the universities of the Anglo-Saxon world.[10] His plans for a Catholic Sisters College were, it seems, much more than a response to the local need for qualified teachers, important as this undoubtedly was, but seemed to be a recovery of a wider Catholic tradition of women's higher education which, he claimed, had been set back by the Protestant reformers.

Closer to home, the Sisters of Notre Dame de Namur had already established Trinity College in Washington D.C. in 1897 as an institution for the higher education of women.[11] It had power to offer collegiate degrees and was registered by the University of the State of New York. Located near Catholic University campus, it was one of fifteen Notre Dame foundations with similar educational aims and is evidence of a growing self-confidence in the Catholic educational community. The ambitions of the Sisters of Notre Dame were fundamental to this shift.[12] It is, of course, possible that Shields's conversations with the Sisters of Notre Dame in the US had brought to light the congregation's work abroad and that, through his usual meticulous attention to detail, he saw the Scottish model of teacher training—in which the Sisters of Notre Dame had an important locus—as a suitable example for the US. The first steps in the realization of Shields's vision of a Catholic Sisters College were the correspondence courses he started in 1905 in response to requests

10 For specific examples of the role of women in higher education in Italy, see Shields, "Teachers College of the Catholic University of America," 314–37.
11 Trinity College is the "parent" of Trinity Washington University, whose website notes the achievements of the Sisters of Notre Dame de Namur in establishing the current institution: https://discover.trinitydc.edu/mission.
12 Sisters of Notre Dame, "The Institute of Notre Dame de Namur," *Catholic Educational Review* 1 (March 1911): 223–30.

from sixty religious congregations. Given the overall lack of opportunity for female participation in the life of Catholic University, this was a welcome move that facilitated further discussion about the best and most appropriate ways to develop the initiative.[13]

Shields would surely have been cognizant of the considerable efforts the teaching congregations / religious orders were already making to support the academic and professional formation of their teaching staffs.[14] Many congregations had, for all intents and purposes, the equivalent of "training schools" (or normal schools) in their novitiates where the teaching sisters followed a "systematic course of study" designed to prepare them for the classroom.[15] Although the superiors of the teaching congregations often had the well developed resources of their own community to hand, they also

13 "In 1905, in response to requests from some sixty different teaching communities, correspondence courses were opened by University professors for the benefit of the Sisters who were denied the privilege of residence instruction." Shields, "Teachers College of the Catholic University of America," 315.

14 Buetow, *Of Singular Benefit,* 191–92. Buetow includes details from the School Manual for the Use of the Sisters of St. Joseph of Carondelet, published in 1883–84. The detailed guidance found therein would not be out of place today. For example: "Teaching chronological tables is not history," and "Begin each new lesson with conversation on objects or pictures illustrative of the reading lesson, to awaken interest and develop the idea."

15 Cf. Thomas Shields, "Catholic Teachers and Educational Progress," *Catholic World* 83, no. 493 (April 1906): 94; in addition, see James A. Burns, "The Development of Parish School Organization," *Catholic Educational Review* 3 (May 1912): 431:

> Again, the science of pedagogy had gained but a slight foothold in the curriculum of the training-schools of the communities, previous to the Council. Their plan of study comprehended the thorough going over again of the studies that had been already seen in school, but there was little besides. The old idea, still obtained very widely, that anyone could teach well any subject that he had thoroughly mastered himself. Catholic training-schools were notably behind the public normal schools in this respect.

See also Joseph Barbian, "The Catholic Normal Schools of the Holy Family," *Catholic Educational Review* 5 (February 1913): 123–31.

recognized the importance of wider support if they were to offer sufficiently rigorous formation to the novices. Appropriate measures were readily available in a succession of weekend classes in various locations, in which deeper study of educational topics was on offer.[16] Interestingly, various congregations, following the Third Council of Baltimore, had begun to offer a summer school to their members; indeed, some dioceses had organized events for both religious and lay teachers in the summer months.[17] Such events are examples of the energy that the Third Council of Baltimore had generated and remind us again that Shields was not working in an educational vacuum—far from it.

In 1907 Shields published *The Education of Our Girls,* a curious book in the form of a fireside chat on the extent to which women should have access to higher education.[18] This short volume was written in the wake of the launch in 1905 of the Catholic Correspondence School (for teaching sisters) and it is reasonable (in hindsight) to see the Correspondence School as a "trial" for the much more adventurous initiative of a full training college. As a marker of its ambitions to develop its presence in the field of education, Catholic University had already established an Institute of Pedagogy in 1902, the first Catholic institution to have a dedicated department of education under the Faculty of Philosophy, with Rev. Dr. Edward Pace as its

16 "A group of teachers from every Catholic school in the Archdiocese of Philadelphia, except two whose situation renders them inaccessible, assemble every Saturday morning during the school year in the Catholic High School to attend lectures on education. The course this year is on the psychology of education. Thirteen different teaching orders are represented at these lectures; the average attendance is about five hundred." Shields, "Catholic Teachers and Educational Progress," 95–96.
17 James A. Burns, "The Development of Parish School Organization," *Catholic Educational Review* 3 (May 1912): 419–34. This article offers a host of interesting insights into the more general thinking on teacher formation and school development following on the Third Council of Baltimore.
18 Thomas Shields, *The Education of Our Girls* (New York: Benziger Brothers, 1907). A review of the book by Sr. Antonine of Holy Cross Academy is available in the *Catholic University Bulletin* 14 (1908): 57–62.

first dean, in the same year as Shields's appointment as an instructor in psychology.[19] There was, therefore, an appetite for further reform in this field and Shields (along with Pace) was willing and able to provide the intellectual ballast and practical energy for such an endeavor. In 1911, the first Summer School for women teachers took place, which foreshadowed the Catholic Sisters College of 1914.[20]

The Catholic University Summer School

Shields was fully aware that suitably robust ways of forming prospective and serving teachers would be necessary if the Catholic community were to be served by Catholic schools of the highest standard.[21] In the practical matter of actually establishing something concrete on the Catholic University campus, the Catholic Sisters College *as a discrete institution* was foreshadowed by the first Catholic University Summer School of 1911.[22] This was a response to consistent requests from sisters to have access to the degree-level teaching of Catholic University.[23] It was initially located in the

19 Buetow, "The Teaching of Education at CUA: 1889–1966."
20 Wohlwend, "The Educational Principles of Dr. Thomas R. Shields," 33.
21 Perhaps the greatest obstacle in the way of the development of our high schools is to be found in the difficulty of securing the adequate preparation of a sufficient number of teachers for the work. The Educational Department of the Catholic University has taken this matter in hand and through the Sisters' College it has already made a splendid beginning. In the near future all of our Sisterhoods will be able to secure the best training that the age affords for their future high school teachers. Thomas Shields, "Survey of the Field (The High School)," *Catholic Educational Review* 2 (December 1911): 943.
22 Shields had already invited female religious sisters to spend time studying on campus at the Catholic University of America when the male students were on vacation. No women were formally admitted to the campus of Catholic University until 1929–30. See Murphy, "Thomas Edward Shields: Religious Educator," 146–47.
23 "The need of such an institute has long been keenly felt by our teaching Sisters, and they have frequently importuned the University authorities to open to

convent of the Benedictine nuns at Brookland, not on campus, as Catholic University was not yet a coeducational site. Shields was, unsurprisingly, one of the many academic staff of Catholic University involved in teaching the courses of the Summer School.[24]

In 1914, in response to the growing numbers of those who wished to participate in the annual Summer School, Archbishop John Joseph Keane of Dubuque offered the facilities of St. Joseph's College in his diocese for Summer School participants, thus providing a twin-campus solution to the happy logistical challenge of meeting the needs of the increasing number of teachers interested in further formation.[25] Staff from the college, along with teaching faculty from St. Thomas College and St. Paul Seminary (St. Paul, Minnesota) offered their services to supplement the work undertaken by the staff of Catholic University.[26] All such activities pointed toward a more national role for Catholic University and its Sisters College in

---

them, in some becoming way, the doors of this great central Catholic school." Thomas Shields, "The Sisters' College," *Catholic Educational Review* 2 (October 1911): 743.

[24] The Sisters' College which opened on Oct. 3 was solemnly inaugurated on Saturday, Oct. 7, by His Excellency, the Most Rev. Diomede Falconio, Apostolic Delegate. The exercises took place in St. Benedict's Convent, Brookland, where the students of the College were assembled. His Excellency offered the Mass of the Holy Ghost, assisted by Very Rev. Dr. Thomas E. Shields, and Rev. Dr. William Turner as deacons. The Rt. Rev. Rector addressed the students and faculty on the significance of the occasion, and beautifully depicted the future usefulness of the new college in the cause of religion and Catholic education in this country. Patrick McCormick, "Current Events–Sisters College," *Catholic Educational Review* 2 (November 1911): 854.

[25] A detailed report of the academic, social, and cultural activities of the Dubuque Summer School is given by Sr. Mary Clara, BVM, "Dubuque Extension of the Sisters College," *Catholic Educational Review* 8 (September 1914): 153–60.

[26] The twin campus model also helped defray the costs of travel for those who lived far from Washington. Cf. Thomas Shields, "Summer Session of the Sisters College, Dubuque Extension," *Catholic Educational Review* 7 (February 1914): 163–69; Unsigned, "Catholic University Summer Schools for 1914," *Catholic Educational Review* 7 (April 1914): 289–305.

the desire of the Catholic Church in America to have schools and teachers of the highest quality.

Shields's overall aspiration was, however, to go further and create a dedicated center for specialization in Catholic teacher formation that was aligned to Catholic University and supported financially by a wide range of people. It would, he hoped, extend its reach across the country and be the site where the academic, religious, and professional pathways of teacher formation would converge.[27]

The final lines of *The Education of Our Girls* constitute the most important early indicators of the scale of Shields's long-standing ambition to establish a dedicated institution for the education of teachers:

> Here, under the shadow of the Catholic University, there will arise within a few years a Catholic Teachers' College for women, to which the various teaching orders will send their most gifted members to receive the highest training that the age affords and to carry back with them to their several communities a knowledge of the latest developments in science and of the most approved methods of teaching.[28]

There is no lack of ambition here. In fact, Shields's words seem like a premonition of what was to come. His writings at this time are replete with energy and a marked determination to bring about the changes he thought necessary if Catholic schools were to live out their divine mission.

Bearing all of this prior ambition in mind, the stated scope of the inaugural Summer School in 1911—"to base educational theory

---

27 "A training college for our Sisterhoods in the immediate vicinity of the University is in contemplation and this project cannot be realized too soon in view of the tremendous interests that are at stake. In the meanwhile there is much that may be done towards the end for which this noble project is being carried forward." Shields, "The University and the Training of Primary Teachers," 590.

28 Shields, *The Education of Our Girls*, 290–91.

and practice on Catholic principles"—was unsurprisingly ambitious and demanding.[29] The timetable for the participants was intense, with classes scheduled from eight in the morning until six in the evening, with a break of two hours from twelve noon until two in the afternoon. Two hundred eighty-four teachers attended: 255 were religious (from 23 orders or congregations) and 29 were lay women.[30] (It was open only to teaching sisters and lay women teachers.)

Academic credits from the Summer School counted toward degrees from the planned Catholic Sisters College. These intensive courses were designed to offer an experience of scholarly community. Shared study and a shared table would, it was hoped, boost the formation of the participants and thus, in practical terms, improve the life of Catholic schools. To do this, the curriculum had to combine robust academic content with the sharing of practical experiences.

The Summer School of 1911 offered a challenging curriculum consisting of the following programs:[31]

- Education, with units in Principles of Education, History of Education, Psychology of Education, Methods of Teaching Religion, Primary Methods, Physical Defects of Children, Methods of Training the Backward Child, Methods of Study, Methods of Teaching History, Methods of Teaching Algebra and Geometry, and Methods of Teaching English;
- Philosophy, with units in General Psychology and Logic; Sciences, with units in Algebra, Geometry, Astronomy, Physics, Chemistry, and General Biology;
- Languages, with units in English (Literature), English (Themed Writing), Latin, French, German, Spanish, Church History, and American Constitutional History;

---

29 Unsigned, "The Summer School: The Catholic University of America," *Catholic Educational Review* 1 (May 1911): 466.
30 Patrick J. McCormick, "The Summer School: Report of the Secretary," *Catholic Educational Review* 2 (September 1911): 658–61.
31 "The Summer School," 467–71.

- Art with a unit in Special Instruction in Free-Hand Drawing; and
- Music, with units in the Art of Singing and the History of Printing.

The courses were taught by a staff of twenty-two: ten priests, eleven lay men, and one lay woman. Shields's topics were "Principles of Education," "Primary Methods," and "Methods of Study"—and he was lauded by some attendees for his "his widely known erudition, experience and contagious enthusiasm."[32] One attendee summed up the academic atmosphere in words that encapsulated the thinking of Shields himself:

> Catholic philosophy as well as common sense are employed in the analysis of rival theories of Psychology. Later, it is forcibly brought home to us how all the ideals of education in ancient times lacked the one supreme element and how Christianity has supplied the touch-stone for all systems which are but "broken lights" of the System of the Master.[33]

The academic flavor of the Summer Schools would have been quite unlike the formational experiences offered to teachers in state schools. This was clearly intentional, as Shields, along with the other faculty of the Catholic University, was adamant that the reality of Catholic education—his commitment to learning from the sciences notwithstanding—had to be different in kind, not just degree, to that offered elsewhere. Otherwise it was no more than an addendum to a system based on what he would categorize as false educational ideals.[34]

---

32 Ursulines of Ursuline Convent, Cincinnati, Ohio, "The First Session of the Summer School," *Catholic Educational Review* 2 (September 1911): 656.

33 A Sister of Saint Dominic, "Our First Year at the Sisters College," *Catholic Educational Review* 3 (May 1912): 440. See also, A Sister of the Congregation of Notre Dame, "The Second Summer Session of the Sisters College," *Catholic Educational Review* 4 (September 1912): 152–57.

34 There were also voices calling for women's colleges to be concerned with

The second Summer School in 1912—now called the "Summer Session of the Sisters College"—featured an increased number of students. This may have been a testament to the success of the initial venture. The number of courses increased, leading to a mix of new and existing offerings along the broad liberal and practical frameworks established in 1911.[35] Subsequent Summer Schools were organized on similar lines.[36]

All in all, the Summer School was an intense experience that sought both breadth and depth. In some ways its structure recalls the plans of study for seminarians discussed at the Third Plenary Council of Baltimore.[37] In fact, the merging of cultural and professional formation in the Summer School would mirror, to a greater or lesser extent, the scope of seminary studies; indeed, it could also be argued that the increased attention to the formation of teachers was in some ways an intentional *complementary pathway* to the seminary formation of prospective priests.[38] It was on this foundation—the

---

the formation of homemakers as life in the home in the new industrial age was affording more leisure time to both men and women. It was the duty of educated women to ensure that the home returned to being a place of productive communal activity. See Sr. Mary Ruth, "The Curriculum of the Woman's College in Relation to the Problems of Modern Life," *Catholic Educational Review* 14 (September 1917): 109–24.

35 See "Summer Session of the Sisters College," *Catholic Educational Review* 3 (April 1912): 355–64 for the courses of instruction. For further data on the list of attendees and courses available at the 1912 Summer School, see Patrick J. McCormick, "The [Second] Summer Session of Sisters College (Report of the Secretary)," *Catholic Educational Review* 4 (September 1912): 158–61. An extensive overview of the program for the 1913 Summer School is available at "The Third Summer Session of the Sisters College," *Catholic Educational Review* 5 (April 1913): 338–55.

36 Cf. Patrick J. McCormick, "The Summer Session of Teachers College: Report of the Secretary," *Catholic Educational Review* 6 (September 1913): 169–75.

37 Priestly formation was seen as the key to successful Catholic parishes; similarly, ambitions for Catholic schools had to be based on teacher formation of the highest quality. See Cassidy, "Catholic Education in the Third Plenary Council of Baltimore."

38 It is a fact not unworthy of notice and perhaps rich in significance that the

retention of the cultural inheritance of the Church and the introduction of insights from psychology and biology—that the Catholic Sisters College would be built.

The Catholic Sisters College

The Board of Trustees of Catholic University formally incorporated the Catholic Sisters College on April 22, 1914. It was to be "separated and distinct from the University, but affiliated with it."[39] This arrangement allowed for the granting of Catholic University degrees while simultaneously respecting the independence of the college to set its own curriculum, albeit within the context of Catholic University's institutional commitment to be aligned to the Holy See. The curriculum of the college would be grouped under the following headings: Religious and Moral Instruction, Educational Courses, Philosophy, Mathematics, Science, Languages, Ancient and Modern History, Letters, Art, and Music.[40]

Given his commitment to the progressive development of educational thought, Shields was not initially unaware of the challenges inherent in the construction of suitable formation and training courses, and, in due course, specialized training centers for Catholic teachers:

> The difficulty which confronts our Catholic schools is that we have neither sufficient money nor sufficient candidates in the teaching profession to permit of their attending a teachers'

---

founder of the Normal School of the Holy Family, at St. Francis, Wisconsin, was the same man to whom the well-known Seminary of St. Francis owed its origin. Neither can there be any doubt but that in the mind of the founder of the twin institutions there existed a nexus and a casual interdependence. The two institutions were planned on converging lines, each being destined in its own way to promote the interests of the Catholic Church in the field of education. Barbian, "The Catholic Normal Schools," 123.

39 "The Catholic Sisters College," 437.
40 "The Catholic Sisters College," 438.

training school in the shadow of the Catholic University. The experience of the past fifty years shows clearly enough that the teachers in our elementary schools cannot do their work effectively if they remain isolated from the higher centers of learning, but it also shows that they cannot remain truly religious in character if they draw their inspiration and their uplift from institutions that are non-religious or anti-religious in character.[41]

In highlighting both the lack of suitable candidates and financial resources, we see the practical reality he (and the wider Church) faced when seeking to align teacher training with university study.[42] This challenge remains with us today.

In practical terms, the building of a new site on the Catholic University campus was, unsurprisingly, an onerous task. In December 1911, fifty-seven acres of land adjoining the campus was purchased as the site of the new building. The proximity of the new site to the campus was significant in that it allowed academic staff to be involved fully in the new venture and thus to bring the benefits of their scholarship to the future teachers.[43] Following much fundraising, the existing teachers college was reopened as "The Catholic Sisters College" in 1913 before being formally affiliated to Catholic University in 1914.[44]

41 Shields, "The University and the Training of Primary Teachers," 590.
42 The preparatory document for the 2015 conference in Rome marking fifty years of *Gravissimum Educationis*, the Declaration on Christian Education, raised similar challenges for the present day. See Congregation for Catholic Education, *Educating Today and Tomorrow*, sec. III, 1. j, k.
43 "It is proposed that the same faculty that teaches in the University proper shall also conduct the courses in the Sisters College. The proximity of the institutions makes this plan feasible and it is desirable in the present situation to keep the instruction in the Sisters College on the same high plane that is maintained throughout the other departments of the University." Thomas Shields, "The Sisters College," *Catholic Educational Review* 3 (January 1912): 9. The same volume also has reproductions of the topographical maps of the proposed new site.
44 Elias, "Thomas E. Shields: Progressive Catholic Religious Educator," 79.

The search for the funds to support the new institution was not the only issue to concern Shields.[45] He was also aware that bringing together different teaching congregations on one campus did not come without potential challenges, not least in how to maintain the unique charism and identity of the individual congregations when they were all part of one body of students. While the development of a diverse scholarly community of teaching sisters was without doubt a "good thing," a sense of shared educational mission could be weakened if the rich pastoral traditions of each congregation were perceived to be secondary to the ambition of Catholic University to be a national provider. In a letter from 1915, Shields explained the issue he had faced in his many years of preparation (starting in 1895) for the Sisters College, lamenting the religious orders' "conservative" nature, which, he said, had made it almost impossible on some occasions to get members of two communities to come together to listen to a lecture on educational matters.[46] To address this potential obstacle to his long-standing plans, Shields proposed that each congregation have its own house to which the sisters could repair when not in classes. In an arrangement similar to the Roman model of seminarians staying in national colleges while attending classes in pontifical universities, it was hoped that a suitable accommodation between the life of the Catholic University and the congregations would thus be found. In this way, the hopes and ambitions expressed at the end of *The Education of Our Girls* would finally be realized.[47]

45 Shields saw the Catholic Sisters College as a major part of the life of the Catholic community and not just a body related to the work of schools. To this end, he pleaded for all Catholics to make a financial contribution to the college by joining the Sisters College League: "It is to be hoped that membership of the League will increase rapidly." Thomas Shields, "The Catholic Sisters College," *Catholic Educational Review* 12 (June 1916): 16.
46 Thomas Shields, "Letter to Sister Josephine," June 1912, cited in Murphy, "Thomas Edward Shields: Religious Educator," 145. Murphy also notes that Shields made no mention of others involved in this work, thus giving the impression (again) that he was not a person comfortable with sharing organizational responsibilities.
47 *The Education of Our Girls* was published in serial form in 1905 and as a book

Conclusion

Available records from the early years of the initial teachers college / Summer School and the 1914 Catholic Sisters College offer powerful insights into the breadth and depth of the curricular material on offer. The documents remain important historical markers of how to educate prospective teachers in a vibrant scholarly community. These are signs to both the Catholic and the wider educational community that the Catholic understanding of education was much more than set of "Sunday school"-style activities but a much more robust process emergent from a scholarly framework, open to new ideas but also rooted in the Church's own spiritual and cultural heritage.

Despite his success in bringing to fruition what had been his heart's desire, the Catholic Sisters College was to prove another burden on Shields's health. In the 1921 Shields Memorial Issue of the *Catholic Educational Review*, the Rev. Patrick J. McCormick made clear the scale of the task Shields had willingly undertaken:

> To direct the academic affairs of a college, as is usually required of the Dean, would have been simple as compared with his task. He was called upon, however, to organize what for this country and time was an entirely new sort of institution. The choice of professors, the organization of studies, in short, the whole academic program, was to be largely arranged by him.[48]

With hindsight we can say that Shields had taken on too much. Establishing a new college from scratch while trying to maintain a heavy schedule of travel, talks to multiple audiences, and a plethora of writing commitments would test even the most robust of constitutions. Nonetheless, there was some continuity of mission from

---

in 1907. It was clear that Shields had seen a Sisters College as one of the key axes for the desired and necessary reform of Catholic education.

48 McCormick, "Shields, First Dean of the Catholic Sisters College," 265.

the original Summer School to the Catholic Sisters College. Shields made this clear in a 1915 article in which he talks about the thirteen thousand plus alumnae of the Sisters College (which opened in 1911) and the Catholic Sisters College, which was formally incorporated in 1914.[49] In addition to the increased numbers of graduate alumnae, Shields was content that the academic and pastoral ambitions for teacher training that he had long nurtured were beginning to be realized:

> Religion is found at the heart of the whole process and, one of the most conspicuous results of the movement inaugurated by the Sisters College, is seen in the rapid process that is being made towards the unification and standardization of our Catholic educational institutions of all grades.[50]

While this comment could be seen as the marking of one's own homework, the available feedback from the wider Catholic educational community would suggest that something positive was indeed stirring in Catholic University's mission to educate teachers.

The college manifested Shields's single-minded determination—not unreasonable in the circumstances—to align academic and professional training in a single institution for the whole country. In thinking along such lines, Shields was at one with the original mission of Catholic University to be the desired point of reference for Catholic intellectual life in US.[51] In his attempts to formalize

49 Thomas Shields, "The Summer Session of the Sisters College," *Catholic Educational Review* 9 (January 1915): 36–42. In an article from 1916, Shields refers to the "fifth year of the Catholic Sisters College." Given that the eponymous institution had been incorporated in 1914, it is not possible to mark five years of its existence in 1916. It seems, therefore, that Shields saw the 1911 Summer School as the real "beginning" of his work, with the change of name in 1914 as solely a legal matter. See Shields, "The Catholic Sisters College."
50 Shields, "The Summer Session of the Sisters College," 39.
51 Truly, since this great University of higher studies not only brings increased glory to your country, but promises salutary benefits in the propagation

the training of teachers across the country we can glimpse shades of a Napoleonic approach to organization, which made a virtue of centralization and top-down planning.[52] While this might seem to go against the important Catholic social principle of subsidiarity, we can also recognize the potential advantages—at least in the short term—such an arrangement had for the growing (in number and influence) Catholic population.

---

of sound doctrine and in the protection of Catholic piety, we are justly confident that the American faithful in their liberality will not disappoint you in bringing to magnificent completion the work they have so generously begun. 7. As the University at Washington is established by this letter, we desire that no other institution of this nature shall be undertaken by anyone without consulting the Apostolic See. Leo XIII, *Encyclical Letter Magni Nobis (On the Catholic University of America)* (March 7, 1889): 6.

52 Shields sees centralization as a force in history that can be seen in, for example, economics, industry, and internationally focused research. He evaluates it in a broadly positive light: "Cooperation is rapidly displacing competition along all lines of human endeavour." Shields, "The University and the Training of Primary Teachers," 587.

CHAPTER 8

MEANS OF REFORM 2: AFFILIATION OF SCHOOLS

Chapter 8 explores the School Affiliation Program. In broad terms, a university-school affiliation program, while of necessity practical in its design and orientation, is, in some ways, a reflection of the communitarian nature of the Church. On the other hand, such a program could also be framed as a means of centralization and, therefore, a challenge to the development of various local initiatives. The latter frame thus makes the school, in a sense, subservient to the university. Both frames run through the Catholic University Affiliation Program, which Shields saw as essential to the success of his Master Plan.

The Affiliation Program in Operation

The theology of communion proposes a spirit of cooperation and the fostering of profound spiritual bonds.[1] It is hence a theme ripe for development and application to multiple ecclesial contexts. One

---

1 "From this sacramentality it follows that the Church is not a reality closed in on herself; rather she is permanently open to missionary and ecumenical endeavour." Congregation for the Doctrine of the Faith, *Letter to the Bishops of the Catholic Church on Some Aspects of the Church Understood as Communion* (May 28, 1992), 4.

such example of fostering unity-in-diversity is found in the original vision of The Catholic University of America as set out by Leo XIII in 1889:

> We urge you all, on the other hand, to be sure that your seminaries, colleges and other Catholic institutions be affiliated with the University as suggested in its statutes, but, however, without impairment of their autonomy.[2]

The prime intention of Leo XIII was to integrate seminary training into the intellectual atmosphere of Catholic University. While this is a laudable aim in itself, the flexibility of his comments helpfully left ample space for the possible inclusion of Catholic schools in a process of affiliation. The question of retaining, and not crushing, the autonomy of the affiliated institutions was also highlighted, thus showing an awareness, in principle at least, of the potential stifling effects of overcentralization. Furthermore, the widely used American term "Et Pluribus Unum"—which appeared on the first Great Seal of the United States in the late eighteenth century—might have been part of the raison d'être of Catholic University as a gathering point for Catholic educators in America. Shields's dream was that from its lecture halls a host of committed, qualified, and pious teachers would emerge, secure in their knowledge of both Catholic doctrine and sound pedagogy, who would then seek to transform Catholic education with their informed and faith-filled professional practice. At the heart of this idealistic vision lay the importance of ongoing cooperation between schools and Catholic University, teaching sisters and academics. When we apply the theology of *communio* to educational models, we ought to find more than standard examples of collaborative working arrangements, but rather a shared mission among people as relational beings with the said mission having both "vertical (communion with God) and horizontal (communion

---

2 Leo XIII, Encyclical Letter *Magni Nobis* (*On the Catholic University of America*), 4.

with people)" dimensions.³ Even though educational institutions are driven initially by the energy and vision of their founding personnel and immediate successors, their future shape and mission should be able to shift as appropriate to address new challenges. This is one example of how a spirit of communion can underpin organic change and offer support for initiatives like a university-school affiliation program. It is within these broad parameters that we can locate the Affiliation Program of the Catholic University.

As already noted, Catholic University's correspondence courses and Summer Schools were means of bringing Catholic school teachers closer, and not just geographically, to the heart of its mission.⁴ Catholic University's Affiliation Program, approved by its Board of Trustees on May 8, 1912, was a natural extension of such important initiatives.⁵ It was a response to moves by the education departments of state universities to extend their influence to all schools in their jurisdiction and was the first school standardization program "under Catholic auspices in the United States."⁶

3 "Therefore, within the sphere of biblical anthropology, man is not an isolated individual, but a *person*: a being who is essentially relational. The communion to which man is called always involves a double dimension, that is to say vertical (communion with God) and horizontal (communion with people)." Congregation for Catholic Education, *Educating Together in Catholic Schools: A Shared Mission between Consecrated Persons and Lay Faithful* (September 8, 2007), 8.

4 "For some years many of the Sisters have been pursuing with credit correspondence courses carried on by the Catholic University of America. Last summer they had more than their proportion of teachers in attendance at the University Summer School, and this notwithstanding the great distance and the heavy expense involved in travel. Several of their academies and high schools are about to affiliate with the University." Thomas Shields, "Catholic University Extension Work in Texas," *Catholic Educational Review* 3 (February 1912): 127. In this article, Shields is referring to sisters working in Texas, but he clearly sees the need for new models of teacher formation.

5 Murphy, "Thomas Edward Shields: Religious Educator," 141.

6 Watrin, *Founding and Development of the Program of Affiliation*, v.

Following on his already strong views on how new ways of understanding pedagogy needed a robust doctrinal base if they were to be effective in Catholic schools, Shields quickly picked up on the perception that Catholic schools needed more substantial means of support than that proposed by the state universities.[7] Working with Pace (see chapter 1), he put in place plans for Catholic University's High School Affiliation Program. The success of the venture came from Shields's desire—as always the fruit of diligence and attention to detail—to make wider theory and aspirations come to life.[8] The actual work on the ground was carried out by teaching sisters under the guidance of Shields and Pace.[9]

The Affiliation Program had two principal aims: a) to help Catholic schools increase their educational standards and b) to encourage Catholic high school graduates to continue their education at Catholic University.[10] It was an attempt to influence and direct the life and culture of the Catholic school system. It was also driven by the seeming inability of existing professional associations and networks to offer adequate support to teachers. In practical terms, the Affiliation Program consisted of reports, school inspections, and examinations designed to standardize the work of Catholic high schools along the lines designed by Catholic University.[11]

7 "Shields and Pace saw an attempt by the non-Catholic universities to dominate the whole public school system and to control all the primary and secondary schools within the radius of their influences, whether such schools were Catholic schools or state institutions." Murphy, "Thomas Edward Shields: Religious Educator," 139.
8 "Shields's contribution seemed to have been the realization of many of Pace's ideas. Shields's organizational ability, vitality, and Pace's prestige and influence were an exceptionally fortuitous combination at that time." Murphy, "Thomas Edward Shields: Religious Educator," 138.
9 Elias, "Thomas E. Shields: Progressive Catholic Religious Educator," 79.
10 For more on this, see Leo McVay, "Dr. Shields and Affiliation," Thomas Shields Memorial Issue, *Catholic Educational Review* 19 (April 1921): 269–73.
11 For precise details of some of the demands placed by Catholic University on prospective affiliated schools, see Watrin, *Founding and Development of the Program of Affiliation*, 198–201.

For all intents and purposes, the Affiliation Program was an extension of the work of the teachers college. By the end of the first year, fifty-two schools—all run by female religious—had joined the program, and its central office moved to the Catholic Sisters College when it opened in 2014. What this shows is Shields's desire to achieve another practical outcome of the work of the Sisters College: the newly formed sisters were, in reality, its *extended arm*, having the aim of making a positive impact on the curriculum and methods of individual schools.[12] In this way, one of the original aims of Catholic University as set out by Leo XIII (see above) was realized, although Leo himself had probably not envisaged Catholic University's work with schools.

The coming together of Catholic University and schools was providential as it offered a new vision of cooperation and mutual growth.[13] The Affiliation Program was made more robust by the related process of accreditation, itself a stronger and more concrete term than affiliation, thus offering a neat symmetry between the theological / ecclesiological notion of the former with the more institutional tones of the latter. The affiliation-accreditation dynamic offered ample space for the complementary talents of Shields and Pace to forge a new initiative as a counterforce to the many powerful

12   Murphy, "Thomas Edward Shields: Religious Educator," 136–43.
13   Doctor Shields's marvelous ability to see the reign of law in the realm of life, together with its unity and coordination, has left its impress here as well as elsewhere on things educational in the Catholic system. Every school or college can become affiliated to the University in such a manner that its local conditions, needs, and aims will be strengthened and adapted to wider applications, losing nothing of its individuality, its freedom, and its special purpose for the pupils it serves. It is this characteristic of the process of affiliation that gives it vitality and natural growth. It is this factor that keeps its uniformity from becoming sameness; that mutually protects the necessary law of divergence and the equally essential law of unification. The definite aims and unchanging principles of true education are thus enriched and ennobled. The spirit of affiliation is identical with the spirit of true Catholicism, namely sound cooperation. McVay, "Shields and Affiliation," 273.

secular voices and trends in American education.[14] In 1916, Shields noted as follows:

> As a direct result of the Sisters College nine colleges and more than one hundred and thirty of the leading high schools conducted by the teaching Sisterhoods of the United States have been affiliated to the Catholic University. This does not include the colleges and high schools conducted by men, whether secular, diocesan clergy or members of religious orders, that have been affiliated with the University.[15]

Shields's use of the phrase "direct result" links the Sisters College unambiguously with the Affiliation Program. The practical outcome was evident in arrangements for the curriculum, with school examinations essentially driven by the demands of Catholic University.[16] We see here how affiliation as a concept soon become more centralized, with the central direction of the life of affiliated schools becoming increasingly the norm. To what extent this arrangement reflects the principles of subsidiarity is a matter worthy of further reflection.

Another feature of the Affiliation Program was the examination system, which involved "tabulated results"—based on common examinations—allowing each school to compare its performance with other schools. This brought in its wake what were, in effect, school league tables that would, claimed Shields, promote a "healthy rivalry"

---

14 "Affiliation was one of the plans that united Shields and Pace in the early years. Pace had been aware in the 1890's of the need for Catholic professional schools, organizations, and new texts if the Catholic teachers and schools were to maintain their own identity in view of the growing secular trend in American education." Murphy, "Thomas Edward Shields: Religious Educator," 138.

15 Shields, "The Catholic Sisters College," 14.

16 "The program for all these secondary schools is outlined by the University and the written examination of all the pupils is conducted under the direction of the University and all the examination papers examined in detail by University professors." Shields, "The Catholic Sisters College," 14.

in schools, which would in turn foster the "enthusiastic cooperation of pupils and teachers."[17] This is another example of the uniformity that underpinned and was driven by the Affiliation Program but is less convincing as a method to improve standards. "Healthy rivalry" is not necessarily a bad thing if adopted with nuance; nonetheless, there is the danger of an *un*healthy rivalry emerging if the perceived status of schools is based on examination results alone; this could lend itself to some form of professional jealousy and envy, as well as a sense of pride among the high-performing schools. Of course, this might have been driven by the desire to ensure that any underperforming schools would have partners in other schools who could offer advice and support in the quest to raise standards.

While we can see some unity of purpose being achieved through the accreditation process, what is more difficult to discern is the degree of autonomy afforded to each school in its curriculum choices. In other words, the "unum" seemed strong but the "pluribus" is less explicit. Of course, it is possible that Shields wished to stress the success of the initiative and thus highlight closer alignment between the schools and Catholic University. In any case, the reality of school life, and the traditional independence of the teaching congregations would suggest that there might have been a substantial degree of local decision-making.[18]

17   A feature of the system which is accomplishing much grows out of the tabulated results which are furnished to each school in which it may learn how its work compares with all the other schools offering the same course. Thus, the number of schools taking English I is given, the total number of pupils, the general average of all these pupils, the average of each school receiving the report, and the rank of each school as compared with all the others. Of course, no school is furnished with information concerning the standing or percentage attained by the pupils of any other school in the system. This promotes a healthy rivalry, together with a genuine and enthusiastic cooperation of pupils and teachers. Thomas Shields, "The Sisters College and the High Schools Affiliated with the Catholic University," *Catholic Educational Review* 15 (February 1918): 104.
18   See also Shields, "The Sisters College and the High Schools Affiliated with

Overall, the Affiliation Program was much more than an administrative maneuver to unite schools around a center of higher education. It was underpinned, implicitly at least, by the important notion of divine filiation: all the baptized are united by divine grace to the Fatherhood of God.[19] In applying this theological point to the Affiliation Program, we discern not just the formation of an educational collective but a living organism animated by the sacramental life of the Church. In this way, schools became the "sons and daughters" of Catholic University, drawing inspiration from it but also, as all children do, developing their own place in the family circle.

Conclusion

The Catholic Sisters College and the Affiliation Program were formidable outlets for Shields's remarkable reservoirs of intellectual and practical energy. Both were key planks in his desire to extend the influence of Catholic University across America and thus act as a bulwark against the perceived influence of secular universities and colleges on educational policy. Indeed, the Affiliation Program was a means to ensuring that the intellectual life and practical wisdom that Shields sought to embed in the college had a positive impact on schools across the country.

The Affiliation Program underwent some review and reorganization in 1938–39 owing to a perception that its development was not keeping up with the demands facing the Catholic school system at that time.[20] This does not necessarily negate the work done by Shields and others in setting up the program but does serve as a reminder of how new institutions and processes, no matter how

---

the Catholic University." This article has a slightly defensive tone as it is responding to an article that, in Shields's view, had underplayed the significance of the Sisters College and the Affiliation Program.

19 *Catechism of the Catholic Church*, § 1303.
20 Rita Watrin describes the period from Shields's death in 1921 until 1937 as the "static years." Watrin, *Founding and Development of the Program of Affiliation*.

lauded and well grounded in their initial years, often need regular refreshing in order to retain vitality in the longer term. The teachers college and Affiliation Program were Shields's particular contribution to developing the original papal vision for Catholic University. His own experience of visiting and working with teaching sisters in their schools encouraged him to do his utmost to help align their work with the intellectual resources of Catholic University.[21] Shields's apparent confidence in the knowledge and methods taught at this institution encouraged him to find new ways to increase the opportunities for teacher formation and thus build a constituency of well-formed Catholic University graduates ready to serve in schools in the United States of America.

21 McVay, "Shields and Affiliation."

PART V

THE *CATHOLIC EDUCATION SERIES*

CHAPTER 9

TEXTBOOKS AND READERS FOR CHILDREN

Long before the Second Vatican Council, Shields had been intent on the reform of Catholic educational methods in line with the emerging scientific principles—or the "new knowledge"—of his time. Alongside the establishment of the Catholic Sisters College (see chapter 8), Shields saw the provision of high-quality classroom resources as another staple of his Master Plan for reform of Catholic education. Shields's classroom material, consisting of a set of dedicated textbooks and readers, were a means to implement the educational vision that emerged from his study of new ideas. As such, this body of work is not ancillary to but rather fully part of his wider mission to improve teacher formation and pupil learning. Shields saw new textbooks, well-formed teachers, and valid methods as a complete educational package. If one element were missing, the Master Plan would fall short.[1]

The textbook as a genre of educational literature was, for all intents and purposes, one of the principal curricular resources available for teachers in America around the turn of the twentieth

1 "Teachers, methods, text-books, all must be gradually transformed in the light of our present knowledge. The task is difficult and time will necessarily be required for its successful accomplishment." Shields, "Notes on Education," 475.

century.[2] The publication of textbooks specifically for Catholic schools in the US in the late nineteenth and early twentieth centuries is evidence of a more general desire to improve the educational experience of children and support the role of the school in both the religious formation of pupils and the development of a confident Catholic presence in society.[3]

Shields's *Catholic Education Series* was published by the Catholic Education Press, which he had founded in 1906.[4] His initiative in developing a series of textbooks and readers for children would face competition; for example, from other contemporaneous publishing initiatives like Sr. Mary Doyle's series of *Standard Catholic Readers*, written explicitly to support the practice of inexperienced teachers.[5] Sr. Doyle was the principal of the Holy Name Normal School in

2 In early modern English culture, the particular genre of "ABCs with Catechism" was a popular means of direct religious instruction in the mainstream Protestant tradition and embedded unapologetically in the teaching of literacy. Such texts were often the only reading material available for children and hence were instrumental in developing the child as a reader. For more on the child as reader and the importance of genres such as ABCs and primers in the religion-literacy nexus in the early modern period, see Edel Lamb, "A Good Child is One that Loves His Book: Literacy, Religious Instruction and the Child as Reader," in *Reading Children in Early Modern Culture* (Cham, Switzerland: Springer, 2018): 29–70.

3 The important role given to education, broadly understood, in Christianity reflects the nature of the Church itself as a teaching organization, a movement called to communicate universally its message. See chapter 1 for more on this theme.

4 The original name of the Catholic Education Press was the Catholic Associated Press.

5 "Every progressive educator is constantly finding new ideas of presentation through his experience. While the majority of our teachers are well equipped for their special work, there are, nevertheless, many of the inexperienced who are not yet resourceful in attracting and maintaining the interest of the child. It is hoped that to such teachers the methods presented in this volume will prove especially helpful and stimulating." Sr. Mary Doyle, *Standard Catholic Readers by Grades, First Year* (New York: American Book Company, 1909), 3. There is ample scope for further comparative studies of textbooks and readers in Catholic schools during this period.

Seattle and her work acknowledges the support of Bishop John Lancaster Spalding, the noted advocate for reform. Shields also claimed that his textbooks and readers were essential for the pedagogical development of teachers as well as for the instruction of pupils.[6] The originality of Shields's resources stems from their status as *component parts* of his Master Plan. As such, the *Catholic Education Series* exemplifies how his wider academic work on concepts such as plasticity, mental growth / development, adjustment, and correlation could be brought to life in classroom material.[7] It is not stretching matters to say that the focus on the textbook as the recommended resource could lead to a conflation of syllabus, understood as the particular material to be taught in a given subject, and curriculum, understood as the overarching structure of the organization of knowledge. As we will see, Shields did tend to veer in this direction.

As has already been established, Shields argued that we must allow children to profit from humanity's rich intellectual and cultural heritage.[8] Central to this project was the importance of literacy,

---

6   Shields's work traveled beyond the boundaries of the US. The Guild of Catholic Teachers, formed in Glasgow (Scotland) in 1934, published a syllabus called *Religious Knowledge: A Course for Young Children*, which makes explicit reference to his work. Scottish Catholic Archives, Religious Education 4/5 (1939), 8.

7   "Shields seems to have been the first who, while giving religion a central place, successfully utilized in his readers the best to be taken from the new psychologies prevalent in his time." Buetow, *Of Singular Benefit*, 196.

8   Shields, *Teachers Manual of Primary Methods*, 216–29. These pages offer some initial thoughts on why reading is the core skill for meaningful education. On p. 244 of the same book, Shields positions the *Catholic Education Series* as part of the context method of teaching reading, not the phonics method. Page 260 then sets forth lists of words related to *Religion, First Book* and *Religion, Second Book*. Chapter 19 (pp. 260–72) takes this further by providing specific guidance on *Religion, First Book*. The lists of words do not begin with specifically religious words but instead remind the reader of the words necessary for understanding the stories in the book. Further guidance is offered on the use of charts. Chapter 18 (pp. 245–59) deals with how to teach spelling. Chapters 22 and 23 (pp. 326–74) are replete with highly detailed and very precise instructions to teachers.

traditionally defined as the ability to decode and comprehend patterns of words and ideas, and hence make sense of the world we inhabit. Literacy so understood is at the heart of any worthwhile educational endeavor. It is hard, however, to disentangle the drive for literacy found in authentic Christian educational movements from wider theological aims: the early monastic schools, for example, were driven by this noble ambition. The reason for this coupling of literacy and human formation should be obvious since, for the Christian, the human person is most fully alive when all the human senses are engaged in the search for and deep appreciation of truth, beauty, and goodness.[9]

Shields emphasized the importance of language in the process of thought development. Education was a much more dynamic and interactive process than the simple absorption of teacher-presented facts: effective thought development, to use his term, required something much more subtle.[10] From the first time the child enters the school, no effort should be spared in ensuring that all relevant material is integrated fully into his or her mind. There is no higher purpose set for the school as an educational institution, and all of the various methods and resources employed in the educational process are means to this vital end.

Shields was also very much aware of how textbooks, indeed any material for use in the classroom or lecture hall, could be grounded in mistaken educational ideas and thus serve only to distort, not enhance, the child's educational journey. His ire was especially directed at textbooks that promoted and exemplified the so-called Culture Epoch Theory.[11] For Shields, this theory of humanity's

---

[9] For some parallel thoughts on the importance of reading in early Protestant communities, see Edel Lamb, "A Good Child is One that Loves His Book."

[10] "A clear line of distinction should be drawn between thought accumulation and thought development; the former leads to erudition, the latter is an integral part of education." Shields, *Teachers Manual of Primary Methods*, 182.

[11] The *APA Dictionary of Psychology* defines Culture Epoch Theory as follows: "The theory, formerly influential but now largely discredited, that all human cultures pass through the same stages of social and economic organization in

progress from the savage to the sophisticated had wrought havoc on educational philosophy. He had, unsurprisingly, identified a series of available educational texts that he judged guilty of importing this scientifically discredited theory into educational thought and practices.[12] A wider exploration of this genre need not detain us further at this point: suffice it to say that Shields spoke of "the utter brutality of this class of child literature" and that "it is high time that every energy were bent to its extirpation before our people become wholly brutalized through its pernicious influences."[13] His emphasis on protecting "our people" (meaning the Catholic population) from such allegedly malign influences propelled him to devise, write, publish, and promote his own series of textbooks and readers, which, he claimed, were underpinned by a scientifically valid methodology and solid Catholic doctrine.[14]

Writing in the *Catholic University Bulletin* in 1909, Shields set out his thoughts on the value of textbooks in Catholic schools. His advocacy of high-quality textbooks is nuanced a little by the crucial reminder that, on the one hand, excellent classroom resources cannot compensate for a poor teacher, and on the other, a textbook with defects can still be an effective educational instrument when placed in the hands of a capable teacher. A successful classroom experience

---

the same order. In most versions of the theory, this involves progress from a hunting-based society through pastoral, agricultural, and early industrial epochs to the modern developed world, with each stage being seen as more complex, organized, and secular than previous stages." American Psychological Association, *APA Dictionary of Psychology* online, https://dictionary.apa.org/cultural-epoch-theory.

12 Shields, *Philosophy of Education*, 91–92. Shields aims his fire principally at the Industrial and Social History Series edited by Dr. Katherine Elizabeth Dopp of the University of Chicago. The series appeared first in 1903 and was directed at children of primary school age. The author of the series claims inspiration from John Dewey.
13 Shields, *Philosophy of Education*, 96–97.
14 For some thoughts on how contemporary Catholic schools should explore the issue of curriculum reform in Catholic schools, see Franchi and Davis, "Catholic Education and the Idea of Curriculum."

for pupils came from the harmonization between the teacher's own choice of methods and the methods underpinning the textbook, both of which had to be "as free as may be from the violations of the laws governing the child's unfolding life."[15]

In particular, the textbook had to exemplify the important pedagogical principle of curricular correlation and thus be a marker against a premature leap into overt subject specialization. Reflecting his view more generally that liberal studies were always prior to professional education, Shields was an advocate of much greater integration of curricular material for young children, with specialization best reserved for older pupils. His passion for correlation via the textbook stemmed from what he saw as the essential pedagogical insights arising from science, which had to be woven into pupil material.[16] Shields, while eager to address lacunae in people's appreciation of science and nature, also sounded a warning bell over the effects of poorly formulated catechesis and related issues, such as loss of respect for the family and a poor understanding of national traditions. Such phenomena, he thought, could only have baleful consequences for social cohesion.[17]

Drawing on this emerging body of "new knowledge," Shields ambitiously framed the *Catholic Education Series* as a complete and integrated curriculum, not simply as a successor to catechetical (or

---

15 Shields, "Notes on Education," 156.
16 "The development of the natural and physical sciences have in our day completely transformed the world in which we live. The children in our schools must be prepared to enter this arena." Shields, "Notes on Education," 157.
17 There is a growing realization of the facts that our children are losing reverence for old age, for their parents, for family and national traditions, for religious beliefs, that there is an enormous increase in juvenile crime in our cities, that there is a general decay of patriotism, a growing tendency to dishonesty in public office, an increasing disregard for the law, and that the family is suffering greatly from the loosening of its bonds. Shields, "Notes on Education," 158.

Similar words could easily be uttered—and often are—by Catholic and other educators today!

religion) texts already in use in Catholic schools. The *Catholic Education Series*, properly taught, would be the optimal educational resource for improving the knowledge and character of children in Catholic schools.[18] Shields was, to be sure, quite scathing about existing school-based catechetical texts that were, he claimed, "cast in the driest of catechetical forms and completely isolated from all the other subjects of the curriculum."[19] Reform of such material was pressing if they were to become examples of good doctrine and grounded in methods wholly aligned with the laws of human development.[20]

The *Catholic Education Series* was designed as an example of how correlation (see chapter 4) could be applied to a curriculum with religion at its core.[21] To recap, the school curriculum, according to the mind of Shields, should be structured around five pathways: science, letters, institutions, aesthetics, and religion. The pathways serve to support the teacher's planning, teaching, and assessment. To be clear, Shields's resources were designed to exemplify a new method of teaching that would lead the child inductively from a sense-induced knowledge of the world to knowledge of God as

18 There was a similar commitment to textbook-based reform in other Christian traditions. See George Herbert Betts, "The Curriculum of Religious Education," *Religious Education* 15, no. 1 (1920): 5–22. Like Shields, Betts emphasized the importance of religion as the core of the curriculum.
19 Shields, "Notes on Education," 159–60.
20 On the importance of good educational resources, see Pius XI, *Divini Illius Magistri*, 80:

> For the mere fact that a school gives some religious instruction (often extremely stinted), does not bring it into accord with the rights of the Church and of the Christian family, or make it a fit place for Catholic students. To be this, it is necessary that all the teaching and the whole organization of the school, and its teachers, syllabus and text-books in every branch, be regulated by the Christian spirit, under the direction and maternal supervision of the Church; so that Religion may be in very truth the foundation and crown of the youth's entire training; and this in every grade of school, not only the elementary, but the intermediate and the higher institutions of learning as well.

21 Pius XI, *Divini Illius Magistri*, 428.

reflected in the doctrines and life of the Catholic Church. The five pathways are similar to the beams that keep a physical structure in place during the construction process. The extent to which this educational scaffolding supports the teacher is dependent, however, on a number of factors, not least the ability of individual teachers to shape curricular material to suit the needs of the pupils.[22] Shields was supportive in principle of affording some liberty to teachers in their choice of material, albeit with a careful eye on the professional balance between the level of theoretical knowledge acquired through higher studies and actual classroom experience.[23]

Shields was confident that his *Catholic Education Series* was a highly satisfactory example of how to apply new methodological knowledge to the project of Catholic education. He valued the opinion of well-qualified teachers on the shape of his new material but was also confident that his method and the associated material he produced was in line with new insights on how children learn. Shields was aware of the intellectual and cultural currents swirling around education in his time and he saw his contribution to Catholic education as timely, necessary, and providential. In other words, Shields saw his Master Plan as part of a divine vocation to reform Catholic education in America and save it from the harmful effects of progressive thinking. The structure of the *Catholic Education Series* offers more evidence of this sureness of vision.

22 The concept of scaffolding is present in much contemporary educational literature. For an overview of its history as an educational term, see Anna Shvarts and Arthur Bakker, "The Early History of the Scaffolding Metaphor: Bernstein, Luria, Vygotsky, and Before," *Mind, Culture, and Activity* 26, no. 1 (2019): 4–23.

23 The teacher needs both a clear comprehension of fundamental principles and experience in the actual work of teaching before she can prudently dispose with guidance in determining the details and the general character of the children's work. No amount of theoretical knowledge without experience nor any amount of experience without clear knowledge of fundamental principles gives the teacher the right to determine the lines along which the minds and hearts of the children committed to the care of the school are to be developed. Shields, "Notes on Education," 476.

CHAPTER 10

THE *CATHOLIC EDUCATION SERIES*: STRUCTURE AND AIMS

Shields's textbooks and readers were designed to be the complete curriculum for Catholic schools. If they were to be successful in raising standards in Catholic schools, they had to be taught by teachers who were themselves furnished with up-to-date knowledge of effective methods.

A Complete Curriculum

Shields had intended to write a complete series of textbooks and readers as the means to implement his educational principles in the life of the Catholic schools of America. The original plan was for an eight-volume collection but an excessive workload and his (probably related) premature death in 1921 thwarted the realization of this ambition. We can only speculate on what the complete series over eight grades would have looked like.[1] There was an attempt by another author—Sister Mary Verone Wohlwend, SND—to continue this cycle but, it seems, with limited success.[2] The following table

---

1 Wohlwend, "The Educational Principles of Dr. Thomas E. Shields," 60.
2 Wohlwend, "The Educational Principles of Dr. Thomas E. Shields," 63: "It

shows the works completed, the date of publication, and which of the planned texts were unfinished ("x") at the time of his death.

Grade	Text-Book	Reader
1	*Catholic Education Series, First Book*, 1908, with a second edition in 1917	
2	*Catholic Education Series, Second Book*, 1909	
3	*Catholic Education Series, Third Book*, 1910	*Catholic Education Series, Third Reader*, 1908
4	*Catholic Education Series, Fourth Book*, 1918	*Catholic Education Series, Fourth Reader*, 1915
5	x	*Catholic Education Series, Fifth Reader*, 1915
6	x	x
7	x	x
8	x	x

It is worth noting that the *Catholic Education Series, First Book* was originally titled *Religion, First Book*.[3] This change in nomenclature addressed a perceived misunderstanding (we are not told who had misunderstood this) of the purpose of the book.[4] The original title

was the privilege of the writer, under the direction of Dr. Johnson, to compile units of religion for grades five through eight."

[3] Thomas Shields, preface to *The Catholic Education Series, First Book* (Washington, D.C.: The Catholic Education Press, 1917), 3.

[4] The book is named Religion, consequently, not because it deals with religion exclusively, but because religion is the most important element which it contains and because all the other elements of the child's mental content are made subordinate to religion, both in arrangement of material and in emphasis. Religion thus becomes the basis of the child's education,

was intended, obviously, to underline the importance of religion to the child's educational journey; the revised title was a way to emphasize that the book was not solely about strictly religious formation (or school-based catechesis) but was intended to be the only resource used in the class and hence be a complete manual for the wider education of the child, albeit revolving around religious principles and practices.

The series is arranged thematically: for grades 1 and 2 there is one combined textbook and reader; for grade 1 the focus is aesthetical, concentrating on moving from the familiar to the abstract, and in grade 2, attention is given to the divine law and the operation of free will. The textbook for grade 3 explores redemption and the Church's sacramental system, with close attention given to figures from the history of salvation; the associated reader aims to develop a proper understanding of conscience. The textbook for grade 4 is on the liturgy, with the reader exploring the rise of Christian civilization after the time of the Emperor Constantine (AD ca. 280–337). There is a reader for grade 5 that has a focus on the classics of literature but there is no companion textbook.

Shields argued that an inadequate understanding of the nuances of pedagogy are the cause of a cultural and educational dissonance.[5] To give two examples, he described art and music provocatively as "holiday attire which is put on for a brief period each day and laid aside before the 'serious' matter of the programs are taken up."[6] He has a similarly negative position toward the teaching of literature if

---

the germ from which all else is made to unfold, and this is as it should be in a Catholic education where everything should be made to lead to God and be used as a means of attaining eternal life. Shields, "Notes on Education," 161–62.

5 There might be a link here to Pope Benedict XVI's diagnosis of an "educational emergency" and its possible deleterious effects on the Church and society. See Benedict XVI, "Letter to the Diocese and City of Rome on the Urgent Task of Educating Young People," January 21, 2008.

6 Shields, "Notes on Education," 158.

approached in such a fragmented and unsophisticated way.[7] It should come as no surprise that the teaching of religion is not spared a similar judgment, with the available material (essentially catechisms) derided as out of touch, abstract in content, and essentially of little or no value to the great mission of authentic Catholic education.

In light of this hard-hitting analysis, revised textbooks had to be a showcase for the principle of correlation. This was essential to ensure the necessary unity of curricular content, which is especially important for the progress of younger children. For the teaching of religion, the textbook must awaken in some way the child's interest in the subject, instead of beginning, as noted above, with abstract formulations of theological principles. The only way in which to offer the child a clear and fruitful understanding of these same theological points is through attractive, concrete presentations of doctrine in embodiments that touch the child's imagination and, hence, arouse enthusiasm. This was a core feature in the preparation of the textbooks for the elementary grades of Catholic schools.[8]

Shields compares his teaching approach with that of the established Baltimore Catechism. Unsurprisingly, the Baltimore Catechism uses the standard question-and-answer format that he regards as a prime example of a dry, abstract pedagogy, and that, he believes, too often fails to raise the child's interest in the subject matter. There is no recognition, however, of the potential for teachers to use the Baltimore Catechism (or similar texts) imaginatively. Perhaps the general atmosphere in Catholic schools would not have been conducive to such initiatives. By way of contrast, *Catholic Education*

---

7 "Our schools seem to be pervaded by a deathless superstition concerning the teaching of literature. The children are given fragments from a hundred authors and it is devoutly believed that these samples will suffice to cultivate a lasting taste for the authors in question." Shields, "Notes on Education," 159.

8 And if we look beneath the surface and find that the text-books of secular instruction present truths in concrete embodiment to the young child and avoid abstract statement, while Christian Doctrine is presented in purely abstract formulations with verbal explanations of the unintelligible words, our difficulty is increased. Shields, "Notes on Education," 403–4.

Series, First Book uses a stock of images and ideas that are already familiar (or should be) to the child. Before looking at *First Book* in more detail, it is important to explore the wider issue of how teachers work with textbooks.

Textbooks and Teachers

The teacher's role in early education is to be the primary resource for the children. It is her role, acting *in loco parentis*, to promote, for example, children's language skills and be proactive in their physical, cultural, emotional, and religious development.[9] The importance of the teacher's role in early education demands the highest competence and best professional training.[10] Through this valuable work, the teacher is called to offer material for thought development that will stand the child in good stead in the future:

> The work in the primary grades has not heretofore received the attention that it deserves from psychologists and educators. It has been left, in large measure, to the guidance of young women with limited academic and professional training. All that was demanded of the primary teacher was, that she keep the children interested and that at the end of the year she send them up into the higher grade with a reasonable ability to call words. The

---

9 Shields, *Teachers Manual of Primary Methods*, 198.
10 In the old days the most incompetent teacher in the school was assigned to the baby class and the efficiency of the teacher was recognized by promoting her to a higher grade. Academic content, rather than professional training, was the standard by which a teacher's value was rated, and in this fact may be found the reason for assigning the poorest teacher to the lowest class. Anyone was supposed to be able to make the children recite their a, b, c's and to hear them spell their words of one or two syllables, but today all this is changed. The fact is now generally recognized that a successful primary teacher is not easily obtained, and that the highest professional training is needed in the lowest grades. Shields, *Teachers Manual of Primary Methods*, 218.

thought development was supposed to belong to a later stage. The consequences of this neglect of primary work by those competent to deal with it are very serious.[11]

What are we to make of this comment? Is it a veiled criticism of the educational level of the primary teachers of his time or is it, rather, an expression of a different reality: the many processes involved in thought development are too complex for any one individual to grasp and that, in consequence, textbooks are a necessary vade mecum for the teacher? If this is the case, the textbook then is no longer just a resource for the child but also the handbook which governs and directs the action of the teacher.[12] This is a strong statement of principle and, despite the possibly problematic (or tone-deaf) language about the ("limited") training of some teachers, actually calls for primary education to be afforded a much higher professional status. As children mature, they grow in knowledge and develop an independence from the textbook and the teacher. For Shields, primary education is not simply a refined form of childcare but the essential first step in a lifelong educational journey. The use of wrong methods in the early years of education will have serious consequences in later life. To use a contemporary phrase, Shields "pulls no punches" in his view of the importance of the teacher's competence in the early years of education—going so far as to encourage the removal of incompetent teachers—and of why teachers at this stage need the support system of high-quality and authoritative textbooks if the young child is to receive the best possible educational experience.[13]

11 Shields, *Teachers Manual of Primary Methods*, 231.
12 There is more than a hint here of the approach adopted by the Catechism of the Council of Trent (a.k.a. the Roman Catechism). This important document was expressly written as a manual for parish priests who were perceived, rightly or wrongly, to need both an accessible doctrinal primer and hints on teaching methods. See Franchi, *Shared Mission*, 50–53.
13 "Clearly, if the teacher's methods are faulty, they should be corrected, or she should be removed from the school. This is particularly true in the primary

Shields emphasized unity and harmony in the teaching process, with the ultimate test being how the teacher's chosen method is in line with the style and methodological preferences expressed in or even demanded by the author of the textbook.[14] This reminds us of the importance placed by Shields on the actual composition of textbooks. So-called "supplementary work," either oral or written, prepared at the teacher's behest, should be a preparation for the material in the textbook and not an alternative site of knowledge.[15] This planting of seeds by the early years teacher is a silent task and she might never gather the fruits of her hidden but invaluable labor. Although the textbook is central to the educational process, the teacher has the ability to make the material come alive by encouraging the pupils to think and by using well-phrased questions to allow pupils to explore issues in an age-appropriate way. This marks a move away from mere memorization toward an allegedly more active, or engaging, form of teaching.[16]

Excellence in method does not, on the whole, come easily to teachers. It demands prior academic and practical training of the highest quality, followed by ongoing collegial support. The judicious use of textbooks, therefore, is an aid to thought development in the hands of a good teacher, and Shields is quick to recommend his own *Catholic Education Series* as an example of how to translate

---

grades where, admittedly, so much depends on method." Shields, *Teachers Manual of Primary Methods*, 218.

14 Shields offers an interesting example. He says that teachers who wish to teach primary reading by the phonics method should not use the *Catholic Education Series* because this series "was constructed with the explicit purpose of preventing the development of those things which are the central aim of the phonic method, hence, their use, as the basis of teaching the phonic method, must necessarily prove a failure." Shields, *Teachers Manual of Primary Methods*, 219. He does not seem to be open to a blend of different sources.

15 "The business of supplementary work of all kinds is to supplement; it should prepare for the thought and the language of the text-book; its effect should be to heighten the interest in the central theme; it must never lead in a divergent direction." Shields, *Teachers Manual of Primary Methods*, 201.

16 Shields, *Teachers Manual of Primary Methods*, 239.

material suitable for thought development into works that are accessible to children.[17]

Shields agreed that the methods and ideals underpinning the textbook should be "tested carefully and conscientiously by competent teachers."[18] We see here an overt affirmation of the professional judgment of the teacher and, possibly, an appreciation of the supportive value of what is often described today as a "community of practice," with teachers supporting each other in many, often implicit, ways. (This might have been quite a common practice in the "normal school" activities of the novitiates of teaching congregations.) Any errors in practice identified should be corrected and, if necessary, a more suitable way forward should be found.[19] On the other hand, he also believed that no teacher should be permitted to declare autonomy in how she uses the material, as so doing would destroy the unity and authority on which the curriculum depends.

To enhance correlation, Shields underlined the importance of "securing symmetry in the text-book."[20] This brings about the proper order, or sequencing, of teaching and should ideally be accompanied by a similar commitment to "order" in the supplementary work of the class.[21] The textbooks must reflect sound educational principles and be able to catch the interest of children.[22] The thought material

17 "The teacher who studies the *Catholic Education Series* of primary text books can scarcely fail to observe the manner in which the method of thought development is embodied in them. The Questions, the Thoughts for Us, and the Lessons for Life constantly direct the attention of teacher and pupil to this aspect of the books." Shields, *Teachers Manual of Primary Methods*, 188.
18 Shields, *Teachers Manual of Primary Methods*, 200.
19 Shields, *Teachers Manual of Primary Methods*, 210.
20 Shields, *Teachers Manual of Primary Methods*, 202.
21 See Shields, *Teachers Manual of Primary Methods*, 202, where Shields cites the example of children's literature, describing it as "abundant," but stating that it has not been developed with any distinct view to Christian aims.
22 "It is curious to note how some of the books used in our schools were prepared, and particularly, in regard to the introduction of new words. Size, sound, appearance and arbitrary standards seem to have dictated the choice

found therein, as well as resting on a sound scientific basis, must also "be the seeds of truth which the Saviour of men brought into the world."[23] Given the importance of the textbook in the mind of Shields, it is no surprise that the author of the textbooks assumes a great (and sacred) responsibility for both content and methods employed. The writing of such important material cannot, however, be the work of the solitary genius dispensing knowledge to a wide constituency. Although Shields's tremendous work ethic and productivity might suggest a predilection for the solitary academic life, he was also rightly renowned for his work in the lecture hall and beyond.

Material intended for use in the class, if it is to be of lasting value, needs input from a wide range of qualified professional voices—the philosopher, psychologist, teacher, clergyman, and school leader, and, in particular, the massed ranks of classroom teachers:

> It is only right and proper that the author of a text-book which is to go into the hands of generations of the little ones of the fold of Christ should bring to the task adequate preparation and give to it sufficient time and thought to insure against grave errors. Moreover, the text-book should call forth comment and criticism from the philosopher, and the psychologist, from the professional educator, from bishop, pastor and principal, as well as from the rank and file of the teachers who may use the book. It should, accordingly, express the wisdom of the many rather than the intelligence of the one. The authorship of the primary text-books used in our schools is, therefore, a matter of the highest importance.[24]

Shields hence offered a rationale for textbooks based on the collective voice of the teaching traditions of the Church community. In stressing the importance of the textbook as a pupil resource,

---

rather than consideration of the usefulness or meaning of words to the child." Shields, *Teachers Manual of Primary Methods*, 243.
23 Shields, *Teachers Manual of Primary Methods*, 238.
24 Shields, *Teachers Manual of Primary Methods*, 200.

teachers manual, and curriculum guide, he lauds the collective wisdom of the educational community as opposed to the intelligence of the solitary scholar. Nonetheless, and despite this attachment to the "many," when Shields lays out the qualities needed in the "author" (singular) of the textbook—high qualifications in psychology and being at home in Catholic ideals and theology—he seems to be describing himself.[25]

Conclusion

The important role played by the teacher in bringing the textbook to life underpins the plentiful guidance found therein. It is helpful that the series offers support in knowledge and methods so that the content—the fruit of Shields's tireless scholarly work—can come to life in the classroom. Shields, perhaps aware of the novel approach he was adopting in his overall package, wished to ensure that practitioners on the ground did justice to his intentions. As such, the teachers (be they religious or lay) were being explicitly trained in his method. While this is not prima facie an unreasonable expectation, it could also be unhelpful in the longer term if it led to a rigid adherence by the teaching profession to one person's pedagogical vision.

Of course, the importance of religion to the curriculum in the Catholic school might justify such a top-down approach, especially since it seems that teachers were regarded essentially as conduits of

---

[25] The author should be known; his qualifications and his position should stand as a guarantee for his work; he should know Catholic ideals and Catholic theology, not in a superficial way but thoroughly and intimately; otherwise he cannot give to Catholic doctrines and practices the proper place in the unfolding mind of the child. His qualifications as a psychologist and an educator should give us assurance that he is not bringing a tyro's skill to bear upon a task which concerns the moral, religious and intellectual life of the multitudes of our children who congregate in our classrooms to be formed in the image of Jesus Christ. Shields, *Teachers Manual of Primary Methods*, 200.

material of which they had little to no part in shaping. We must also bear in mind that if the majority of young teachers in Shields's time were members of female religious congregations, such a centralized approach, filtered through their vow of obedience, would seem quite normal.

Shields did not question the need to *communicate* knowledge, and he would have little time for those who would dismiss material because of a perceived lack of relevance to the life of the child. Shields's commitment to educational reform arose from his desire to communicate in more fluent and scientifically verified ways the Catholic religious tradition—doctrine, history, arts—to the young people of the Church. Nonetheless, his claim that the *Catholic Education Series* was a complete curriculum for children is undercut somewhat by his advocacy of Justine Ward's initiatives in the field of music, unless of course he regarded Ward's material as being so closely related to his own work that it was, in his mind, part of the overall package on offer.[26] Furthermore, there is no indication in his series of any material for sports, games, or any other form of physical activity. This undercuts the idea that his work offers an integrated program of human formation. What are we to make of this? Perhaps it is a sign, no more and no less, of the pressure of his multiple duties overwhelming his ability to hold so many roles at the same time as opposed to an attempt to exaggerate the scope of his work.

---

26 See chapter 11 for more on music.

CHAPTER 11

THE *CATHOLIC EDUCATION SERIES*: A STUDY IN KNOWLEDGE AND METHOD

The *Catholic Education Series*, although unfinished, was one of the principal means by which Shields sought to extend his pedagogical vision. This section offers an analysis of two books from the series: *Catholic Education Series, First Book* and *Catholic Education Series, Fourth Book*. Published in 1908, *First Book* is an important text because it was the first resource for pupils written by Shields and thus could be said to represent the initial freshness and energy of his approach. It also benefits from a high level of guidance from the author to the teacher, both in the text and in another publication (*Teachers Manual of Primary Methods*), on the best way to use the text for maximum benefit. *Fourth Book*, by contrast, was the final book he wrote but lacks a similar level of guidance for the teacher. The theme of *Fourth Book* is the Mass—"the source and summit of the Christian life"[1]—and presents an opportunity to explore how Shields applied his pedagogical insights to this most important of doctrines.

---

1 Vatican Council II, Dogmatic Constitution on the Church *Lumen Gentium* (November 21, 1964), 11.

Catholic Education Series, First Book

While Shields accepts that the repetition of material can be helpful, this way of working must avoid the trap of staleness and aridity. His preferred inductive approach is to present, for example, the work of creation over a series of lessons and activities and therein encourage the teacher to plant the seeds of the workings of the divine plan in the mind of the child.[2] Shields's series aims to bring together insights from psychology and religious thinking in a way that is attractive for pupils and, crucially, accessible to teachers. Most importantly, *First Book* is, for Shields, an example of a way of teaching that is wholly in line with the (inductive) methods of teaching practiced by Jesus. In *Teachers Manual of Primary Methods*, he further illustrates his preferred "method" with developed examples, one of which he calls the "Idea of the Shepherd." Shields selected the image of the shepherd owing to what he described as its "simplicity." Recognizing that most young children have no real idea of the life and work of a shepherd—perhaps as true then as now—he makes the point that the idea of the shepherd is so central to the Church that it merits

---

2   In Lesson VII of the Baltimore Catechism the question is asked "Why is Jesus Christ true God?" and the answer is given "Jesus Christ is true God because He is the true and only Son of God the Father." In the lesson "A Welcome to Jesus" which we are considering, the Father of Jesus is presented as the Creator of all those things that the child knows and loves. Thus the Divine Sonship of Jesus is presented in a concrete and germinal form instead of in an abstract form which could not be assimilated by the child. Shields, "Notes on Education," 279.

See also Shields, "Notes on Education," 283:

> In presenting the idea of Creation it will be observed how often it has been repeated, but each time in a new setting and in action rather than in any passive embodiment. Again, the Divine Sonship is not presented in a single statement which the child is required to repeat over and over again until it is engraven on his memory, but each statement of Creation carries with it the thought of the Divine Sonship, for it is the Father of Jesus who gives the birds their songs, who makes the trees grow, who sends the sunshine and the rain, etc.

some further development.

First Book (for children age six or thereabouts) is where the Idea of the Shepherd is introduced as part of a wider "nature scene." Arguing that this image is one of "love and sweetness," with the figure of Jesus at the center, he then introduces the "Mother Idea": both the shepherd and the mother share the qualities of motherly love, tenderness, and watchfulness.[3] The focus seems to be on the cultivation of a sense of home, reminding the child that the school is an extension of these domestic surroundings.[4] This intentionally fosters the building of bridges between home and school, while simultaneously fostering a slowly emerging Christocentricity to the curriculum.[5]

As noted above, Shields favored a fivefold pedagogical approach with science, letters, institution, aesthetics, and religion as the determined curricular pathways. We would, therefore, expect his first printed resource for schools to be an example par excellence of this way of structuring classroom material. This is not quite the case, however, because the structure of *First Book* does not, on an initial reading, easily align with the five preferred pathways. Matters are not helped by the absence of a contents page and the lack of clear signposting in the actual text itself. One can only imagine the reaction

---

3 Shields, *Teachers Manual of Primary Methods*, 190.
4 The sense of home is developed and extended in the texts for second grade. The "Idea of the Shepherd" is the fulcrum for activities designed to foster a "higher phase of development" that looks beyond the home to interaction with other social groups. Shields, *Teachers Manual of Primary Methods*, 191. *Second Book* moves from a nature study focused on "Mother Milkweed" to the story of David and the reintroduction (with greater depth) of the Shepherd Idea, located now in the Nativity story. There is deliberate repetition of the details of the story in order to "secure development and detail." Shields, *Teachers Manual of Primary Methods*, 192.
5 "Our Saviour taught His followers to clothe God with the attributes of Father; He never referred to Himself as the Father, but as the Shepherd. He sometimes goes further and points to His love for His followers in the quality of mother love, as when, weeping over Jerusalem, He said 'How often would I have gathered you under My wing even as a hen gathereth her chickens.'" Shields, *Teachers Manual of Primary Methods,* 190.

of a teacher, whether newly qualified or experienced, when handed this text as the sole classroom resource for a year!

When we start to study the material in *First Book* more closely, however, some light begins to appear. Shields emphasizes progression-in-unity by grouping similar themes across the five parts of the book, starting with nature, moving on to home life, and then including an explicit religion lesson based on an adapted gospel story. The final theme of music rounds off the section. Interspersed throughout the text are color plates of gospel scenes from famous artists and black and white etchings of secular scenes. Shields explains the rationale for including works of art to accompany the stories: half-tone pictures of nature scenes that are not unfamiliar to the child leaves some room for the child to make an imaginative response to the scene depicted. Scenes from the Bible—often from the "old masters"—that are more remote from the experience of the child require full color so that they can make a deeper impression on the child's imagination.

In the preface to the second edition of *First Book,* which was published in 1917, Shields explains the structure of the text. It is divided into five parts, each of which is intended to explore "the great instincts that determine the child's relationship of dependence upon his parents," with a view to developing the Christian character of the child.[6] At the end there is a very practical section titled "Suggestions for Teachers," in which he makes the aims and structure of the text much more explicit:

> It is a reader, a nature study book, a book of instruction on home life, an elementary text-book of religion, and an art book dealing with the three-fold root of the aesthetic faculty, viz., form, color, and rhythm. These five lines are not dealt with separately, but are woven into organic unity.[7]

---

6 Shields, preface to *First Book,* 4.
7 Shields, "Suggestions for Teachers," in *First Book,* 98.

The incipient "integrated curriculum" proposed by Shields is highly experiential and requires substantial levels of pupil movement and activity. As any experienced teacher of young children would surely attest, such an approach requires a high level of organization and planning if matters are not to descend into a form of unregulated classroom chaos. Hence his repeated emphasis on the importance of teacher formation, as only well-educated teachers who are at home in the science of pedagogy, would be able to make the text come truly alive in the classroom.

Returning to the question of teacher support, the *Teachers Manual of Primary Methods* was written in response to requests from teachers on the best way to maximize the benefit to pupils of the material in the *Catholic Education Series*.[8] Yet Shields had already admitted in 1909 that the scaffolding present in *Religion, First Book* (as it was then called) was inserted after requests from schools that were contemplating use of the book.[9] At the very least this shows some evidence of a dialogic approach to the writing of the textbooks. We can only speculate on what the actual concerns of the teachers were at this time, but the requests strongly suggest that further teacher development was necessary if they were to remain abreast of the pedagogical developments upon which Shields drew so heavily. Furthermore, it is possible that Shields's enthusiasm for pedagogical

---

[8] To derive the full benefit from the use of these books the teachers have felt the need of a manual of method which would set forth the principles of method involved and the aims which the authors of these primary text-books sought to attain. The present volume is an answer to requests frequently expressed by the primary teachers who have been using the *Catholic Education Series* with good results, but who feel that much more might be achieved through a better understanding of the methods employed. Shields, *Teachers Manual of Primary Methods*, 8–9.

[9] "However, in compliance with the numerous requests that have reached us from schools that contemplate using this book, we shall present here a somewhat detailed account of the work of the first grade as we should like to see it carried out where *Religion, First Book*, is in the hands of the children." Shields, "Notes on Education," 475.

A STUDY IN KNOWLEDGE AND METHOD

reform might have made him assume too much of his intended readership, thus revealing a gap between his expectations and the reality of a teaching profession that was perhaps lacking in professional confidence.

Whatever the truth of the situation outlined above, both *Teachers Manual of Primary Methods* and the 1909 article in the *Catholic University Bulletin* offer a comprehensive guide to *Catholic Education Series, First Book*. Shields clearly intended this first book of the series to be like rows of carefully planted educational seeds.[10] To achieve this is no small task and shows without question the attachment of the author to his own understanding of how the human brain developed. *First Book* is designed, therefore, as a single resource that, in the hands of a well-trained teacher, will set the pupil on the right path from the outset.[11] It is the children's first printed educational resource, laying the foundation for no less than their intellectual, aesthetic, and religious development.

There are some key features woven throughout the text. There is a strong emphasis on the nurturing life of the home. There is also an assumption (not unreasonable given the times in which it was written) of the mother as primary caregiver and the father as the primary (if not the sole) economic provider. This familial unity is introduced through a story that explores the family life of some robins, the protagonists of the story. The aim is that the children, with teacher support, make the connection between the family unit of the robins and the life they experience at home. Shields expresses a hope that the building of confidence between parents and children in the early years of a child's life will act as a shield against moral dangers in later life.[12]

---

10 Shields, preface to *First Book*, 3–7.
11 Lesson content and vocabulary were selected to match the child's stage of development. Shields, *First Book*, 104–10 contains a list of words that the child should know at this stage.
12 "The habit of bringing to their parents all their concerns and of reposing complete confidence in them in all their necessities and of giving expression

In line with the preface to the 1917 second edition of *First Book*, the contents pages of the *Teachers Manual in Primary Methods* clearly lay out the themes of the five parts of *First Book*: Love (Part I), Nature Study (Part II), Domestic Study (Part III), Religious Lesson (Part IV) and Songs (Part V).[13] The five parts share a common internal structure, beginning with a nature study (to be dramatized by the children), a domestic study (to be lived out at home), a religion lesson, and ending with music (two songs). See the table opposite.

Curiously, the fivefold structure mentioned earlier is not fully reflected in the structural arrangements of *First Book*. There is no specific mention of one of the pathways, that of "letters," but there is an assumption that letters and sounds are taught explicitly. As this text is a reader as well as a textbook (the distinction is important), at the end of the first year in school the child should be able "to recognize without difficulty from six to eight hundred words" as well as write and spell most of them correctly.[14] He recommends six weeks to two months work with blackboard and chalk so that children are able to recognize eighty-three words as the basis of the vocabulary in the *First Book*.[15] Shields goes so far as to give precise instruction on the already established "action method" of teaching letters, as this promotes an association between visual and motor areas of the brain.[16] Evaluation of the success or otherwise of his methods for teaching literacy is beyond the scope of the present volume. McMahon's study, however, declares that "The *First Book* fails as a beginning reader."[17] He offers as reasons for this evaluation

---

to their love having been thus built up in early childhood will not fail to be a safeguard against many moral dangers in later years." Shields, *First Book*, 167.

13 Shields, *Teachers Manual of Primary Methods*, 15. A similar structure is laid out for *Second Book* (with seven parts) and *Third Book* (with four parts).
14 Shields, "Suggestions for Teachers," in *First Book*, 98.
15 Shields, "Suggestions for Teachers," in *First Book*, 99.
16 Shields, "Suggestions for Teachers," in *First Book*, 100. See also Shields, *Teachers Manual of Primary Methods*, 43–50, for further thoughts on how to enlarge the child's spoken and written vocabulary.
17 McMahon, "The Shields Method," 165.

Themes	Part I	Part II	Part III	Part IV	Part V
Nature Study	Looking for Breakfast (Mr. and Mrs. Robin); Building a Nest	The Babies' Breakfast (birds); Home from the Market (Father Robin)	Summer; Breakfast on the Grass; The Rescue	The Broken Wing	The Apple Tree (continues into the Domestic Study…)
Domestic Study	The Nest of Mother's Arms; Father's Welcome Home	The Two Mothers; The Family Breakfast	A Visit to the Country	The Sick Child	The Apple Tree (continued from Nature Study)
Religion Lesson	The Home of Jesus; A Welcome to Jesus; A Secret; The Tired Teacher; The Little Children; A Sweet Lesson	Jesus Feeds the People	The Savior (Storm at Sea)	Jesus Heals the Sick	Our Home in Heaven; The Mother of Jesus; The First Christmas
Songs	It is Love; Jesus' Love	The Father's Love; Dearest Lord, We Thank You	Come to Me; Little Robin, Never Fear	The Mother's Prayer	Christmas Carol; Lullaby

that the words presented are too difficult for young children and that *First Book* could not be used in a class until children had an improved vocabulary. McMahon had the advantage of having interviewed teachers in the Thomas Edward Shields Memorial School (established in 1922) about how they had worked with the *Catholic Education Series*. Their verdict was clear: the underlying principles were sound but "the details are found wanting in many ways," noting also that Dr. Shields died before the course "was tested in the crucible of intelligent practice."[18] In fairness, it should also be pointed out that, as we have seen above, Shields did acknowledge the feedback received from teachers prior to publication. McMahon also records the view of the sister in charge of the school that the sequence of lessons in *First Book* was erroneous and that the home story should come before the nature study "because experience proved that children of this age were more familiar with home than with nature." The sister had no problem in changing the order of the lessons and, after doing so, "the changed order has yielded better results."[19]

First Book was reviewed at length by Sr. M. Magdala in the 1915 edition (vol. 9) of the *Catholic Educational Review*.[20] She described the book as a positive contribution to Catholic education. Some of the terms used in the review capture the essence of her response: we read that the books have "an utter absence of the trivial,"[21] and "this principle of simplicity pervades the contents of this complete little text-book."[22] The review accords with Shields's insistence on the importance of correlation and that religion should not just be ancillary to, but at the heart of, the educational experience of the child in the Catholic school.

John Francis Murphy summed up the approach of the *First Book* as a major step forward for Catholic schools in America, while recognizing that the pace of change might have been overwhelming, not just for the hard-pressed teacher but for the young pupil.[23] From a twenty-

18 McMahon, "The Shields Method," 162–63.
19 McMahon, "The Shields Method," 163.
20 Sr. Mary Magdala, "Discussion" of *The Catholic Education Series, First Book*, by Thomas Shields, *Catholic Educational Review* 9 (January 1915): 72–77.
21 Magdala, "Discussion" of *First Book*, 72.
22 Magdala, "Discussion" of *First Book*, 75.
23   No questions and answers, separate lists of prayers, or rules of the church, found even in first grade catechisms up to the last decade, were in the

first century perspective we can recognize how the *Catholic Education Series* would have had a substantial impact on the teachers and pupils in Catholic schools. How this doctrinal and pedagogical approach underpinned *Catholic Education Series, Fourth Book* will be explored below.

Catholic Education Series, Fourth Book

The theme of *Catholic Education Series, Fourth Book* is the Mass. The text revolves around an exploration of the parts of the Mass, with much interesting material on related issues such as church architecture, the liturgical year, and the importance of vestments.[24] Shields offers a very practical approach but it remains rooted, unsurprisingly, in his wider educational ideas. Shields's thoughts on the liturgy chime with the mood of the nascent "liturgical movement," which saw liturgical revival as a crucial marker of the Church's spiritual and corporate nature. This movement—inspired by the wider atmosphere of *ressourcement*, which called for a return to biblical and patristic sources in theological study—paved the way for the liturgical reforms of Vatican II.[25] Shields, therefore, was very much working according to the spirit of the times.

---

book. The print was large, well-spaced, with thirty-one illustrations within the eighty-six pages of student text, and eleven hymns with musical accompaniment. It may have been overwhelming to a first grader, but it represented a major break in the pattern of religion textbooks for the teachers. Murphy, "Thomas Edward Shields: Religious Educator," 115.

24 Pope Francis takes a similar (practical) approach to liturgical formation. "The theme is vast and always deserves an attentive consideration in every one of its aspects. Even so, with this letter I do not intend to treat the question in an exhaustive way. I simply desire to offer some prompts or cues for reflections that can aid in the contemplation of the beauty and truth of Christian celebration." Francis, *Desiderio Desideravi*, 1.

25 For an excellent introduction to the modern liturgical movement, see Keith F. Pecklers, "The History of the Modern Liturgical Movement," *Oxford Research Encyclopedias*, September 3, 2015, online at: https://oxfordre.com/religion/display/10.1093/acrefore/9780199340378.001.0001/acrefore-9780199340378-e-19.

Because the liturgy is the pinnacle of the Christian life, how catechetical and educational texts explore and set out its history and doctrine reveals much about their doctrinal appropriateness.[26] One of the important (if largely forgotten) post–Vatican II documents on liturgy, *Eucharisticum Mysterium*, summed up the importance of correct liturgical teaching as follows:

> Those who have charge of the religious instruction of children, especially parents, parish priests and teachers, should be careful when they are introducing them gradually to the mystery of salvation, to give emphasis to instruction on the Mass. Instruction about the Eucharist, while being suited to the age and abilities of the children, should aim to convey the meaning of the Mass through the principal rites and prayer. It should also explain the place of the Mass in participation in the life of the Church.[27]

This comment leaves no room for doubt about the importance of the Mass in catechetical instruction for children. Whether such instruction takes places in the home, in a parish setting, or in a school, the demands are the same. What is noticeable is the sense of educational perspective it offers, in particular the reminder that teaching must be suited to the "age and abilities" of the child and that the core educational material is found in the actual texts of the Mass.[28] All of

---

26 An important text for any study of the pedagogical implications of liturgical renewal is Romano Guardini's *The Spirit of the Liturgy*, originally published in 1930. While a relatively short book, its seven chapters offer insights into why the renewal of the liturgy was not a process at arms lengths from the wider renewal of the Church. It was first published in 1918 and thus captures some of the reforming energy that surely had influenced Shields.

27 Sacred Congregation of Rites, Instruction on the Worship of the Eucharistic Mystery *Eucharisticum Mysterium* (May 25, 1967), 14. https://adoremus.org/1967/05/eucharisticum-mysterium.

28 This accords with some recent thinking exploring children as religious practitioners. See Faith Glavey Pawl, "Minding Children in the Study of Liturgy: Philosophical Reflections on Children as Religious Practitioners," *TheoLogica*:

this is at one with the direction of travel proposed by Shields in *Fourth Book*.

In the book's short preface, Shields explains that *Fourth Book* is closely aligned to the material found in *Third Book*, where the focus is on "types and figures of the Old Testament" and the "the transition from the old to the new dispensation." *Fourth Book* is focused on the Mass as the "central source of grace" enabling the child to live a worthy life on earth.[29] *Fourth Book* also complements the material in *Fourth Reader*, where "the child will learn something of the great work which the Catholic Church has accomplished among men."[30]

The aims of *Fourth Book* are proposed unambiguously: the child will be taught how to give worship to God and that all human endeavors should be offered to God.[31] Shields also makes the important claim that the art that had been explored in the preceding texts in the *Catholic Education Series* now finds it fullest expression in the liturgy. The focus here is no longer on traditional religious art but on church architecture, the importance of the altar, and the need to find beauty and meaning in the objects related to worship.

The actual text of *Fourth Book* is rooted in an academically rigorous yet pastorally sensitive appreciation of the rites of the Mass. The structure of the volume does, however, raise some questions about method: there is little to no guidance on how the material presented should be taught in class. There are no attempts to "signpost" chapters or offer further direction for teachers. It is possible that Shields was of the view that teachers would have

---

An International Journal for Philosophy of Religion and Philosophical Theology 4, no. 1 (2020): 6–29.

29 Thomas Shields, *Catholic Education Series, Fourth Book* (Washington, D.C.: Catholic Education Press, 1918): 5.

30 Shields, *Fourth Book,* 5.

31 "In the Fourth Book in Religion the child will be taught how to worship God worthily, both as an individual and as a member of an organized society. He will there learn that the best of all human achievements should always be directly offered to God, and that in this way alone work from man's hands may grow in perfection." Shields, *Fourth Book,* 5–6.

already been sufficiently familiar with his favored methods—this was the final textbook to be written although others had been planned—and that further guidance, rightly or wrongly, was not necessary.

The structure of the book is simple. Each chapter consists of a long passage in prose explaining the stated topic matter and ending with a set of comprehension questions. In other words, it is a traditional reading and comprehension approach, supplemented by poems and hymns at the beginning and end of each chapter. Photographs of church buildings are scattered throughout the book with, it seems, little thought given to their purpose, save to exemplify forms of church architecture explained in the accompanying text. It is curious that the long and important sections on the parts of the Mass contain no illustrations, given that there is ample scope for accompanying photographs, sketches, or diagrams of various parts of the liturgy. The book does not offer indications of recommended further activities. All of this suggests that the teacher had to supplement the text with her own material.

Given Shields's commitment to the fivefold pedagogical pathway (see above), it would seem reasonable to assume that this crucial pedagogical approach would be woven through a text dealing with the most sublime of Christian mysteries. It is possible to group the material according to this preconceived plan (see opposite), although how this can be accomplished is not made obvious owing to the lack of general teacher direction, or scaffolding, in the text.

In looking more closely at how *Fourth Book* uses each of the five pathways, we can discern a subtle yet no less effective example of correlation in which history and art in particular are employed to give shape and meaning to the Mass.

Religion is, unsurprisingly, the intentional common thread throughout *Fourth Book*. What distinguishes *Fourth Book* from *First Book* is the "direct entry" into explicitly religious material. The material seems to assume a class in which all the students are Catholic, with teachers who are well schooled in both doctrine and method. There is no attempt to smooth the path of entry with reference to

Science	Letters	Institutions	Aesthetic	Religion
The focus on different styles of Church architecture and the means of construction is rooted in an understanding of science.	There are no recommended vocabulary lists but the use of reading comprehension tools is a driver of literacy.	There is a development of the Church as a Eucharistic community, which emerges from Judaism.	The inclusion of poems and hymns is the principal means of developing the aesthetical senses, along with a focus on appreciating the beauty of church architecture.	The text is explicitly religious throughout. Unlike *First Book*, there is no attempt to enter the religious domain through nature.

the family and nature, as in *First Book*. There is no sign of introducing liturgy with reference to the importance of the table and common meals in family life, as might be expected in an experiential approach to teaching liturgy. In other words, *Fourth Book* is a clear, unapologetic, and direct example of catechesis in a school setting.[32]

The text of *Fourth Book* is dotted with poems and hymns having, in most cases, explicitly religious themes. This is complementary to the stories and poems of *Fourth Reader*, although there

---

[32] Shields's work seems to reflect the urgency for effective catechesis that Pius X had articulated in the 1905 encyclical *Acerbo Nimis*:

> Now, if we cannot expect to reap a harvest when no seed has been planted, how can we hope to have a people with sound morals if Christian doctrine has not been imparted to them in due time? It follows, too, that if faith languishes in our days, if among large numbers it has almost vanished, the reason is that the duty of catechetical teaching is either fulfilled very superficially or altogether neglected. Pius X, *Acerbo Nimis*, 16.

Of course, Shields had a different view on the effectiveness of teaching the Catechism of the Council of Trent and the Baltimore Catechism for young children.

is a common theme of written words as the principal means of communication, with little indication of whether stories should be read to or by the children.

The focus on church architecture is intended to show how science, broadly understood, can contribute to structural beauty, which is essential to the Christian understanding of the world. The chapter entitled "House of God" places the sites of Christian worship in the context of Jewish worship patterns. The earliest Christian churches, in turn, were designed to be sacred spaces marked by beauty where the baptized could gather for worship.[33] The chapter on "The Basilica" includes a good deal of historical material, suitably adorned with photographs, with special mention of the Roman basilicas of St. John in Lateran, St. Paul Outside the Walls, and St. Peter. (There is no mention of St. Mary Major, the other member of the "big four" group of Roman basilicas.) A sense of dynamism and transformation is evident in the claim that the original Roman (non-Christian) basilicas were modified so as to become a "suitable building in which to carry out the ceremonies of Christian worship, and to make it express, in every possible way, the mysteries of Christian faith."[34] The chapter on "The Gothic Cathedral" offers Shields a platform for some important "pedagogical" insights on the importance of the fine arts for the gradual rise of Christian places of worship as a specific genre of architecture.[35] He is particularly attracted to Gothic forms as a pinnacle of artistic and architectural achievement.[36] Photographs of some of the great European church

33 Shields, *Fourth Book*, 53–57.
34 Shields, *Fourth Book*, 77.
35 For a thousand years, the thoughts and skill of Catholic peoples throughout the Western world were devoted to the development of the fine arts, so that they might produce worthy offerings for the House of God and express with eloquent beauty the truth of the faith. Mosaics in the walls of the church, in the ceilings and in the pavements, reproduced many of the great scenes of the Old and New Testament. Shields, *Fourth Book*, 99.
36 "The laity, the religious order, and the secular clergy, all united in the twelfth and thirteenth centuries to build such splendid cathedrals as Notre Dame of

buildings—Westminster Abbey and Gloucester Cathedral (England), Giotto's Tower attached to the cathedral in Florence (Italy), and the cathedrals of Rheims, Amiens, and Notre Dame (France)—are more than adornments to the text but are designed to imprint on the mind of the children the actual reality of church architecture. While the buildings themselves are wonders of engineering and represent major scientific advances, Shields lauds them as works of art and sites of aesthetic significance from the hands of artists who were motivated by nothing else than the "beautifying of the House of God."[37]

The chapter headed "What the Gothic Cathedral Taught the People" is essentially an encomium to the educational properties of this form of architecture. Because the Gothic cathedrals predated the printing press, their walls and stained glass windows served as catechetical instruments on which, for example, the great feasts were explained pictorially to the people.[38] There is also evidence for a particular form of correlation in that the cathedrals were sites that showed how the Old Testament figures prefigured the coming of Jesus Christ and that this "typology" is crucial to the Christian's sense of being part of the People of God.[39] Furthermore, the use of art as a catechetical instrument was, in a sense, always age-appropriate, as both adults and children could enjoy and learn from the feast of color and images that surrounded them as they worshipped.[40]

Paris, Chartres, Rheims, Brouges, and Amiens, buildings which were never surpassed and which continue to be the wonder of the world." Shields, *Fourth Book*, 93.

37 Shields, *Fourth Book*, 195.
38 Shields, *Fourth Book*, 123.
39 Melchizedek was interesting in himself, but he becomes far more interesting as the type of Jesus Christ, Who is also both Priest and King. Through Abraham and Isaac, God set apart His Chosen People. These two characters are consequently full of interest. But, in the incident in which Abraham is about to sacrifice his son Isaac, we are taught to see how greatly God the Father loves us, since he is willing to sacrifice his son upon the cross for our salvation, even as Abraham was willing to sacrifice Isaac in obedience to the voice of God. Shields, *Fourth Book*, 117.
40 John Paul II fully understood the power of Gothic art for the portrayal of the

Regarding the teaching of letters, we have very little material that is explicitly shaped to achieve this important end. There is no equivalent to the vocabulary list in *First Book*. With the text aimed at fourth grade (children of around ten years of age), the assumption seems to be that the pupils will, by and large, be sufficiently literate to work with the text, albeit, one would assume, with varying levels of support from the teacher. The sole form of literacy exercise suggested, as already noted, is the classic reading comprehension test: what is noteworthy in the questions is that they demand a close reading of the text in order to formulate an answer—which is not a bad thing and perhaps we need more of this approach today—but it did not appear to encourage wider reflection on issues arising from the written material. From an educational perspective, Shields was eager to ensure that the children were given the "solid food" of facts to allow for deeper and more meaningful reflection in later years. Of course, there might also be the expectation that the teacher herself would encourage such reflection through, for example, suitable open questions and other supplementary material.

To the children of Catholic schools in the early years of the twentieth century, institutional awareness—knowledge of their identity as Catholics—would have been high. In the first place, the roll of Catholic schools would have been nearly 100 percent Catholic and the schools would have been staffed mainly by teaching sisters. The parish clergy would be an ubiquitous presence in the wider life of the school community. In this respect, the educational air the children breathed would be both implicitly and explicitly Catholic. Nonetheless, Shields detected a need to open their horizons and offer them the possibility of learning more about the *institution* of the Church through his material.[41]

Christian story. See John Paul II, "Letter to Artists," April 4, 1999, 8: "How is one to summarize with a few brief references to each of the many different art forms, the creative power of the centuries of the Christian Middle Ages?"

41 The root of "institution" is the Latin *institutionem*, meaning some form of arrangement or body that has been established for a specific purpose. Further

Fourth Book's many photographs of church buildings in Europe are indicators of a strong family story that runs through the ages. It is this catechetical thread that is at the center of the curriculum and to which all other domains of learning must, in the spirit of correlation, refer. Shields is offering wide angles of understanding in his promotion of institutional belonging. In the first place, he communicated to his young readers an explicitly historical portrayal of the life of the Church. The first photograph in *Fourth Book* is of St. Peter's Basilica in Rome, no doubt a marker of the *romanitas* he desired to convey. His further comments, noted above, about other Roman basilicas would be of a piece with this mindset. Shields seems almost to be teasing those who had leveled charges of a lack of patriotism toward Catholics (see above) by doing his best to help young American Catholics glimpse the life of the Church in other sites, especially in the Catholic hub of Rome.[42] The important principle of correlation is again to the fore because it is through knowledge of a) the Church's journey from Jewish worship to the Christian Eucharist and b) the development of particular forms of architecture that housed and adorned the Eucharist that institutional belonging is fostered. Shields is proposing the Church as a family whose journey and particular abodes can be tracked through the ages—he is, in fact, telling the family story.

Fourth Book deals with aesthetics through study of both church architecture and church music. We have mentioned church architecture above and we now explore Shields thoughts on the teaching of music.

Shields is clear that a knowledge and appreciation of church music is not simply about developing a keen aesthetic sense,

---

consideration of the Church as an institution brings us into the realm of ecclesiology, the study of the Church. While the Church can, for sure, be explored through an institutional lens—its body of doctrine, canon law, educational institutions, and way of approaching wider society demands no less—this needs a complementary focus on the many layers of spirituality and human stories that are woven into its history.

42 It could also be argued that by showing the life of the Church outside America in this way Shields was fuelling the charge that Catholics either lacked patriotism or had split loyalties.

important as that might be.[43] The role of music in the liturgy was to allow the people to be involved actively in a way that the other arts—painting, sculpture, and architecture—might not allow.[44] What is important is music's capacity to foster an appreciation of that which is sacred and not simply to be a vehicle for the display of musical talent.[45]

Nonetheless, Shields was not advocating a free-for-all in matters musical: the Church has developed its own musical style in the form of Gregorian Chant, which, he claims, is the "handmaid of devotion."[46] He agrees with Pius X's determination to exclude from the life of the Church all music that is not in harmony with the liturgy.[47] There is more than a hint here of the ways of thinking articulated by the liturgical movement with respect to the desire to bring the riches of the Mass closer to the congregation and thus foster devotion through the activation of the senses. As one noted scholar associated with the liturgical and catechetical renewal movements, Josef Jungmann, SJ (1889–1975), wrote in 1936: "Lived but above all prayed, dogma will prove to be the best school; and so far as prayer is concerned, the prayer of the Church—the liturgy—takes first place."[48]

We see in Shields's observations on music in the liturgy a foreshadowing of the postconciliar move toward liturgical reform *and* an alignment with the liturgical reforms of Pius X.[49] This would suggest

43 "It would be a mistake, however, to use the Fourth Book in Religion primarily as a means of teaching the fine arts." Shields, *Fourth Book*, 6.
44 Thomas Shields, "Musical Education in Catholic Schools," *Catholic Educational Review* 15 (January 1918): 3–11.
45 "From the days of the apostles, the Church has always made use of music both to arouse and to give expression to the feelings and emotions appropriate to her sacred offices. She does not employ music in her churches to entertain her children nor to exhibit musical art in its various stages of perfection." Shields, *Fourth Book*, 290.
46 Shields, *Fourth Book*, 294.
47 Shields, *Fourth Book*, 292.
48 Jungmann, *The Good News*, 114.
49 "It should be borne in mind that the true solemnity of liturgical worship depends less on a more ornate form of singing and a more magnificent

that Shields was drinking from the same stream of liturgical renewal in order to enhance, widen, and deepen the participation, properly understood, of the people in the Mass. As a practical scholar, it is no surprise to find that he favored a complete system of musical instruction in Catholic schools, and his 1918 article, "Musical Education in Catholic Schools," outlines in detail a method for classroom implementation of such instruction.[50] Because this article is contemporaneous with *Fourth Book,* it would seem to be a reliable guide on how to integrate his theory into the daily life of the class. Essentially, he is advocating the use in Catholic schools of the Catholic Education Music Course developed by Justine Ward (1879–1975), a convert to Catholicism, who later wrote a biography of Shields.[51]

In the article, Shields proposed that grades 1–4 would focus on the training of voices and how to read music and that grades 5–8 would emphasize the appreciation of both secular vocal music and ecclesiastical music. Grades 5–8 would also be when instrumental instruction begins. The course would provide foundations for a more developed program running through high schools, which would be college / university accredited, of course, by Catholic University. This level of organization is of a piece with Shields's tendency to centralize, but his willingness to collaborate with Ward—who offered a level of musical knowledge he lacked—also reveals a desire to be more collegial when necessary.

It is worth mentioning that Ward's influence on music education remains strong. Shields asked her in 1910 to become involved in developing a course for children on music.[52] She was the foundress

---

ceremonial than on its worthy and religious celebration, which takes into account the integrity of the liturgical celebration itself, and the performance of each of its parts according to their own particular nature." Sacred Congregation of Rites, Instruction on Music in Liturgy *Musicam Sacram* (March 5, 1967), 11. https://adoremus.org/1967/03/musicam-sacram.

50 Shields, "Musical Education in Catholic Schools," 3.

51 Ward, *Thomas Edward Shields.* This is very much a record of Shields from the perspective of a close collaborator, admirer, and friend.

52 The obituary of Mrs. Ward in the *New York Times* describes her as a "pioneer"

of the first School of Liturgical Music of The Catholic University of America in 1929. The website of the Department of Music of Catholic University gives ample space to extolling the "Ward Method" of teaching music.[53] The website also recognizes the role of Shields in the development of Ward's career: in the tab headed "Philosophy of Education," it is noted that Ward took Shields's thoughts on educational philosophy and transferred them to the teaching of music.[54]

Returning to the text of *Fourth Book*, what is striking is the assumption that the teachers will know what to do with the material he presents. The contents does not have a heading for "Hymns" but does have one for "Poems," with forty-nine separate examples. There is a heading for "Psalms," but only two—Psalms 116 and 99—are included in the list. This seems to be an uncharacteristic lack of attention to detail, and another indicator, perhaps, that the vast amount of work he had foisted upon himself had eventually taken its toll.

In the preface of *Fourth Book*, he notes that (mostly) liturgical hymns will be used at the start and end of each chapter in order to allow the children to express in song the curricular material that the chapter develops.[55] While this is another welcome sign of correlation,

---

in the teaching of music. Her fame was such that the Ward Method of teaching music is renowned internationally. See *New York Times*, "Justine Ward, Who Developed Music-Teaching Method, Dies" (November 29, 1975), 30. https://www.nytimes.com/1975/11/29/archives/justine-ward-who-developed-musicteaching-method-dies.html.

53 Some general information on the Ward Method can be accessed on the website of Catholic University here: https://music.catholic.edu/faculty-and-research/areas-of-research/ward-method-studies/ward-method/history/index.html. More than ten volumes of Ward Method books are listed on the website of The Catholic University of America Press, https://www.cuapress.org/search-results/?contributor=ward-method.

54 https://music.catholic.edu/faculty-and-research/areas-of-research/ward-method-studies/ward-method/philosophy-education/index.html.

55 Shields, *Fourth Book*, 7: "Hymns, mostly liturgical, are employed at the beginning

it remains unclear why such an important teaching strategy lacks any form of obvious teacher support. There might be good reasons for this, such as teacher familiarity with the music, given that there is no musical notation in the book. Furthermore, many of the teachers had possibly availed themselves of the Catholic Education Music Course, which Shields had mentioned in the article from 1918 cited above. Nonetheless, it again seems curious that there is no mention of Ward's influence on his musical theories, not least on how he addressed the composition of hymns for use in the classroom.[56] We must also consider the informal and often undervalued networks in schools in which teachers support each other quietly, sharing experiences, skill, and knowledge for the benefit of the pupils. Whatever the truth of the situation, music would have a strong presence in Shields's work for pupils.

Overall, *Fourth Book* is a content-heavy offering that can be shaped according to Shields's five preferred pedagogical pathways. Bearing in mind that the material was aimed at children in the fourth grade, and therefore around ten years of age, it would be interesting to have independent accounts of how teachers and pupils coped with the material. It might well be that immersion in the Shields Method since first grade had enhanced the knowledge and skill levels of the pupils; that is, that they had been suitably enriched by this exposure to robustly Catholic ideas and images following their initial grounding in the early books of the series.

---

and end of each chapter to aid the child in finding poetical and musical forms of expression for the thought that is gradually being developed in his mind, hence, the hymns are always consonant with the prose text."
56 Ward, *Thomas Edward Shields*, 151. Mrs. Ward describes an early meeting with Shields over lunch. He asked her opinion on the music he had included in two of his books for children. She quotes her verdict on the quality of the music in direct speech: "They are simply appalling—impossible.... The music is pretentious, cheap, complicated. It is much too difficult for little children to sing." From this encounter sprang Mrs. Ward's engagement with liturgical music and her role as a close collaborator of Shields.

Conclusion

The two examples offered in this chapter show both the benefits and limitations of the so-called Shields Method, as found in two books of the *Catholic Education Series*. The contrast between *First Book* and *Fourth Book* is striking. There seems to be a general imbalance between both texts on the amount of curricular content on offer and the level of support available for teachers. The lack of teacher direction in the later text is a possible indicator of Shields's satisfaction with teacher competence, since by then the Catholic Sisters College was already operating well and offering streams of well-qualified teachers to the Catholic schools network.

While *First Book*, unlike *Fourth Book,* contains a detailed set of instructions for the classroom teacher, in both texts, there is every effort to construct material that corresponds to Shields's own understanding of child development theories. This would build the teachers' knowledge base of what would have been largely new ideas to them. Shields succeeds overall in aligning his interpretation of research into pedagogical issues with the production of practical materials for classroom use.

Crucially, Shields is also very aware of the reality of human nature. He is not blind to the reality of sin, and remarks, rightly, that one of most difficult tasks facing teachers is that of "developing in the children a correct knowledge of sin and a right attitude towards it."[57] This is no less the case today. His ideas for developing a distaste for sin, so to speak, seem remarkably contemporary: there is no space, he argues, for threats of hell or other forms of divine punishment. What is important is to stimulate the child's mind to embrace that which is good.[58] His *Catholic Education Series* aimed to do just that.

57 Shields, *Teachers Manual of Primary Methods*, 193.
58 "In developing the idea of sin, on the other hand, our chief concern is to prevent the idea from realizing itself in action. The matter must therefore be so presented as to stimulate mind and heart and action in an opposite direction." Shields, *Teachers Manual of Primary Methods*, 194. See also the same source at 196: "The children are shown the seven capital sins in their true

Future studies on Shields will ask if his particular educational project is transferable in any way to contemporary Catholic education settings or whether it was a way of working that was of its time and cannot easily, if at all, be replicated today. Some initial thoughts on this matter will be offered in the conclusion. It is also important to ask whether the ways of codifying knowledge and preserving cultural capital as exemplified in his textbooks and readers could be classified as examples of children's literature. For sure, his *Catholic Education Series*, although it had shortcomings, deserves recognition for serving as a showcase for his scholarly endeavors and personal energy.

---

colors; these sins, hideous in themselves, egg on the wicked old man, who is made to inspire the children with fear and dread, to destroy the child Jesus, and the result is his own misery and untimely death."

CONCLUSION

Evaluating Shields's Contribution to Catholic Education

The conclusion will tie together some of the thematic strands that are, in a sense, still hanging from Shields's tapestry. In so doing, it will also identify a number of areas that contemporary educators might wish to revisit in light of Shields's ideas and ideals.

Part 1 of the conclusion is an evaluation of Shields's Master Plan for reform. Part 2 looks forward, exploring how Shields's legacy is a potential source of influence for necessary reform in the theory and practice of contemporary Catholic education. Three areas have been selected for comment in part 2, each of which can draw from Shields's work: i) the processes of Catholic teacher formation; ii) the curriculum in Catholic schools, and iii) the dialogue between religious education and catechesis.

Shields's Master Plan: Success, Failure—or Something in Between

It is to be expected that such a vast panorama of action, as envisaged by Shields, would come complete with bumps and inconsistencies, as well as successes, along the way. Shields's attachment to the insights emergent from so-called progressive thinking was a means to an end, with the end being the child's commitment to the life of the Church. In this respect it is not wholly accurate to describe

Shields as a Progressivist or even a Catholic Progressivist, given his clear and unapologetic articulation of the divine mission of Catholic education. Shields, for sure, sought to integrate elements of progressive thinking into the theory and practice of Catholic education but saw this dialogic process as a way of *confirming* the Church's own educational traditions, especially the teaching methods of Jesus as recorded in the gospels. Given this interesting approach, Shields could be described as someone who actually sought to obstruct Progressivism's path into the world of Catholic education.

Shields's educational vision and mission seemed to take for granted a generally solid Catholic piety in the home. He was, unsurprisingly, wedded to the view that the school had to be an extension of the home and that the early years of school must offer a homelike experience to children. The same way of thinking underpins the traditional concept of the parents as the primary educators of children—a mainstay of Catholic thinking on education—with teachers acting *in loco parentis*. Yet this attachment to traditional home-school partnerships also raises questions. For example, then as now, if a child comes to school from what we could describe as a "disordered" family life—and how we can we safely assume that such disorders, more or less serious, did not exist at his time of writing (or any time)—to what extent can the authority of the home be seen as a model for the life of the school?

Similarly, if a particular family's pattern of religious practice is not consistent—for example, if only one parent is a practicing Catholic—does this damage in any way the home-school transition process, when the school, in Shields's vision, is an essential part of a shared religious vision? Some might also argue that Shields's views on family life and the role of women in the home are not aligned to contemporary reality, undercutting his more general position on education. Chapter 27 of *Philosophy of Education* requires careful reading in this respect. We see here a fine balancing act between the importance, as he saw it, of women as homemakers set alongside a desire for their higher education and cultural formation "in the pursuit of literature and art, and in the wider intellectual and moral interests that are shaping the course of advancing civilization."[1] Of course, these are perennial questions for educators and not unique to Shields's time, but they do need posing.

Shields did achieve some success in what we can safely describe (using contemporary language) as *measurable* outcomes: the Catholic Sisters College was built, his textbooks and readers were put into circulation, and the *Catholic Educational Review* continued until long after his death in 1921, ceasing publication in 1969. The deeper question is whether his work has enjoyed long-term or deeply rooted influence on the theory and practice of Catholic education in the US. It is curious that his reputation was very strong at the time of his death, as seen in the plaudits afforded him in the Memorial Issue of the *Catholic Educational Review*, yet so little mention is made of his work in later years.[2] It is not always clear why this is the case, and we can only speculate on the reasons for his reputational shift.

In the first place, Shields left no identifiable "school" of followers, despite the many admirers of his work dotted throughout America, and especially within Catholic University. While Shields was one of the early reform-minded scholars to emerge from Catholic University, we can tentatively conclude that his work increasingly became like the proverbial leaven that became hidden in subsequent stages of reform. In other words, educational reforms continued apace but his influence receded. More critically, it could also be the case that his life's work—and the work of those of a similar mind—were soon regarded as a hiatus in Catholic educational thought and "normal service" (that is, the use of the catechism) was eventually restored to schools. To what extent this could be true remains a moot point.

In this light, a more general examination of developments in Catholic education in America in the years after Shields's death might

---

1 Shields, *Philosophy of Education*, 290. See also John Sullivan, "Edith Stein: Education for Personhood," in *Lights for the Path* (Dublin: Veritas, 2022), 115–49.
2 See Thomas Shields Memorial Issue, *Catholic Educational Review* 19 (April 1921): 289–92.

offer further clues to possible reasons for his apparent "demise." Buetow described the years between 1918 and 1957 as involving a "maturing process" for Catholic education in America; the early energy around the development of the first Catholic schools and the understandable excitement at the foundation of Catholic University now had to address a cluster of new challenges, including the problematic socioeconomic conditions in America following the financial crash of 1929 and perceived weaknesses in the provision of public education.[3] The time and effort spent in addressing such political realities might have limited the resources available for the implementation of the reform plans mapped out by Shields.

Furthermore, the publication in 1929 of Pius XI's *Divini Illius Magistri* gave a universal voice to the Church's desire to retain and strengthen the religion-education nexus and oppose all moves to weaken the Christian duty to educate from the perspective of faith.[4] This document is still (at the time of writing) the Church's sole encyclical on education. The focus on educational reform from the universal perspective of the Church, as found in the encyclical, allied to the commitment to Catholic educational reform specifically in the US—driven principally by Catholic University—made for a powerful amalgam of forces, in which the role of Shields's former doctoral student, Rev. Dr. George Johnson, cannot be underestimated.

In 1938, Johnson was charged by the bishops of the United States to set up a Commission on American Citizenship, which gave him a valuable opportunity to "direct the fashioning of proximate educational goals."[5] Johnson formulated five such goals for what he described as "Christian education in American democratic society": physical fitness, economic literacy, social virtue, cultural development, and moral perfection.[6] It is curious that explicit religious formation was omitted from the list, although it would surely have

3 Buetow, *Of Singular Benefit*, 218–80. Chapter 5 of the book is titled, "1918–1957: Maturing Process."
4 Pius XI, *Divini Illius Magistri*.
5 Buetow, *Of Singular Benefit*, 231.
6 Buetow, *Of Singular Benefit*, 231.

been woven throughout all five elements. Further important developments followed. Johnson's *Better Men for Better Times*, an outline of curricular principles for the Catholic school, was published in 1943. In 1944 the Commission on American Citizenship devised a three-volume program, *Guiding Growth in Christian Social Living*, which drew on Johnson's work to offer guidance to schools for the development of their curricula.[7] It is possible, even reasonable, to conclude that the new direction promoted by the American bishops used up some, if not all, of the ecclesial energy that could have been expended on the development and expansion of Shields's vision of reform.

Another possible reason for the lack of a dedicated group of followers around Shields was his tendency to work alone and to control, as far as he could, all aspects of his programs of study at Catholic University. This commitment, while admirable up to a point, dissipated the energy required for the more general development of his own writing and research.[8] It could also be a sign of an unhappy perfectionism that reflects a possible lack of trust in others' ability to discharge their responsibilities effectively, stemming from an overattachment to the value of one's own scholarly conclusions. This attitude is not uncommon in university life.

There is also the conundrum of how to achieve the proper balance in academia between research and teaching, the latter term now extended by rather loose terms such as "knowledge exchange" and "public engagement." Some, of course, might commend Shields for showing a desire to loosen himself from the possibly restrictive bonds of the academic ivory tower so as to become a more practice-minded reformer, but this direction of travel did have implications for his development as a scholar. The lack of theoretical development mentioned above was, therefore, an understandable consequence of his zeal to implement practical reforms and a desire not to let his work gather layers of dust on library shelves. Murphy offers an important perspective on the source of the problem:

---

7 See Buetow, *Of Singular Benefit*, 237–39, for more on this.
8 Murphy, "Thomas Edward Shields: Religious Educator," 130.

His later writings represented no further development of his thought, but only extensions from this period. He entered next into public debate with Catholic leaders on the national level, but did not remain in that arena. Instead he became increasingly involved with the establishment of a college for sisters, his own journal of education, and his publishing house. It would be almost as if his powers of analysis, which on the farm in Minnesota had resulted in something practical, needed to produce another invention or tool.[9]

Murphy's observation about Shields's later work as simply "extensions" of his earlier writing rings true when his body of work is evaluated as a whole. There is a good deal of repetition of material, not so much in the actual words used but in the similarity of ideas presented in different outlets. Diligent readers of Shields's work will soon come to see the truth of this statement.

Shields's personality and personal history is also a factor to consider in any evaluation of his work. It is possible that his own negative experiences as a child colored his view of educational methods and institutions, leading to an overreaction when he began to discover and see merit in the new ways of framing educational methods. In other words, Shields had the zeal of the convert in his desire to apply new thinking to Catholic education, with reform being overtaken by a single-minded desire to overturn what he saw as the damage done by flawed methods.

We saw in chapter 7 how much time and energy the establishment of the Catholic Sisters College required but such was the importance Shields rightly placed on its success that he did not spare himself in doing all he could do make it work. Given that the Catholic Sisters College closed its doors in 1964, is this evidence of success (it lasted 50 years) or some form of failure? If the latter, why?

9 Murphy, "Thomas Edward Shields: Religious Educator," 117.

In retrospect, CSC [Catholic Sisters College] was not able to fulfil Shields's vision. The lack of an appreciable endowment and CSC's inability to convince more religious communities to build houses of study hampered financial stability and growth potential. Despite these drawbacks, CSC provided an environment that allowed sisters to study and practice the principles of education while respecting their religious commitments. CSC played a significant role in improving professionalism in Catholic education in the early to mid-twentieth century.[10]

Drawing on the comment above, it would also be unwise simply to pin the blame for the demise of the college on the effects of Vatican II (which had just begun before the college closed its doors) or on diminishing numbers of religious in the teaching congregations. Paradoxically, the college's success in the initial years might have developed a cadre of highly capable sisters, fully capable of implementing suitable pedagogical reforms in the various congregations' own internal teaching processes. Murphy also comments on the lack of financial stability, the perennial ghost at the feast when new educational initiatives are proposed and developed.

More broadly, the closure of the college is a reminder that educational initiatives in the Church often successfully meet the needs of particular times but then require replacement by similar bodies when cultural dynamics and trends evolve. While this might seem to be a faintly absurd policy of like-for-like replacement, it does offer the opportunity for fresh energy, fresh faces, and fresh minds to address the new challenges of each age, thereby helping the Church's educational mission to evolve and develop without losing sight of the core mission.

Finally, the *Catholic Educational Review* became a major drain on Shields's energy. Anyone involved in editing and managing professional publications will be aware of the time, commitment, and

10 Anello, "Intellectual Formation," 104.

patience necessary for success. Although the *Review* was cofounded with Pace, it seems that the bulk of editorial and administrative duties, not to mention the writing of articles, fell on Shields.[11] Murphy quotes 1914 correspondence from Shields to a Sr. St. Ignatius in which Shields attributed the source of his anxiety regarding the journal's future as stemming from Pace's inability to contribute meaningfully to its development and its slower than expected growth in circulation.[12] The latter is surprising given the level of interest shown, in the early years at least, in the work of the Catholic Sisters College, which would seem to be a fertile breeding ground for the widening of the readership of the *Review*. The *Review* ceased publication in 1969, and it is not unreasonable to state that a publication in a specialist field that had a lifespan of around sixty years was a success.

In sum, it is wholly reasonable to assert that Shields's work of reform was a success, albeit with some qualifications as noted above. The broad range of scholarly initiatives he began surely demonstrate considerable intellectual energy and practical skill. Nonetheless, it is possible for one individual to take on too many roles, even if for the best of reasons, and Shields's life shows how this can often have both detrimental personal health consequences and block the development of initiatives from like-minded colleagues.

11 Murphy, "Thomas Edward Shields: Religious Educator," 132–36.
12 The Review is now giving me more anxiety than any of the other large affairs that rest on my shoulders. There are several reasons for this. The hierarchy, the Sisters, and an organized body of instructors are now responsible for the Sisters College. Of course, I retain my place as Dean, but this is only one office in an organized institution. With the Review the case is otherwise. While Dr. Pace's name appears as one of the editors, he is so overwhelmed with work that he has not been able to give it much attention, and the whole responsibility, financial, and otherwise, rests on my shoulders. It is not growing as fast as I should wish and so I am devising plans to extend its circulation and to secure advertising, both of which are necessary for the maintenance of the Review. Thomas Shields, Letter to Sister St. Ignatius, cited in Murphy, "Thomas Edward Shields: Religious Educator," 134.

We now turn our gaze forward to assess the extent to which Shields's ideas could influence contemporary discussion on the reform of Catholic education and serve as seeds of a new research agenda in the field.

Looking Forward

Developing the Catholic Mission in Education

Shields was in many ways a scholar immersed in the often high-octane debates prevalent in educational circles in the early years of twentieth-century America. This does not mean that his insights should be regarded today as a mere historical curiosity or exhibits in a museum of ideas. For sure, every age, including our own, requires scholars with the vision and energy of Shields if the mission of Catholic education is to be up to date, intellectually coherent, and culturally fluent. In other words, Catholic education should be fit for purpose, no matter the context. It is hence necessary to explore the extent to which Shields's ideas might be able to inspire Catholic educators today. Drawing from his voluminous output, I propose to focus on three contemporary themes that could be suitably reenergized by referring to Shields's work. The selected themes are as follows: i) processes of Catholic teacher formation; ii) the curriculum in Catholic schools, and iii) the dialogue between religious education and catechesis. The thoughts set out below are not intended to be exhaustive but are simply inflected summaries of Shields's thought intended as further contributions to current debates.

Processes of Catholic Teacher Formation

A key plank of any system of teacher formation is the valuing of the academy as the site of the necessary intellectual refinement that should precede and accompany more practical initiatives. Catholic teacher formation can draw profitably from the energy generated in institutions of Catholic higher education to develop programs of study suitable for the needs of the present age. This commitment to intellectual refinement must also be accompanied by suitable means for the spiritual-pastoral formation of teachers throughout their careers.

The discussions above compel us to consider the extent to which the formation of Catholic teachers is challenged by issues of identity, religious practice, and professional commitment among those who aspire to be teachers. There are important questions around the processes necessary for their academic and pastoral formation. Shields's development of the Sisters College might offer some examples of how a suitable way ahead could be forged.

In recent times, the Congregation for Catholic Education has included reflection on the broad aims of teacher formation in some of its general educational documents. Nonetheless, serious study of the myriad issues around formation is still pressing.[13] This may, of course, suggest a desire to leave issues around teacher formation—given their complexity and political sensitivity—to the mind of the local church and its partners in providing education.[14]

The *Directory for Catechesis* proposed the formation of a range of institutes for catechists, including "Higher Institutes," which would be "true *university institutes* in terms of the organisation of studies, the duration of courses, and the conditions for being admitted."[15] This would seem to be an articulation for the present age of Shields's vision of academically robust teacher formation, even though the *Directory* has a focus on catechists, not on the teaching profession. Given the overlap between catechesis and education, and the strongly catechetical flavor of Shields's model of education (see above), it is right to consider the extent to which the "Shields

---

13 Cf. Congregation for Catholic Education, *Educating to Intercultural Dialogue in Catholic Schools: Living in Harmony for a Civilization of Love* (October 28, 2013), 76–80; Congregation for Catholic Education, *Religious Dimension*, 62–63 and 96–97.
14 See Rymarz and Franchi, *Catholic Teacher Preparation*.
15 Pontifical Council for Promoting New Evangelization, *Directory for Catechesis*, 156.

model" of teacher formation, located primarily in a college affiliated to or integrated within a Catholic university, is one that could successfully be exported to the Church of the twenty-first century. It is important to bear in mind that in many but not all countries, Catholic institutions offer initial degrees in education, so in some respects that destination has been reached. The issue then becomes one of ongoing professional support available at the appropriate level and how a Catholic university qua university has a role in advancing the status of the profession, and what this means for breadth and depth of study.

Essential to debates on how best to harmonize the work of Catholic institutions globally is a commitment to value the local and be shy of overly centralized options.[16] Nonetheless, some shared understanding of how teacher formation should be organized across the Church would seem essential for a Church that is truly *catholic* in its self-understanding and ways of working. The common search for shared understanding offers the "solidarity" of the center to the "subsidiarity" that emerges from local reflections and initiatives.

Shields's work was geared chiefly toward a cadre of sisters from teaching congregations, whose community life would normally offer the important spiritual-pastoral support they needed. The sister-led model of Catholic education is no longer a predominant feature of the Church's educational mission, so it is imperative to develop a mature understanding of the lay nature of the apostolate of teaching. Programs in Catholic universities (or associated bodies), therefore, become conduits for the application of a contemporary understanding of the lay apostolate in a way that reflects the curricular provisions outlined above. These programs will then become beacons of how to apply the Catholic Intellectual Tradition to education.

---

16 See Leonardo Franchi and Richard Rymarz, eds., *Formation of Teachers for Catholic Schools: Challenges and Opportunities in a New Era* (Singapore: Springer, 2022). This volume offers both an overview of Catholic teacher formation programs in the Anglosphere and critical reflection on some of the challenges they face today.

The Curriculum in Catholic Schools

Wide-ranging discussion on the nature and structure of the curriculum in Catholic schools is essential if the school is to be a dynamic and evolving site of learning. In some cases the term "Catholic curriculum" is employed to capture, successfully or otherwise, the foundational curricular vision of the Catholic school. Discussion on the nature and content of the curriculum should be intense and passionate, but must be one that opens, not closes, doors. Of course a school that is truly Catholic will have its doors already open to young people of all traditions. Its Catholic identity stems primarily from the anthropological and philosophical vision at the root of its curriculum and mission, not the religious affiliation of teachers and pupils. The curriculum, to be clear, is the site where knowledge and understanding of Catholic thinking is communicated in an age-appropriate way to pupils, suitably framed as a dialogical process or "encounter" that seeks to understand the longings of humanity for the "good life."[17] This leads to the vital question of what is being encountered. In the strictly religious sense of the term, the encounter is between the human person and the divine person of Jesus: flowing from that is the related encounter with inherited knowledge and social practices that afford students "a rich cultural and scientific heritage preparing them for professional life and fostering mutual understanding."[18] The priority of knowledge in the curriculum, therefore, is not and cannot involve a denial of the importance of professional skills and preparation for life. On the contrary:

> The Catholic Curriculum, to be clear, is powered by the union of faith and reason, focuses on embedding skills in knowledge and encourages students to live a life of wisdom and discernment.

17 "Catholic identity should be a *place of encounter*, a tool promoting the convergence of ideas and actions." Congregation for Catholic Education, Instruction *The Identity of the Catholic School for a Culture of Dialogue* (January 25, 2022), 84.
18 Congregation for Catholic Education, *The Identity of the Catholic School*, 29.

This is similar to broader wisdom traditions in education but, crucially, defines wisdom as the Logos—the Word of God: It is a universal invitation to critically explore the best of humanity, as expressed for example in the arts and sciences.[19]

Offering the treasures of human knowledge to new generations as the mission of the Catholic school today, as always, would seem to be a matter of educational justice. There is scope for discussion on how this can be achieved.

With respect to methods of teaching in Catholic schools, which should always be included in curricular discussions, the importance placed by Shields on the textbook might seem rather quaint in an era marked by the easy availability of multimedia presentations and all manner of electronic aids to study. Shields's *Catholic Education Series*, however, is more than simply a textbook for religious education class. It offers a model of curriculum wherein the main aims of learning are clustered around a common and explicitly religiously conditioned worldview. This raises questions such as: Should we now be aiming for a blended learning approach that combines textbooks ("hard copies") and online approaches that might offer more flexibility and responsiveness?

Deeper questions can also be raised as to the extent to which the integrated curriculum approach offers a suitably vigorous articulation of the domains of knowledge relevant to the school of today. Furthermore, would textbooks or other resources designed specifically for young people—a mainstay of Shields's method—and which contained material which was explicitly religious in content and appearance, enhance or diminish the Catholic school's dual responsibility to offer a curriculum which meets the needs of both young Catholics and students from other religious and philosophical traditions who inhabit Catholic schools? This is another matter requiring open and honest discussion.

19 Franchi and Davis, "Catholic Education and the Idea of Curriculum," 105.

The Dialogue between Religious Education and Catechesis

Finally, we come to a theme that is not explicitly addressed by Shields but does merit revisiting in light of his work. Catholic schools, for sure, need a strong religious education curriculum if they are to flourish educationally and pastorally. Religious education as a domain of knowledge will always influence and be influenced by forces from outside its domain, not least the desire for curricular integration implicit in commonly used terms such as "interdisciplinarity." Contemporary religious education theorists and practitioners, in line with Shields's approach, are also called to engage curiously and positively with a broad range of educational ideas and also to engage with wider scholarly networks. This would seem to be one way in which to broaden the appeal of the Catholic educational tradition.[20]

The current thinking in the Church is that religious education in the school is part of but not synonymous with catechesis, the latter being a matter that concerns the wider Church.[21] If school-based religious education is not necessarily the optimal site for catechesis, it is essential to ask what the purpose of religious education in schools actually is. Essentially, the response is a commitment to a knowledge and understanding of the Catholic worldview. This involves, of course, serious study of the Church's theological and pastoral traditions that seeks to locate this inheritance in a wider cultural framework. We see an example of this approach in the treatment of history and art in Shields's textbooks (see chapter 11). Another example is the importance Shields placed on music as part of the child's religious and

---

20 Some interesting material has been published on the influence of Catholic thinking on domains of knowledge. Cf. John Piderit and Melanie Morey, eds., *Teaching the Tradition: Catholic Themes in Academic Disciplines* (Oxford: Oxford University Press, 2012); Convery, Franchi, and Valero, *Reclaiming the Piazza III: Communicating Catholic Culture*.

21 Cf. Congregation for Catholic Education, *Educating to Intercultural Dialogue in Catholic Schools*, 76–80; Congregation for Catholic Education, *Religious Dimension*, 62–63 and 96–97.

cultural formation. The importance of this issue is such that wider and deeper discussion of how to articulate and give practical examples of authentic religious education has become pressing. Shields's position on the religious formation of children in the school would not be problematic in a school where the vast majority of children experienced a well-layered "Catholic" identity—this would have been more likely in his day—but might be rather more difficult to foster in a school where the makeup of the pupil population is less uniform. This sociological reality, well documented in contemporary studies on issues related to religious affiliation and practice, cannot be put to one side when we discuss curricular matters.[22] It might be an opportune time to think more closely about the role of the family and parish in the catechesis of the child and not rely on the timetabled religious education class in the school as the primary, or even sole, catechetical opportunity.

To shift the primary catechetical focus from the school to the family and parish is not to abandon young children to a diet of secularist ideology in schools. The key point, to return to the idea of the Church as an "educational movement" highlighted earlier, is to rediscover how "divine pedagogy" guides the life of the Church in general terms but also the life of the local church:

> Revelation is the great educational work of God. In fact, it can also be interpreted through a pedagogical lens. In it we find the distinctive elements that can lead us to recognise a *divine pedagogy*, one which is capable of profoundly influencing the Church's educational activity.[23]

The extract above is taken from chapter 5 of the *Directory for Catechesis*, which is headed "The Pedagogy of Faith." Chapter 5 is found in part two of the document and is titled "The Process of Catechesis." It is

22 See, for example, Stephen Bullivant, *Mass Exodus: Catholic Disaffiliation in Britain and America since Vatican II* (Oxford: Oxford University Press, 2019).
23 Pontifical Council for Promoting New Evangelization, *Directory for Catechesis*, 157.

here that we find a sustained reflection on revelation, salvation history and divine pedagogy. There is a focus on the importance of grace and beauty, the latter recalling Shields's stress on church architecture and religious art in his textbooks and readers. The underscoring of beauty around and in the liturgy recalls Vatican II's teaching on the importance of liturgy in the life of the parish, which "must be fostered theoretically and practically among the faithful and clergy" if Sunday Mass is to become the center of parish community life.[24] If the catechetical formation of young Catholics is primarily set in the parish, the life of the parish then becomes the place where families are encouraged to deepen their mission as primary educators of their children. Granted, this model of parish formation is not always widely available, and there is still a place for some form of catechesis in the Catholic school. Nonetheless, careful and creative consideration of the best way to organize the Church's educational mission for young people remains a priority.

Final Thoughts

The present study is not a complete biography of Shields but rather a critical exploration of his contribution to the reform of Catholic education at a particular moment in history. There remains scope for a much more finely grained study of Shields's life and work. In particular, access to his correspondence with teaching sisters and others in the world of education would fill out the lines drawn in the present volume and no doubt bring to the fore his clearly substantial networks and contacts.

Book-length studies of the work of figures like Pace and Johnson would complement the present study and bring to wider audiences the importance not just of individual inspirational figures but the need to create and support institutions like Catholic University, which offer a serious scholarly platform for the research from which Catholic education must draw.

---

24 Vatican Council II, *Sacrosanctum Concilium*, 42.

Shields's dynamism and vision made a substantial difference to teacher formation.[25] After his death, a model school for the Catholic Sisters College—St. Anthony's Parish School of Brookland—was set up, using the *Catholic Education Series* as its core classroom texts.[26] Some initial information on the school's mode of operation, and on how it worked with the *Catholic Education Series,* is available in McMahon's chapter on the Shields Method.[27] McMahon also notes that he had the opportunity to interview the staff—who are "trained to pick the plums out of the Shields basket of hints"—about the Shields Method. Their verdict is instructive: "All agree that that fruit has been worth the planting," but interestingly also note that "the hammering out of improvements through daily trial, are necessary with a method which was never fully tested by its author."[28]

The school still exists and is now called St. Anthony Catholic School. According to the school's website it was originally founded under the auspices of the Benedictine Sisters but was renamed the Thomas E. Shields Memorial School after Shields's death in 1921.[29] The "new" school was opened by Fr. George Johnson of Catholic University, who was a doctoral student of Shields's. The Dominican Sisters were invited to lead the school in its early years, but in 1927 they were called to other duties and the Benedictine Sisters returned

---

25 There are many complimentary remarks from his former students in the Thomas Shields Memorial Issue, *Catholic Educational Review* 19 (April 1921): 289–92.

26 St. Anthony's Parish School of Brookland will hereafter be used as a model school for the Catholic Sisters' College of the Catholic University, under the direction of our Department of Education. The curriculum will be based on the Catholic education series of the late Very Rev. Dr. Thomas Edward Shields, former Dean of the Catholic Sisters' College and editor of The Catholic Educational Review. The new school will be in a true sense of the word a memorial to Dr. Shields, to the carrying out of whose educational ideas it will be devoted. "Model School: Catholic Sisters College," *Catholic University Bulletin* 29, no. 1 (January 1923): 3.

27 McMahon, "The Shields Method," 162–63.

28 McMahon, "The Shields Method," 181–82.

29 See the school's website at https://stanthonyschooldc.org/history.

to direct the school's activities according to the original Benedictine spirit. This suggests that the influence of Shields was in hiatus and that by 1927 it was already waning.

What Shields described as "correlation" is now encompassed by terms like "interdisciplinary learning."[30] As the methods of religious education (as proposed by Shields) must be informed by advances in the empirical data generated by the sciences, so too contemporary education must evolve in line with critical engagement with evidence. Given the high level of information increasingly available about how humans best learn—and what this means for the art of teaching—it is incumbent upon all educators to continue to "seek the truth" and reform practice accordingly following the latest advances in the science of learning. While not all of Shields's ideas have stood the test of time, what remains important is his energy, dedication, and determination to see new knowledge and ways of working not necessarily as threats but as opportunities for growth.

---

30 Other terms currently in vogue are "cross-curricular learning" and "multi-disciplinary learning."

BIBLIOGRAPHY

Alexander, Thomas. Introduction to *A Common Faith*, by John Dewey. 2nd ed. New Haven: Yale University Press, 2013.
Anello, Robert. "Intellectual Formation for Professionalism in Catholic Education: Catholic Sisters' College, Washington, D.C." *U.S. Catholic Historian* 35, no. 4 (Fall 2017): 79–104.
Anonymous. "The Teachers Institute." *Catholic Educational Review* 1 (January 1911): 74–76.
———. "The Summer School: The Catholic University of America." *Catholic Educational Review* 1 (May 1911): 466–72.
———. "Summer Session of the Sisters College." *Catholic Educational Review* 3 (April 1912): 348–64.
———. "The Third Summer Session of the Sisters College." *Catholic Educational Review* 5 (April 1913): 338–55.
———. "Catholic University Summer Schools." *Catholic Educational Review* 7 (April 1914): 289–305.
———. "The Catholic Sisters College." *Catholic Educational Review* 7 (May 1914): 437–44.
———. "Model School: Catholic Sisters College," *Catholic University Bulletin* 29, no. 1 (January 1923): 3.
Aquinas, Thomas. *De Veritate*, q.11. St. Isidore E-Book Library. Available at: https://isidore.co/aquinas/english/QDdeVer11.htm.
Baglow, Christopher. "A Catholic History of the Fake Conflict between Religion and Science." *Church Life Journal*, May 4, 2020. Available at: https://churchlifejournal.nd.edu/articles/a-catholic-history-of-the-conflict-between-religion-and-science.
Barbian, Joseph. "The Catholic Normal Schools of the Holy Family." *Catholic Educational Review* 5 (February 1913): 123–31.
Benedict XVI, Pope. "Letter to the Diocese and City of Rome on the Urgent Task of Educating Young People." January 21, 2008.

Betts, George Herbert. "The Curriculum of Religious Education." *Religious Education* 15, no. 1 (1920): 5–22.

Bowen, James. *A History of Western Education.* Vol. 2, *Civilization of Europe, Sixth to Sixteenth Century.* London: Methuen, 1975.

———. *A History of Western Education.* Vol. 3, *The Modern West, Europe and the New World.* London: Methuen, 1981.

Boxer, Adam, ed. *The researchEd Guide to Explicit and Direct Instruction: An Evidence-Informed Guide for Teachers.* Woodbridge, UK: John Catt Educational, 2019.

Brelsford, Theodore W. "Editorial Introduction." *Religious Education* 98, no. 4 (Fall 2003): 407–10.

Bryce, Mary. "Four Decades of Roman Catholic Innovators." *Religious Education* 73, supp. 1 (1978): 36–57.

Buetow, Harold. "The Teaching of Education at CUA 1889–1966." *Catholic Educational Review* 65, no. 1 (1967): 1–20.

———. *Of Singular Benefit: The Story of Catholic Education in the United States.* London: Macmillan, 1970.

Bullivant, Stephen. *Mass Exodus: Catholic Disaffiliation in Britain and America since Vatican II.* Oxford: Oxford University Press, 2019.

Burns, James A. "The Development of the Parish School Organization." *Catholic Educational Review* 3 (May 1912): 419–34.

Canons and Decrees of the Council of Trent. Translated by H. Schroeder. Rockford, Ill.: Tan Books, 1978. [Originally published in 1941 by Herder Book Co. (St. Louis, Mo.)]

Cantwell, Thomas. "A Comparative Study of the Theories of Self-Activity and Religion according to the Very Reverend Thomas E. Shields and Monsignor George W. Johnson." Master's thesis, The Catholic University of America, 1949.

Cassidy, Francis P. "Catholic Education in the Third Plenary Council of Baltimore." *The Catholic Historical Review* 34, no. 3 (October 1948): 257–305.

Catechism of the Catholic Church. Vatican City: Libreria Editrice Vaticana, 1993.

Catholic University of America's Commission on American Citizenship. *Better Men for Better Times.* Washington, D.C.: The Catholic Education Press, 1943.

Clement of Alexandria, "The Instructor," in *The Writings of Clement of Alexandria.* Vol. 4, *Ante-Nicene Library Translations of the Writings of*

the Fathers Down to AD 325, edited by Alexander Roberts and James Donaldson, 113–349. Edinburgh: T and T Clark, 1867.
Congar, Yves. *Diversity and Communion*. New London: Twenty-Third Publications, 1985.
Congregation for Catholic Education. *The Religious Dimension of Education in Catholic Schools: Guidelines for Reflection and Renewal*. April 7, 1988.
———. *Educating Together in Catholic Schools: A Shared Mission between Consecrated Persons and Lay Faithful*. September 8, 2007.
———. *Circular Letter to Presidents of Bishops' Conferences on Religious Education in Schools*. May 5, 2009.
———. *Educating to Intercultural Dialogue in Catholic Schools: Living in Harmony for a Civilization of Love*. October 28, 2013.
———. *Educating Today and Tomorrow: A Renewing Passion, Lineamenta*. Instrumentem Laboris. April 7, 2014.
———. *The Identity of the Catholic School for a Culture of Dialogue*. Instruction. January 25, 2022.
Congregation for the Doctrine of the Faith. *Letter to the Bishops of the Catholic Church on Some Aspects of the Church Understood as Communion*. May 28, 1992.
Convery, Ronnie, Leonardo Franchi, and Jack Valero, eds. *Reclaiming the Piazza III: Communicating Catholic Culture*. Leominster: Gracewing, 2021.
Cooling, Trevor, with Bob Bowie and Farid Panjwani. *Worldviews in Religious Education*. London: Theos, 2020.
Corrin, Jay P. *Catholic Intellectuals and the Challenge of Democracy*. Notre Dame, Ind.: University of Notre Dame Press, 2002.
Dansette, Adrian, and James A. Corbett. "The Rejuvenation of French Catholicism: Marc Sangnier's Sillon." *The Review of Politics* 15, no. 1 (1953): 34–52.
Dawson, Christopher. *Progress and Religion: An Historical Enquiry*. Washington, D.C.: The Catholic University of America Press, 2001. [Originally published in 1929 by Sheed and Ward (New York)].
———. *Religion and Culture*. Washington, D.C.: The Catholic University of America Press, 2013. [Originally published in 1948 by Sheed and Ward (New York)].
———. *The Crisis of Western Education*. Washington, D.C.: The Catholic University of America Press, 2010. [Originally published in 1961 by Sheed and Ward (New York)].

De Lubac, Henri. *The Splendor of the Church*. San Francisco: Ignatius Press, 1986.

Dewey, John. "Religious Education as Conditioned by Modern Psychology and Pedagogy." *Religious Education* 69, no. 1 (1974): 5–11. [Originally published in the *Proceedings of the First Annual Convention of the Religious Education Association, Feb. 10–12, 1903* (1903): 60–66].

———. *Democracy and Education: An Introduction to the Philosophy of Education*. Delhi: Aakar Books, 2004. [Originally published in 1916 by McMillan (New York)]

———. *A Common Faith*. 2nd ed. New Haven: Yale University Press, 2013. [First edition published in 1934 by Yale University Press (New Haven)].

Dixon, Robert. "The Influence of Religious Teaching Orders on Catholic Schools in Canada Outside of Quebec." *International Studies in Catholic Education* (December 2019), online. Available at: https://www.tandfonline.com/doi/full/10.1080/19422539.2019.1691828.

Doyle, Dennis. "Thomas Aquinas: Integrating Faith and Reason in the Catholic School." *Catholic Education: A Journal of Inquiry and Practice*. 10, no. 3 (2007): 343–56.

Doyle, Mary. *Standard Catholic Readers by Grades, First Year*. New York: American Book Company, 1909.

Egan, Kieran. *Getting It Wrong from the Beginning: Our Progressivist Inheritance from Herbert Spencer, John Dewey, and Jean Piaget*. New Haven: Yale University Press, 2002.

Elias, John L. "Catholics in the REA, 1903–1953." *Religious Education* 99, no. 3 (2004): 225–46.

———. "Edward Pace: Pioneer Psychologist, Philosopher and Religious Educator." In Elias and Nolan, *Educators in the Catholic Intellectual Tradition*, 49–74.

———. "George Johnson: Policy Maker for Catholic Education." In Elias and Nolan, *Educators in the Catholic Intellectual Tradition*, 103–30.

———. "Thomas E. Shields: Progressive Catholic Educator." In Elias and Nolan, *Educators in the Catholic Intellectual Tradition*, 75–102.

Elias, John L., and Lucinda A. Nolan, eds. *Educators in the Catholic Intellectual Tradition*. Fairfield, Conn.: Sacred Heart University Press, 2009.

Fitzpatrick, Thomas. *No Mean Service: Scottish Catholic Teacher Education, 1895–1995: A Centenary Celebration*. Bearsden: St. Andrews College, 1995.

Franchi, Leonardo. *Shared Mission: Religious Education in the Catholic Tradition.* London: Scepter, 2017.

Franchi, Leonardo, and Robert Davis. "Catholic Education and the Idea of Curriculum." *Journal of Catholic Education* 24, no. 2 (Fall 2021): 104–19.

Franchi, Leonardo, and Richard Rymarz, eds. *Formation of Teachers for Catholic Schools: Challenges and Opportunities in a New Era.* Catholic Education Globally: Challenges and Opportunities in a New Era 1. Singapore: Springer, 2022.

Francis, Pope. *Fratelli Tutti (On Fraternity and Social Friendship).* Encyclical Letter. October 3, 2020.

———. *Desiderio Desideravi (On the Liturgical Formation of the People of God).* Apostolic Letter. June 29, 2022.

Fujikawa, Fumiko Maria Christina. "The Educational Contents and Implications of *The Education of Our Girls* by Dr. Thomas Edward Shields." Master's thesis, The Catholic University of America, 1954.

Gearon, Liam. "European Religious Education and European Civil Religion." *British Journal of Educational Studies* 260, no. 2 (2012): 151–69.

Gibbons, Cardinal James. *The Ambassador of Christ.* Baltimore: J. Murphy & Co., 1896.

Groome, Thomas H. "Remembering and Imagining." *Religious Education* 98, no. 4 (Fall 2003): 511–20.

Groothius, Douglas. "On Not Abolishing Faith Schools: A Response to Michael Hand and H. Siegel." *Theory and Research in Education* 2, no. 2 (2004): 177–88.

Guardini, Romano. *The Spirit of the Liturgy.* Translated by Ada Lane. New York: Crossroads Publishing Company, 1997.

The Guild of Catholic Teachers. *Religious Knowledge: A Course for Young Children.* Scottish Catholic Archives, Religious Education 4/5, 1939.

Gushurt-Moore, André. *Glory in All Things: Saint Benedict and Catholic Education Today.* Brooklyn: Angelico Press, 2020.

Hall, Royal G. "The Significance of John Dewey for Religious Interpretation." *The Open Court* 6, article 2 (1928): 331–40. Available at https://opensiuc.lib.siu.edu/ocj/vol1928/iss6/2/.

Hand, Michael. "A Philosophical Objection to Faith Schools." *Theory and Research in Education* 1, no. 1 (2003): 89–99.

Heft, James L. *The Future of Catholic Higher Education*. Oxford: Oxford University Press, 2021.
Hirst, Paul. *Moral Education in a Secular Society*. Warwick: University of London Press, 1974.
Jackson, Robert. "Religion, Education, Dialogue and Conflict: Editorial Introduction." *British Journal of Religious Education* 33, no. 2 (2011): 105–9.
John Paul II, Pope. *Catechesi Tradendae (On Catechesis in Our Time)*. Apostolic Exhortation. October 16, 1979.
———. *Fides et Ratio (On the Relationship between Faith and Reason)*. Encyclical Letter. September 14, 1998.
———. "Letter to Artists." April 4, 1999.
Johnson, George. "Character Education in the Catholic Church." *Religious Education* 24, no. 1 (1929): 54–57.
John XXIII, Pope. "Address at the Opening of the Second Vatican Council." October 11, 1962.
Jungmann, Josef, SJ, ed. *The Good News Yesterday and Today*. Translated, abridged, and edited by William A. Huesman, SJ. New York: W.H. Sadlier, 1962.
Kathan, Boardman W. "Horace Bushnell and the Religious Education Movement." *Religious Education* 108, no. 1 (2013): 41–57.
Keane, John. "The Catholic Universities of France." *Catholic World* 47, no. 279 (June 1888): 289–97.
Lamb, Edel. *Reading Children in Early Modern Culture*. Early Modern Literature in History. Cham, Switzerland: Springer, 2018.
Lash, Nicholas. "The Church: A School of Wisdom?" In *Receptive Ecumenism and the Call to Catholic Learning: Exploring a Way for Contemporary Ecumenism*, edited by Paul Murray, 63–77. Oxford: Oxford University Press, 2008.
Lehner, Ulrich. *The Catholic Enlightenment: The Forgotten History of a Global Movement*. Oxford: Oxford University Press, 2016.
Leo XIII, Pope. *Immortale Dei (On the Christian Constitution of States)*. Encyclical Letter. November 1, 1885.
———. *Spectata Fides (On Christian Education)*. Encyclical Letter. November 27, 1885.
———. *Magni Nobis (On the Catholic University of America)*. Encyclical Letter. March 7, 1889.
———. *Rerum Novarum (On Capital and Labour)*. Encyclical Letter. May 15, 1891.

Malloy, David. "The American Hierarchy, The Propaganda Fide, and Composition of the Baltimore Catechism." *Records of the American Catholic Historical Society of Philadelphia* 103, no. 2 (Fall 1992): 35–46.

McCormick, Patrick, J. "The [First] Summer School: Report of the Secretary." *Catholic Educational Review* 2 (September 1911): 658–61.

———. "Current Events–Sisters College." *Catholic Educational Review* 2 (November 1911): 854.

———. "The [Second] Summer Session of the Catholic Sisters College." *Catholic Educational Review* 4 (September 1912): 158–61.

———. "The [Third] Summer Session of Teachers College: Report of the Secretary." *Catholic Educational Review* 6 (September 1913): 168–75.

———. Review of *Philosophy of Education*, by Thomas Edward Shields. *Catholic Educational Review* 13 (May 1917): 458–59.

———. "Shields, First Dean of the Catholic Sisters College." Thomas Shields Memorial Issue. *Catholic Educational Review* 19 (April 1921): 265–68.

———. "Shields as Writer." Thomas Shields Memorial Issue, *Catholic Educational Review* 19 (April 1921): 274–76.

McKinney, Stephen J. "A Catholic Vision of Education." In Convery, Franchi, and Valero, *Reclaiming the Piazza III*, 191–210.

McMahon, John. "The Shields Method: Some Methods of Teaching Religion." PhD diss., National University of Ireland. London: Burns, Oates and Washbourne, 1928.

McVay, Leo. "Shields and Affiliation." Thomas Shields Memorial Issue, *Catholic Educational Review* 19 (April 1921): 269–73.

Moran, Gabriel. "Still to Come." *Religious Education* 98, no. 4 (Fall 2003): 495–502.

Murphy, John F. "Thomas Edward Shields: Religious Educator." PhD diss., The Catholic University of America, 1971.

———. "The Contribution of the Human Sciences to the Pedagogy of Thomas E. Shields." *The Living Light* 10, no. 1 (1973): 79–87.

Myers, William R. "John Dewey, God and the Religious Education of the American Public." *Theology Today* 74, no. 2 (2017): 157–71.

Neuhaus, Richard John. "The Real John Dewey." *First Things* (January 1992). Available at: https://www.firstthings.com/article/1992/01/the-real-john-dewey.

Newman, John H. *An Essay on the Development of Christian Doctrine.* Rev. ed. 1989. Reprint, Notre Dame, Ind.: University of Notre Dame Press, 2005. [Originally published in 1845, with a second edition in 1878].

———. "Intellect, the Instrument of Religious Training." Sermon, 1856. *Works of John Henry Newman,* collected by the National Institute for Newman Studies. Available at https://www.newmanreader.org/works/occasions/sermon1.html.

Nolan, Lucinda A. "Bishop John Lancaster Spalding: Prelate and Philosopher of Catholic Education." In Elias and Nolan, *Educators in the Catholic Intellectual Tradition,* 20–48.

Notley, R. Steven. "Reading Gospel Parables as Jewish Literature." *Journal for the Study of the New Testament* 41, no. 1 (2018): 29–43.

Nugent, Walter. *Progressivism: A Very Short Introduction.* Oxford: Oxford University Press, 2010.

O'Donoghue, Tom. *Come Follow Me and Forsake Temptation: Catholic Schooling and the Recruitment and Retention of Teachers for Religious Teaching Orders, 1922–1965.* Bern: Peter Lang, 2004.

O'Hagan, Francis. *The Contribution of the Religious Orders to Education in Glasgow during the Period 1847–1918.* Lewiston, N.Y.: Edwin Mellon, 2006.

O'Hagan, Francis, and Robert Davis. "Forging the Compact of Church and State in the Development of Catholic Education in the late Nineteenth Century Scotland." *Innes Review* 58, no. 1 (2007): 72–94.

Ozoliņš, Jānis T. "Aquinas, Education and the Theory of Illumination." *Educational Philosophy and Theory* 53, no. 10 (2020): 967–71.

Pace, Edward. "Modern Psychology and Catholic Education." *Catholic World* 86, no. 486 (September 1905): 717–29.

———. "The Papacy and Education." *Catholic Educational Review* 1 (January 1911): 1–9.

———. "Homily, Requiem Mass for Thomas Shields." Thomas Shields Memorial Issue. *Catholic Educational Review* 19 (April 1921): 194–200.

Paul VI, Pope. *Populorum Progressio (On the Development of Peoples).* Encyclical Letter. March 26, 1967.

Pawl, Faith Glavey. "Minding Children in the Study of Liturgy: Philosophical Reflections on Children as Religious Practitioners." *TheoLogica: An International Journal for Philosophy of Religion and Philosophical Theology* 4, no. 1 (2020): 6–29.

Pecklers, Keith F. "The History of the Modern Liturgical Movement." In *Oxford Research Encyclopedias*, September 3, 2015. Available at: https://oxfordre.com/religion/view/10.1093/acrefore/9780199340378.001.0001/acrefore-9780199340378-e-19.

Pew Research Center. *Religion and Education around the World, 2018*. Available at: https://www.pewresearch.org/religion/2016/12/13/religion-and-education-around-the-world/.

Piderit, John, and Melanie Morey, eds. *Teaching the Tradition: Catholic Themes in Academic Disciplines*. Oxford: Oxford University Press, 2012.

Pinsent, Andrew. "A Catholic Understanding of Science." In Convery, Franchi, and Valero, *Reclaiming the Piazza III*, 113–28.

Pius X, Pope. *Acerbo Nimis (On Teaching Christian Doctrine)*. Encyclical Letter. April 15, 1905.

———. *Pascendi Dominici Gregis (On the Doctrines of the Modernists)*. Encyclical Letter. September 8, 1907.

———. *Our Apostolic Mandate*. Letter to the French Bishops. August 25, 1910.

———. *Catechism of Christian Doctrine*. Dublin: M.H. Gill, 1914.

Pius XI, Pope. *Divini Illius Magistri (On Christian Education)*. Encyclical Letter. December 31, 1929.

Pontifical Council for Promoting New Evangelization. *Directory for Catechesis*. London: Catholic Truth Society, 2020.

Pontifical Foundation Gravissimum Educationis. "Democracy: An Educational Urgency in Pluricultural and Plurireligious Contexts," 2020. Available at: https://www.fondazionege.org/en/progetti/democracy-an-educational-urgency-in-pluricultural-and-plurireligious-contexts:12237/.

Pring, Richard. *Challenges for Religious Education: Is There a Disconnect between Faith and Reason?* Abingdon: Routledge, 2019.

Rice, Bob, and Nicholas Stein. "The Catechism of the Catholic Church and Ministry with Youth and Young Adults." In *Speaking the Truth in Love: The Catechism and the New Evangelization*, edited by Petroc Willey and Scott Sollom, 461–73. Steubenville, Ohio: Emmaus Academic, 2019.

Rivera, Eleanor. L. "Cultivating the Spirit: Catholic Educators, Primary Educators and Pedagogy in Early Third Republic France." *Paedagogica Historica: International Journal of the History of Education*, published online, February 4, 2022. Available at: https://www.tandfonline.com/doi/abs/10.1080/00309230.2022.2032770.

Royal, Robert. *A Deeper Vision: The Catholic Intellectual Tradition in the Twentieth Century*. San Francisco: Ignatius Press, 2015.

Rymarz, Richard, and Leonardo Franchi. *Catholic Teacher Preparation: Historical and Contemporary Perspectives on Preparing for Mission*. Bingley, UK: Emerald, 2019.

Sacred Congregation of Rites. *Musicam Sacram*. Instruction on Music in Liturgy. March 5, 1967.

———. *Eucharisticum Mysterium*. Instruction on the Worship of the Eucharistic Mystery. May 25, 1967.

Schall, James. *Another Sort of Learning*. San Francisco: Ignatius Press, 1988.

Shahan, Thomas J. *The Beginnings of Christianity*. New York: Benziger Bros., 1903.

———. *The Middle Ages*. New York: Benziger Bros., 1904.

———. *The House of God*. New York: The Cathedral Library Association, 1905.

Shanks, Rachel, ed. *Teacher Preparation in Scotland*. Bingley, U.K.: Emerald, 2020.

Shields, Thomas. "The Teaching of Pedagogy in the Seminary." *Catholic University Bulletin* 11 (1905): 442–49.

———. "Catholic Teachers and Educational Progress." *Catholic World* 83, no. 493 (April 1906): 93–101.

———. *The Education of Our Girls*. New York: Benziger Brothers, 1907.

———. *The Teaching of Religion*. Washington D.C.: The Catholic Correspondence School, 1908.

———. *Catholic Education Series, First Book*. Washington D.C.: The Catholic Education Press, 1908, 1917.

———. *The Making and Unmaking of a Dullard*. Washington, D.C.: The Catholic Education Press, 1909.

———. "Notes on Education." *Catholic University Bulletin* 15 (1909): 65–88; 156–80; 275–99; 400–23; 474–98.

———. "The Catholic Educational Association." *Catholic University Bulletin* 15 (1909): 88.

———. "Catholic Educational Literature." *Catholic University Bulletin* 15 (1909): 663–67.

———. "The University and the Training of Primary Teachers." *Catholic University Bulletin* 16 (1910): 578–87.

———. "University Chronicle." *Catholic University Bulletin* 17 (1911): 88–91.

———. "The Teaching of Religion." *Catholic Educational Review* 1 (January 1911): 56–65.

———. "Fundamental Principles in the Teaching of Religion." *Catholic Educational Review* 1 (April 1911): 338–46.
———. "Correlation in the Teaching of Religion." *Catholic Educational Review* 1 (May 1911): 420–29.
———. "The Sisters' College." *Catholic Educational Review* 2 (October 1911): 742–43.
———. "Survey of the Field (The High School)." *Catholic Educational Review* 2 (December 1911): 925–43.
———. *Teachers Manual of Primary Methods.* Washington, D.C.: The Catholic Education Press, 1912.
———. "The Sisters College." *Catholic Educational Review* 3 (January 1912): 1–12.
———. "Catholic University Extension Work in Texas." *Catholic Educational Review* 3 (February 1912): 126–30.
———. "Teachers College of the Catholic University of America." *Catholic Educational Review* 6 (November 1913): 314–37.
———. "Summer Session of the Sisters College, Dubuque Extension." *Catholic Educational Review* 7 (February 1914): 163–69.
———. "Survey of the Field (Vocational Training)." *Catholic Educational Review* 7 (April 1914): 346–59.
———. "The Summer Session of the Sisters College." *Catholic Educational Review* 9 (January 1915): 36–42.
———. "Survey of the Field (Vocational Education)." *Catholic Educational Review* 9 (April 1915): 289–303.
———. "Survey of the Field (The Cultural and Vocational Aims in Education)." *Catholic Educational Review* 10 (June 1915): 46–56.
———. "The Catholic Sisters College." *Catholic Educational Review* 12 (June 1916): 10–17.
———. *Philosophy of Education.* Washington, D.C.: The Catholic Education Press, 1917.
———. *Catholic Education Series, Fourth Book.* Washington, D.C.: The Catholic Education Press, 1918.
———. "Musical Education in Catholic Schools." *Catholic Educational Review* 15 (January 1918): 3–18.
———. "The Sisters College and the High Schools Affiliated with the Catholic University." *Catholic Educational Review* 15 (February 1918): 97–105.

———. Review of *Schools of Tomorrow*, by John and Evelyn Dewey. *Catholic Educational Review* 16 (November 1918): 344–46.

Shields, Thomas, and Edward Pace. *Twenty-Five Lessons in the Psychology of Education*. Washington, D.C.: The Catholic University of America, 1906.

Shvarts, Anna, and Arthur Bakker. "The Early History of the Scaffolding Metaphor: Bernstein, Luria, Vygotsky, and Before." *Mind, Culture, and Activity* 26, no. 1 (2019): 4–23.

Sister Antonine of Holy Cross Academy. Review of *The Education of Our Girls*. *Catholic University Bulletin* 14 (1908): 57–62.

A Sister of the Congregation of Notre Dame, "The Second Summer Session of the Sisters College." *Catholic Educational Review* 4 (September 1912): 152–57.

Sister Mary Clara. "Dubuque Extension of the Sisters College." *Catholic Educational Review* 8 (September 1914): 153–60.

Sister Mary Magdala. "Discussion" of *The Catholic Education Series, First Book*. *Catholic Educational Review* 9 (January 1915): 72–77.

Sister Mary Ruth. "The Curriculum of the Woman's College in Relation to the Problems of Modern Life." *Catholic Educational Review* 14 (September 1917): 109–24.

A Sister of Saint Dominic, "Our First Year at the Sisters College." *Catholic Educational Review* 3 (January–May 1912): 435–44.

Sisters of Notre Dame. "The Institute of Notre Dame de Namur." *Catholic Educational Review* 1 (March 1911): 223–30.

Sloyan, Gerard. *Shaping the Christian Message: Essays in Religious Education*. New York: Macmillan, 1958.

———. "The Good News and the Catechetical Scene in the United States." In Jungmann, *The Good News Yesterday and Today*, 211–28.

Spalding, John L. "Normal Schools for Catholics." *Catholic World* 51, no. 301 (April 1890): 88–97.

———. *Religion, Agnosticism and Education*. Reprint, St. Athanasius Press, 2018. [originally published in 1902 by A.C. McClure & Co. (Chicago)].

Sullivan, John. "Catholic Universities as Counter-Cultural to Universities PLC." *International Studies in Catholic Education* 19, no. 2 (2019): 190–203.

———. *Lights for the Path*. Dublin: Veritas, 2022.

Taylor, Charles. *A Secular Age*. Cambridge, Mass.: The Belknap Press of Harvard University Press, 2018.
United Nations. *Universal Declaration on Human Rights* (1948), article 18. https://www.un.org/en/about-us/universal-declaration-of-human-rights.
Ursulines of Ursuline Convent, Cincinnati, Ohio. "The First Session of the Summer School." *Catholic Educational Review* 2 (September 1911): 654–57.
Vatican Council II. *Sacrosanctum Concilium*. Constitution on the Sacred Liturgy. December 4, 1963.
———. *Lumen Gentium*. Dogmatic Constitution on the Church. November 21, 1964.
———. *Gravissimum Educationis*. Declaration on Christian Education. October 28, 1965.
Veverka, Fayette Breaux. "Defining a Catholic Approach to Education in the United States, 1920–1950." *Religious Education* 88, no. 4 (1993): 523–42.
Ward, Justine. *Thomas Edward Shields: Biologist, Psychologist, Educator*. New York: Charles Scribner's Sons, 1947.
Watrin, Rita. *The Founding and Development of the Program of Affiliation of the Catholic University of America: 1912 to 1939*. Washington, D.C.: The Catholic University of America Press, 1966.
Weigel, George. *The Irony of Modern Catholic History: How the Church Rediscovered Itself and Challenged the Modern World to Reform*. New York: Basic Books, 2019.
Wohlwend, Mary Verone. "The Educational Principles of Dr. Thomas E. Shields and Their Impact on His Teacher Training Programme at the Catholic University of America." PhD diss., The Catholic University of America, 1968.
Yarnold, Edward. *Cyril of Jerusalem*. London: Routledge, 2000.

APPENDIX

The Psychology of Education (1907)

T. E. Shields

Lesson XXV

Educational Principles in the Teaching
of Christ and of the Church
331–344[1]

I

The artist's freedom and his control of the medium in which he works depend on his knowledge of the fundamental principles upon which his art rests. This is as true of the teacher as it is of the poet or of the painter. No one need, therefore, be surprised to find the teacher who fails to grasp the meaning of the fundamental principles of education, or who fails to embody them in his work in the classroom, remains enslaved to the details of method, to "the letter of the law which killeth."[2]

A full understanding of the meaning of the principles involved and a clear recognition of their validity are indispensable prerequisites to the intelligent handling of any method. In this fundamental course, therefore, we have been occupied chiefly with the derivation from philosophy and science of a number of principles of wide import in the work of education.

---

[1] The numerals in brackets mark the start of each new page in the original publication. The title page for this lesson is p. 331, and the main text begins on p. 332.
[2] See 2 Cor 3:6. The translations of Scripture allusions or quotations are reproduced from Shields's original, but notes such as this are the work of the editor. Shields's quotations resemble the translation of the Douay-Rheims Bible, but many cases (such as this one) do not exactly match.

Now, it is admittedly difficult to grasp the full significance of a principle in its abstract formulation until it has first been seen in a concrete setting. The meaning of these fundamental principles of education will, accordingly, become clearer as they are studied in their concrete embodiment in methods of teaching the various school subjects. Correspondence courses in which they are applied in methods of teaching language, logic, and Christian Doctrine have been prepared by Professors in the Catholic University and are now available for those who may care to profit by them. Other courses will follow in due time.

Nowhere are these educational principles so perfectly embodied as in our Savior's method of teaching and in the organic teaching of the Church. [333]

This theme will be more fully developed in connection with the method of teaching Christian Doctrine. It seems well, however, before bringing this fundamental course to a close, to call attention to the embodiment in the teaching of Christ and of His Church of some of the principles whose philosophic and scientific aspects we have studied in the preceding lessons.

To the faithful believer, the fact that Christ and the Holy Spirit embody these principles in their method of teaching is a clearer proof of their validity than is to be found in all the philosophic and scientific data that have been adduced in their support in these pages. Moreover, love will lead many a devout soul into the inmost meaning of principles contemplated in these divine methods for whom the scientific formulation of the same principles would have but little significance.

II

Principle I.
The center of orientation in educational endeavor has shifted from the logical basis of the body of truth to be imparted to the needs and capacities of the growing mind. (Cf. Les. IV, V)

Principle II.
The relation of truth to the growing mind is similar to that of food to the growing body; in each case, incorporation into the living structure is the end sought. (Cf. Les. VI)

Principle III.
Where the truth is assimilated when it is taken into the mind, the resulting growth is in a geometrical ratio. (Cf. Les. VII)

APPENDIX

These three principles are embodied in every page of the Gospel and they are conscious features of the organic teaching of the Church. There [334] is a striking contrast between our Lord's method and the method employed by the Greek philosophers. Socrates, Plato, and Aristotle spoke to mature minds; they turned the attention of their hearers to the knowledge which they already possessed and which they attempted to formulate in abstract principles. Their teaching was the inscription on the tomb of knowledge, pointing to the life and activity in the past.

Our Lord, on the contrary, addressed Himself to the little ones and to the simple and untutored children of nature. The simple fishermen of Galilee, the shepherds and the tillers of the soil crowded round Him and they received from Him the words of life. He spoke to them of the highest and of the most far-reaching truths, but always in terms of their own experience. To the shepherd He spoke of the sheepfold; to the tillers of the soil He spoke of the vine and its branches, of the seedtime and the harvest, of the wheat and the cockle. He addressed Himself to common human instincts and emotions, to love of life and love of offspring. Everywhere and always He made these simple natural truths the basis of the larger and higher truths which He came from heaven to reveal to men. "All these things Jesus spoke in parables to the multitudes; and without parables He did not speak to them."[3] The capacity of the mind before Him, whether it be that of a little child or that of a doctor of the law, was always the center of orientation in His teaching.

Principle II seems never to have been out of His mind, "Not by bread alone doth man live, but by every word that proceedeth from the mouth of God."[4] "I am the bread that came down from heaven."[5] "Feed my lambs, feed my sheep."[6]

Unless the spiritual truth received be incorporated into the mind so as to bring forth fruit, it will rise up at the last day in condemnation against the wicked servant. This truth He illustrates in numerous parables [335] such as that of the wicked servant who wrapped up the talent in a napkin,[7] and the barren fig tree,[8] etc.

3 Matt 13:34.
4 Matt 4:4.
5 John 6:41.
6 See John 21: 15–17.
7 Luke 19:20–24.
8 Matt 21:19.

That a truth assimilated promotes growth in a geometrical ratio is also implied in many of His parables. "Unless the grain of wheat falling into the ground perish, it remaineth alone, but if it perish, it bringeth forth fruit a hundredfold."[9] He constantly refers to the words of truth which He sows in the hearts of His followers as seeds that are to spring up into an abundant harvest.[10]

The Church, following in the footsteps of her Divine Founder, has from the day of Pentecost to the present hour, gone out to every people and she has spoken to each tribe and to each nation in its own tongue. She has incorporated into her ritual ceremonies and rites that were dear to the peoples whom she converted. She transformed their feast into Christian festivals. Like St. Paul, she makes herself all things to all people that she may save all. She brings salvation to the Jew and to the Gentile, to the philosopher with generations of culture back of him and to the savage in the primeval forest, to the child at his mother's knee, to kings, and to the lawgivers of the empire. In each case she works with the materials she finds incorporated in the individual life until she builds the mind up to a capacity sufficient to receive the higher truths of the kingdom. She lays the obligation upon her bishops and her priests to break the bread of life to her children by preaching to them the sublime mysteries of heaven in language suited to their capacity.

III

Principle IV.

In the acquisition of truth the center of interest is to be found in the dynamic rather than in the static. (Cf. Les. IV)

[336]

Principle V.

Interest arises from partially known truths and it is developed by organizing the previous content of the mind with reference to the truth to be acquired; it should precede and be the measure of acquisition. (Cf. Les. II, XI, XII)

---

9 John 12:24.
10 For example, Matt 13:3–9, 18–30.

Christ constantly warned His followers against a static religion that expressed itself in rigid forms, in the letter of the law that killeth. "It is the spirit that giveth life."[11] In the kingdom all was to be growth and life. He established His Church in a germinal form; it was to develop in freedom. Hierarchy, and government, and liturgy were all to unfold themselves in due season.

There was to be no coercion; desire must ever precede the reception of heavenly truths. "Cast not thy pearls before swine."[12] "Put up again thy sword into its scabbard."[13] "You cannot come to me unless it be given to you by my Father who art in heaven."[14] This interest and desire which was always to precede the reception of revealed truth, Christ aroused by appealing to the previous content of the minds of His hearers. He referred them to their own traditions, to the prophecies, to the figures of the Old Testament. With these He wove the experience of every-day life, the love of the shepherd for his sheep, of the father for his son. And from these dim foreshadowings of the Incarnation He built up an eager interest in the truth which He came to proclaim. To this He added the natural desire to escape pain and disease, to assuage hunger; and to it He also added the love of power and of dominion.

This is well illustrated in the sixth chapter of the Gospel according to St. John, in which the Evangelist tells of the manner in which our Lord announced to His followers the establishment of the Holy Eucharist. "A great [337] multitude followed him because they saw the miracles which he did on them that were diseased."[15] When He had led them out into the wilderness, away from the distractions of the haunts of man, and when He had aroused their interest and their curiosity to such an extent that they even forgot to bring food with them, He added the further incentive of desire by multiplying the loaves and fishes. He escaped from their midst and appeared to His disciples that night walking on the waters, thus confirming their faith and still further arousing their interest in what He was about to do. The interest of the crowd was such that they sought Him everywhere, and, having heard of His appearance on the other side of the lake, they left

---

11 John 6:64.
12 Matt 7:6.
13 Matt 26:52; John 18:11.
14 John 6:66.
15 John 6:2.

their homes and their ordinary occupations to seek Him out and learn what further He had to say to them. When they came to Him, He reproached them with the fact that their cupidity was greater than their interest in His divine power. "Amen, Amen, I say to you, you seek me, not because you have seen miracles, but because you did eat of the loaves and were filled. Labor not for the meat which perisheth, but for that which endureth unto life everlasting, which the Son of Man will give you."[16]

It would, indeed, be difficult to find a more perfect illustration of principle V than that contained in the fourth chapter of St. John, where our Lord announces Himself to the Samaritan woman. He arouses her interest by the breaking of a Jewish custom in asking her for water. He harkens back to Jacob and the Prophets, He awakens her desire to escape from the drudgery of hauling water from the well, He arouses interest in His own personality, "If thou didst know the gift of God, and who he is that sayeth to thee, give me to drink; thou wouldst have asked of him, and he would give thee living water."[17] He then fanned her interest to fever [338]-ish intensity by telling her of her own past, before announcing to her His Messiahship and sending her into the city to awaken the interest of its inhabitants and to bring them to Him.

This antecedent preparation of the content of the mind for the reception of revealed truth is characteristic of the whole history of God's dealing with man. For centuries the Chosen People were prepared by miracles and prophecies and promises for the coming of the Redeemer, and His immediate approach was heralded by angels, by the Wise Men of the East, and by the preaching of the Baptist.

According to the divine promise, the Holy Spirit was to abide with the apostles and their successors, calling to their minds whatsoever Christ had said and showing them the things that were to come. The Church has always insisted upon the necessity of careful preparation before entering upon the contemplation of the sublime mysteries of religion. She insists upon vigils of fasting and prayer before her chief festivals. During the four weeks of Advent she prepares her children for the celebration of Christmas. And during the seven weeks of Lent she prepares them for the celebration of Easter. In each case her ritual carries the mind back to the conditions of the world which led up to the events which she celebrates.

16 John 6:26–27.
17 John 4:10.

APPENDIX

IV

Principle VI.

In any line of human endeavor the model that is in most complete harmony with the experience of the imitator and that embodies his ideal of perfection in a given direction serves to orientate his imitative activity. (Cf. Les. XXII, XXIII)

[339]

Principle VII.

The strength of the imitative impulse is in inverse ratio to the distance which the imitator perceives to exist between his chosen model and his present conscious power of achievement. (Cf. Les. XXII, XXIII)

"Be you therefore perfect, as also your heavenly Father is perfect."[18] "But every one shall be perfect, if he be as his master."[19] The apostles urged the same truth. "For yourselves, know how ye ought to follow us."[20] "To make ourselves an example to you to follow us." "For unto this you are called: because Christ also suffered for us, leaving you an example that you should follow his steps."[21]

The power of imitation was also announced in a negative form by our Lord when He said, "It were better for him that a millstone were hanged about his neck and that he be cast into the sea than that he should scandalize one of these little ones."[22] "Woe to him by whom scandal cometh."[23]

The Church holds up Christ and His Blessed Mother as the perfect models for all her children. But, guided by the Holy Spirit, she insists on the duty that rests upon each one of her children of giving good example, and she has pointed out multitudes of saints from all walks of life so that her children might feel the uplifting influence of this great imitative impulse.

Christ's miracles and His teaching, perfect as the latter was, failed to reach the intelligence of His followers because His own life was too far removed from theirs to be comprehensible to them. They had feared

---

18 Matt 5:48.
19 Luke 6:40.
20 2 Thes 3:7.
21 1 Peter 2:21.
22 Luke 17:2.
23 Matt 18:7.

Jehovah and worshipped Him from afar, and now, notwithstanding the fact that the Son of God took upon Himself human infirmity that man might approach and understand the perfect way, still this was not to be accomplished without miracle. Even His beloved John fled from Him in the hour of peril and Peter denied Him with an oath. The holy women went down to His sepulchre to anoint a dead Christ and not to welcome a risen Savior; Thomas refused to believe in the Resurrection on the testimony of the ten and declared that his assent would wait upon the sensible avouch of his own eyes and the evidence of his sense of touch. And yet, poor, blundering Peter, probably because his frailties brought him so much nearer to his audience, made five thousand converts by his first sermon, many of whom remained to seal their faith with their blood.

[340]

V

Principle VIII.
The presence in consciousness of appropriate feeling is indispensable to mental assimilation. (Cf. Les. XVI)

Principle IX.
Perception determines, in large measure, the mind's power of assimilation. (Cf. Les. XVIII, XIX)

Every page of the Gospel illustrates the way in which Christ employed these principles. He works miracles, not merely to excite the sense of wonder, but to feed the hungry to heal the lame and the blind, to make the dumb to speak and the dead to rise. In fact, He does every legitimate thing within the range of His divine power to create appropriate feeling and to develop suitable percepts in the mind of His followers before announcing to them the glad tidings.

The manner in which these principles are embodied in the ritual of the Church has been sufficiently indicated in Lesson XVI. In fact, the whole liturgy of the Church is built on the principle that spiritual truths must be presented to the mind of man in a concrete setting, so that he may attain to its inner meaning through the perception of analogus [sic.] sensible things.

[341]

VI

Principle X.
The cultivation of the senses fixes the limits beyond which mental development cannot proceed. (Cf. Les. XVII)

Principle XI.
Truth that is assimilated, is rendered functional by the act of expression. (Cf. Les. XX, XXI)

Christ takes His disciples out into the fields, onto the hillsides, into the wilderness, and down by the shores of the sea to illustrate the truths which He preached by a constant appeal to the imagery which filled the senses of His followers. "Behold, I say to you, lift up your eyes, and see the countries; for they are white already to harvest,"[24] "Henceforth thou shalt be a fisher of men."[25]

Dr. Pace, in his article in the Catholic World for September, 1905, on Modern Psychology and Catholic Education, points out how the Church in her organic teaching has embodied these principles. "The Church has always recognized the importance of these processes for the development of intellectual and moral activity. We have only to look at her liturgy. What more forcible appeal could be made to the senses than that which she makes in her ceremonial, in the administration of the Sacraments, in the adornment of her temples, in every prescription of her ritual? Light and color, movement and harmony, stately forms and graceful lines are all combined to impress the eye and ear of him who worships in her sanctuary. The art of the builder, the painter, the sculptor, and the musician is pressed into the service of religion. And religion itself—as doctrine, as historical fact, and as moral precept—is brought home to the mind through the portals of sense. * * * * The Church has never denied that religion and morality have their [342] seat in the heart; that the interior life of thought and will is essential; and that without this life merely external performance is worthless. But she has also insisted, and she still insists, that religion must have its

---

24 John 4:35.
25 Luke 5:10.

outward manifestation, if it is to grow as the mind grows and to become a dominant power as the faculties unfold. This is the philosophy that underlies her whole system of worship—a system which is so ordered as to secure, in the most appropriate forms, the expression of our belief. To kneel in adoration, to bow one's head in prayer, to approach the Sacraments as the ritual enjoins, to share in the various observances which mark the seasons of the ecclesiastical year—what is all this but the concrete expression of our religious life? And this expression, bodily, external, ceremonial as it is, nevertheless is the best means of cultivating sentiments that are of the soul—inward and spiritual and full of the divine life."[26]

VII

Principle XII.

The preservation of unity and of continuity in the developmental processes demand that instincts and reflexes be utilized as the basis of habits. (Cf. Les. XIII, XIV, XV)

Principle XIII.

The preservation of symmetry in the developing mind is necessary both to culture and to productive scholarship. (Cf. Les. IX, XIV)

Principle XIV.

Culture demands the development of the will, of the aesthetic faculty, and the cultivation and the control of the emotions, no less than the training of the cognitive powers. (Cf. Les. XXIV)

Principle XV.

The remedy for materialism is to be found in the methods of study and of teaching no less than in the content of the curriculum. (Cf. Les. XXIV)

[343]

Principle XVI. The power of adjustment to a rapidly changing environment is the measure of vitality. (Cf. Les. X, XXIV)

---

26 Edward Pace, "Modern Psychology and Catholic Education," *Catholic World* 86, no. 486 (September 1905): 721–22; 725–26. The former page range refers to the text before the ellipses; the latter page range to the text after the ellipses. The original publication lacked the closing quotation marks.

The embodiment of these five principles in Christ's method of teaching is so obvious that we will not pause here to point it out. He constantly appeals to emotions and instincts, to the love of parent for offspring, to physical appetites, to human ambitions, to the desires for wealth and power, and He makes these purely human tendencies lift the soul into an understanding of the higher truths. He appeals to the whole man and develops every faculty by which the soul is endowed. He does not let the minds of his followers rest in dry formulae or in the things of sense which He constantly uses to lift up the mind to a view of immaterial truths. He always adjusts Himself to the attitude of His followers and answers the questions that form themselves in their minds.

The embodiment of these principles in the organic teaching of the Church is set forth in some detail by Dr. Pace in the article from which we have just quoted and which every student of this course should study carefully.

VIII

These and similar educational principles have, without being understood by her children, always animated the organic teaching of the Church. They were as clearly embodied in her ritual and in her life during the darkest hours of the ninth century as they were during the brilliant centuries that were adorned by the Fathers or by the Schoolmen.

Those who left the fold of Christ during the sixteenth century carried with them as much of human science as was possessed by those who remained in [344] the bosom of the Church. No longer guided by the spirit of the Church, the reformers abandoned these principles; they suppressed feeling as an unworthy accompaniment of Revealed truth, accusing the Church of idolatry, they extinguished the lights on her altars and banished the incense from her sanctuaries; they broke the stained glass of her windows and the images of her saints; they suppressed her sacraments and her ritual. Ignorant of the laws of imitation, they would have neither guardian angels nor patron saints. Not knowing the vital necessity of expression, they held that faith without works was sufficient for salvation. With the Savior's warning ringing in their ears, "The letter killeth, it is the spirit that giveth life," they accepted the rigid standard of the written word in lieu of the living voice.[27]

---

27 2 Cor 3:6.

Thus, one by one, revealed truths were extinguished in their midst, leaving the descendants of confessors and of martyrs wandering in exterior darkness, where, like the Children of Israel, they were compelled to make bricks without straw. But the day of salvation is at hand. Delving in the natural sciences, the children of this generation have gained a clear realization of some of the laws that underlie the life and growth of the mind, and lifting up their eyes, they find these laws embodied, perfectly, in the organic teaching of the Catholic Church, which, like a cloud by day and a pillar of fire by night, will lead them back into the kingdom.

Research Questions

1. Show fully the embodiment of any one of the above sixteen principles in the Gospel and in the organic teaching of the Church.
2. Why should Catholic teachers be the best teachers in the modern world?

Collateral Reading

Cardinal [James] Gibbons, *The Ambassador of Christ* [Baltimore: J. Murphy & Co., 1896]; Pace, *Modern Psychology and Catholic Education* (Catholic World, Sept., 1905, and reprint, Philadelphia: Catholic Truth Society); [Thomas J.] Shahan, *The House of God* [New York: The Cathedral Library Association, 1905], *The Beginnings of Christianity* [New York: Benziger Bros., 1903], and *The Middle Ages* [New York: Benziger Bros., 1904].

Index

A

Acerbo Nimis (Pius X), 54–55, 197n32
adjustment, 73, 76–79, 85, 90, 95, 167, 250
Affiliation Program, 13, 153–61
anthropology, Christian, 27n7, 86, 155n3
Aquinas, Thomas, 33, 103, 103n25, 120
architecture, 198–99
Augustine, 120

B

Baltimore Catechism, 5, 5n12, 6, 8, 10, 60, 176, 197n32. *See also* memorization
Barrett, Amy Coney, 59n25
Benedict XVI, Pope, 175n5
Better Men for Better Times (Johnson), 213
Billiart Julie Marie de, 134
Bryce, Mary, 13
Buetow, Harold, 12–13, 53n7, 139n14

C

catechesis, 93–95, 97, 101–2, 102n22, 111, 111n46, 175, 197, 197n32, 201, 217–19, 222–24
Catechesi Tradendae (John Paul II), 111

catechetical framework, 101–2
catechisms, 59–63, 83, 110n45, 176, 211. *See also* Baltimore Catechism
Catholic Correspondence School, 140–41, 155
Catholic Educational Review, 8, 16–17, 150, 211, 215–16, 216n12
Catholic Education Series (Shields), 15, 81, 96, 174n4; as complete curriculum, 170–71; Master Plan and, 167; publishing of, 166; structure and aims, 173–83; as study in knowledge and method, 184–207. *See also* textbooks
Catholic Intellectual Tradition, ix, 3, 46–47, 49, 71, 86, 92, 219. *See also Educators in the Catholic Intellectual Tradition*
Catholic Sisters College, 10–11, 19, 96, 118; *Education of Our Girls* and, 15; importance of, 214; Johnson and, 118; as not fulfilling Shields's vision, 215; Pace and, 6; reform and, 18, 135–52; teachers and, 124, 147–48
"Catholic Teachers and Educational Progress" (Shields), 139n15, 140n16

253

Catholic University Bulletin, 15–16, 69, 112n48, 169–70
Catholic University of America, ix, 4, 6, 10–16, 56, 71n6, 120n10, 154
Catholic University of Ireland, 120n10
Catholic University Summer School, 141–47, 155, 155n4
chant, 202
character formation, 107–11
church architecture, 198–99
citizenship, 9, 127, 132, 212–13
Clement of Alexandria, 33
Commission on American Citizenship, 9, 212–13
Common Faith, A (Dewey), 46
conscious life, 73, 83, 99–100
Constantine, 175
correlation, 10, 80–81, 90, 107, 192, 196, 201, 226; *Catholic Education Series* and, 167, 171; church architecture and, 199; curriculum and, 170, 204; development and, 85; gospel and, 95; pedagogy and, 110; textbooks and, 176, 180
"Correlation in the Teaching of Religion" (Shields), 80
Council of Trent, 27n5, 61, 178n12, 197n32
Counter-Reformation, 61
Culture Epoch Theory, 168–69
curriculum, 107–11, 129–33, 173–77, 220–21
Cyril of Jerusalem, 33

D

Dawson, Christopher, 2–3, 31, 45n20
democracy, 40–44, 57–59, 212
Dewey, John, 14, 51n3, 109; catechisms and, 59–60, 83; Catholic response to, 50–65; Neuhaus on, 62n32; Progressivism and, 39–50, 43n15, 48n26, 48n28; schools and, 77
Dicastery for Evangelization, 93–94
Directory for Catechesis (Pontifical Council for Promoting New Evangelization), 93–95, 101–2, 102n21–102n22, 109, 218–19, 223–24
Divini Illius Magistri (Pius XI), 56, 56n18, 78n25, 212
Doyle, Mary, 166–67
drawing, 88

E

ecclesial contexts, 2–9
education. *See* Catholic education
Education of Our Girls, The (Shields), 15, 18, 140–41, 143, 149, 149n47
Educators in the Catholic Intellectual Tradition (Elias and Nolan, eds.), 13
Egan, Kieron, 44
Elias, John, 13, 118
Enlightenment, 26–27
Essay on the Development of Christian Doctrine, An (Newman), 71
Eucharisticum Mysterium (Second Vatican Council), 194

INDEX 255

Evolution and Ethics (Huxley), 70
exclusion, 27n7

F
Fides et Ratio (John Paul II), 103, 103n24
Francis, Pope, 29n14, 193n24
Fruit Lesson, 88
"Fundamental Principles in the Teaching of Religion" (Shields), 113n50

G
gospel, pedagogy of, 95–98, 245–46, 248
Gothic cathedrals, 199
Gravissimum Educationis (Second Vatican Council), 120–21
"Great Commission," 111
Gregorian Chant, 202
Guardini, Romano, 29, 194n26

H
Harper, William Rainey, 51
Herbart, Johann Friedrich, 41n10
Hirst, Paul, 28
Huxley, Thomas, 70
hymns, 204–5

I
Idea of the Shepherd, 185–86
Immortale Dei (Leo XIII), 53, 57–58
Incarnation, 74, 245
inclusion, 27n7, 42
Index Omnium (Shields), 10, 81, 81n33

institution, Church as, 200n41
institutional awareness, 200
intellectual contexts, 2–9
intellectual tradition. *See* Catholic Intellectual Tradition
intelligibility, 110–11

J
"Jack and the Beanstalk," 70–71
Jesus Christ: Catholic education and, 32–33; curriculum and, 220; Incarnation of, 74, 245; as incomprehensible, 247–48; pedagogy and, 96–97, 113, 243, 245–46, 251
John Paul II, Pope, 103, 103n24, 111, 199n40
Johnson, George, 8–9, 118, 212–13, 225
John XXIII, Pope, 32–33
Jungmann, Josef, 202

K
Keane, John, 135–36, 136n2, 142

L
La Salle, Jean Baptiste de, 134
Lash, Nicholas, 30
Lehner, Ulrich, 27n5
Leonine Revolution, 54
Leo XIII, Pope, 4, 53–54, 54n13, 57–58, 154, 157
Lineamenta, 120–21
literacy, 91n59, 166n2, 167–68, 167n8, 190–91, 197, 200, 212

liturgy, 112n49, 175, 193–95, 193n24, 194n26; curriculum and, 108; educational movement and, 30; education and, 29; gospels and, 96; hymns and, 204–5; Jesus Christ and, 92; memorization and, 111n46; music and, 202–3

M

Making and Unmaking of a Dullard, The (Shields), 9, 15, 69n1
Mass, 77, 184, 193–96, 202–3
Master Plan, 18–19, 47, 117, 122, 167, 172, 209–17
Matthew, Gospel of, 32, 111
McCormick, Patrick J., 105n28, 150
McMahon, John, 6, 12, 190–91
McVay, Leo, 157n13
memorization, 56, 83–84, 86n49, 109, 110n45, 111n46, 179
mental development, 75n15, 80, 82–87, 82n36, 249
mental growth, 82–87, 95, 122, 126, 167
methodology, 2n4
Michel, Virgil, 13
Milkweed Lesson, 88
mission, of Catholic education, 98–101, 121, 217
mission statements, 99, 99n13
Montessori, Maria, 40–41
Moran, Gabriel, 48n28
Mother Idea, 186
Munich Method, 12
Murphy, John Francis, 13–14, 53n11, 73, 149n46, 156n8, 192–93, 214

music, 112n49, 201–5, 205n56. *See also* Ward, Justine
"Musical Education in Catholic Schools" (Shields), 203

N

Neuhaus, Richard John, 62n32
New Evangelization, 32. *See also* Pontifical Council for Promoting New Evangelization
Newman, John Henry, 14, 71, 93, 93n2, 120n10
Nicholas V, Pope, 31n19
Nolan, Lucinda, 13
"Notes on Education" (Shields), 15–16, 44–45, 69, 90n58, 110n45, 112n49, 165n1, 172n23
Notley, R. Steven, 113n51

O

Of Singular Benefit: The Story of Catholic Education in the United States (Buetow), 13, 53n7, 139n14, 167n7
O'Hara, Edwin V., 13
On the Liturgical Formation of the People of God (Francis), 29n14
Our Apostolic Mandate (Pius X), 58–59

P

Pace, Edward, 5–8; Affiliation Program and, 156–58, 158n14; catechetical movement and, 8n23; *Catholic Educational Review* and, 216, 216n12; *Catholic Education Series* and, 16; Catholic

INDEX 257

University of America and,
140–41; in Elias, 13; experimental psychology and, 6n14, 90;
liturgy and, 249; Master Plan and,
122; motor processes and, 8n22;
philosophy and, 7n21
"Papacy in Education, The"
(Pace), 8
*Pascendi Dominici Gregis (On the
Doctrines of the Modernists)* (Pius
X), 55–56, 55n16, 58
Paul VI, Pope, 37–38
pedagogy, 2n4, 18, 69, 92–114; of
gospel, 95–98, 243, 245–46, 248;
key features of Shields's, 98–111;
Shield's principles of, 70–87
Philosophy of Education (Shields), 15,
71n7, 101n18, 103–7, 105n28;
history of education in, 130n28;
mental development in, 86n50;
pedagogy and, 70; psychology
in, 84n44; Sabbath in, 86n49;
science in, 132n34; Scotland
and, 108n37; teachers in, 79n28,
131n30; women and family in, 210
phonics, 179n14
Pius X, Pope, 54–56, 55n16, 58–59,
197n32, 202
Pius XI, Pope, 56, 56n18, 78,
78n25, 171n20, 212
plasticity, 73–76, 85, 90, 95, 125,
167
Plenary Council of Baltimore, 4, 18
Pontifical Council for Promoting
New Evangelization, 93–94
Populorum Progressio (Paul VI), 37–38
priestly formation, 146n37

Progressivism: challenge of, 34;
defining, 37–38; of Dewey,
39–48; European *vs.* American,
40–41, 40n6; Pace and, 6; Paul
VI and, 37–38
Progressivist Religious Education
Association, 9
Protestant Reformation, 25,
106n31, 138

R
REA. *See* Religious Education
Association (REA)
readers, 91n59, 165–72, 179n14, 197.
See also textbooks
reading, 166n2, 167–68, 167n8,
190–91, 200, 212
reason, 103–7
Reformation, 25, 106n31, 138
reign of law, 72
religious education, 30; catechesis
and, 94, 222–24; catechisms and,
59–60; defined, 95n7; Dewey
and, 44–48; Progressivism and,
51
Religious Education (journal), 9, 47
"Religious Education as Conditioned by Modern Psychology
and Pedagogy" (Dewey), 47
Religious Education Association
(REA), 9, 43n15, 50–56, 51n4,
52n5, 64–65
religious instruction, 8n22, 12, 47,
60, 80, 86, 94n4, 95, 107–11,
166n2, 171n20, 194
Rerum Novarum (Leo XIII), 54
ressourcement, 84, 84n43, 193

revelation, 223
role-modeling, 86, 86n48
Roman Catechism, 61n28, 178n12

S
sacrament, 62, 112n49, 175, 249–51
St. Anthony's Parish School of Brookland, 225, 225n26
saints, 109
Sant'Egidio Community, 31
scaffolding, 172n22
Scholas Occurrentes movement, 31
science, 7–8, 7n21, 10, 47, 71, 89, 91, 91n59, 96, 113, 132n34, 197
Scotland, 123n14
Second Vatican Council, 27n5, 32–33, 84, 97, 111, 120–21, 193–94, 215
secularism, ix, 27–28
sense training, 87–89, 171
Shields, Thomas: biography of, 11–12; education of, 9–10; institutional reform and, 135–41; Johnson and, 8–9; life and work of, 9–19; Pace and, 6–7, 8n23, 122; pedagogical principles of, 70–87, 241–52; reform plan of, 18–19; works of, 14–17, 14n43
Shields Method, 2, 96, 205, 225
"Sisters College, The" (Shields), 148n43
Sloyan, Gerard, 12, 12n31
Sower Scheme, 12
Spalding, John Lancaster, 4–5, 5n11, 52n5, 136–37, 137n7
Spectata Fides (Leo XIII), 54n13
Spencer, Herbert, 41, 41n9

Spirit of the Liturgy, The (Guardini), 194n26
Standard Catholic Readers (Doyle), 166–67
"Summer Session of the Sisters College" (Shields), 151n51
"Survey of the Field (The Cultural and Vocational Aims in Education)" (Shields), 118n4
"Survey of the Field (The High School)" (Shields), 141n21

T
Taylor, Charles, 27
teacher(s): Catholic Sisters College and, 124, 147–48; culture and, 121–26; curriculum and, 129–33; development processes and, 72; formation, 25, 95, 117–33, 120n10, 217–19; methods, 126–29; reign of law and, 72; role of, 70, 86, 117; self-determination and, 85; sense-training and, 87–88; skills of, 114; textbooks and, 177–82; thought material and, 76
Teachers Manual of Primary Methods, The (Shields), 15, 69, 77n21; *Catholic Education Series* and, 189–90; drawing in, 88n54; God in, 186n5; home in, 186n4; literacy in, 167n8; loving order in, 76n19; memorization in, 82n37; sense training in, 87; sin in, 206n58; supplementary work in, 179n15; teachers in, 177n10, 179n14

INDEX

"Teaching of Education at CUA 1889—1966" (Buetow), 12–13
"Teaching of Pedagogy in the Seminary, The" (Shields), 122n13
Teaching of Religion, The (Shields), 15, 112n48
textbooks, 110n45, 165–72, 177–82. *See also Catholic Education Series* (Shields)
Thomas Edward Shields Memorial School, 191–92
"Thomas Edward Shields: Religious Educator" (Murphy), 13–14
Thomas Edward Shields: Biologist, Psychologist, Educator (Ward), 11–12
"thought material," 76, 82–83
Trinity College (Washington, D.C.), 138, 138n11
Twenty-Five Lessons in the Psychology of Education (Shields), 15, 69, 71n6, 83n39, 83n41, 85n47, 92, 97–98, 112n48, 118n2, 241–52

U

United States Conference of Catholic Bishops, ix

Universal Declaration of Human Rights, 26
"University and the Training of Primary Teachers" (Shields), 123n14, 132n33, 143n27
University of Glasgow, 31n19

V

Vatican II, 27n5, 32–33, 84, 97, 111, 120–21, 193–94, 215
vocation, teacher, 121–26

W

Ward, Justine, 11–12, 81n33, 183, 203, 205n56
Ward Method, 204n53
Watrin, Rita, 13
Weigel, George, 54
Wohlwend, Mary Verone, 14, 173
women, 138, 141n22, 145n34. *See also* Catholic Sisters College; *Education of Our Girls, The* (Shields)

Y

Yorke, Peter C., 13
Yorke Method, 12